The Hitler Myths

The Hitler Myths

Exposing the Truth Behind the Stories about the Führer

Sjoerd J. de Boer

FRONTLINE BOOKS

First published in Great Britain in 2022 by
Frontline Books
An imprint of
Pen & Sword Books Ltd
Yorkshire – Philadelphia
Originally published by Just Publishers, the Netherlands.
Translated by Arnold Palthe.

Copyright © S.J. de Boer 2021

ISBN 978 1 39901 905 7

The right of S.J. de Boer to be identified as Author of this work has been asserted by him in accordance with the Copyright, Designs and Patents Act 1988.

A CIP catalogue record for this book is available from the British Library.

All rights reserved. No part of this book may be reproduced or transmitted in any form or by any means, electronic or mechanical including photocopying, recording or by any information storage and retrieval system, without permission from the Publisher in writing.

Typeset by Mac Style
Printed and bound in the UK by CPI Group (UK) Ltd, Croydon, CR0 4YY.

Pen & Sword Books Limited incorporates the imprints of Atlas, Archaeology, Aviation, Discovery, Family History, Fiction, History, Maritime, Military, Military Classics, Politics, Select, Transport, True Crime, Air World, Frontline Publishing, Leo Cooper, Remember When, Seaforth Publishing, The Praetorian Press, Wharncliffe Local History, Wharncliffe Transport, Wharncliffe True Crime and White Owl.

For a complete list of Pen & Sword titles please contact

PEN & SWORD BOOKS LIMITED
47 Church Street, Barnsley, South Yorkshire, S70 2AS, England
E-mail: enquiries@pen-and-sword.co.uk
Website: www.pen-and-sword.co.uk

Or

PEN AND SWORD BOOKS
1950 Lawrence Rd, Havertown, PA 19083, USA
E-mail: Uspen-and-sword@casematepublishers.com
Website: www.penandswordbooks.com

Apparently, rumours are far more interesting than plain reality
(Sven Felix Kellerhoff, 2003)

Contents

Introduction		viii
Chapter 1	Adolf Hitler, a Jew?	1
Chapter 2	Did Hitler Live in Poverty?	13
Chapter 3	Adolf Hitler, a Hero?	19
Chapter 4	Did Hitler Have a Son?	41
Chapter 5	Hitler the Socialist?	49
Chapter 6	Where is the Blutfahne?	56
Chapter 7	Was Mein Kampf Hitler's Own Work?	59
Chapter 8	Hitler's Second Book	71
Chapter 9	Did Hitler Believe in the Protocols of the Wise Men of Zion?	76
Chapter 10	Did Hitler Create an Economic Miracle?	80
Chapter 11	Hitler, an Artistic Genius?	89
Chapter 12	Did Hitler Suffer from a Sexual Disorder?	109
Chapter 13	Did Hitler Always Get his Way?	135
Chapter 14	Was Hitler Ill?	156
Chapter 15	Did Hitler Really Commit Suicide?	174
Chapter 16	Was the Führer Bunker Really That Strong?	205
Chapter 17	What Happened to Hitler's Remains?	210
Chapter 18	Hitler's Testament	213
Chapter 19	Was Hitler a Demon?	219
Bibliography		234
Index		240

Introduction

A ridiculous biography

Seventy-five years after the death of Adolf Hitler, the wildest stories about him are still circulating. Arranged in sequence, a ridiculous biography has been created full of bizarre incredible 'facts' about the former Führer of Germany that would read something like this:

Adolf Hitler was the homosexual, impotent, demonic and paranoid grandchild of a Jew. As a little boy, a goat bit his penis, leaving him sexually frustrated for the rest of his life. Despite his frigidity, he contracted a venereal disease while living in Vienna and during the First World War, he fathered a child with a French village girl. After the war, he entered into a state of permanent hypnosis because a physician in the military hospital of Pasewalk didn't complete his alternative treatment and in the early 1930s, he murdered his niece Geli, with whom he had maintained an extremely bad relationship.

This weird Austrian managed to grasp power in Germany in order to achieve a number of horrible things, including the almost assembly line murder of six million Jews, although it was said later on he had never issued the order for this. He was, however, responsible for the construction of a fantastic network of highways in Germany.

Discrepancies in his policy are explained away by the fact that, despite his aversion to the Christian faith he has always remained a devout Catholic and this fire-eating, fuming and fretting demon suffered from so many personality disorders and mental diseases that he can be called completely devout and completely opportunistic in the same breath.

The dictator with the one testicle had sex with many well-known women, including Magda Goebbels, on whom he fathered a child, probably forgetting to keep a last shot in the locker as he rarely ever shared his bed with his mistress, Eva Braun. This may have had to do with his addiction to hard drugs, described by his personal physician

Theodor Morell, which caused him to make such weird military decisions that the war could only end in failure.

The allegedly infallible Hitler subsequently committed double suicide with both cyanide and a pistol, after which he called upon a UFO to take him to safer pastures. Providence obeyed and had him transferred to Argentina, not with a UFO but by U-boat, and there he lived for years without both jaws, which were kept in Moscow. After having made Eva Braun pregnant at the last opportunity, Hitler died in 1986 at the age of 97, many years after the end of the Second World War.

An utterly ridiculous story of a life, although every statement made represents a Hitler myth, which is actually presented as a serious possibility in one source or another. Arranged in sequence like this, it becomes instantly clear that not all of them can be true simultaneously but even the lowest conspiracy addict or gossip journalist naturally presents his theories independently of all other possible untrue stories and substantiates them with eyewitness accounts and all sorts of other 'facts' from the past. Preferably sprinkled liberally with a sauce of mystery and conspiracy. Many of the stories mentioned above pop up time and again on the internet, in the form of books or in the written press. Meanwhile, several of these bizarre stories seem to have taken root in our collective memory. Hitler did have Jewish blood, didn't he? And couldn't it be highly likely Hitler used drugs? And why is there still so much uncertainty about what happened with his remains after his alleged suicide?

In response to publications in which Hitler's evil is explained based on a single fact, and being a member of a post-war generation that has very seldom learned anything about Hitler at first-hand, I wanted to find out what the most important myths about the most notorious dictator in Europe are based on. That is necessary because since the emergence of the internet, old discussions about Hitler flare up frequently again, even if they come from obsolete, unreliable sources or dusty books being taken from the shelf once again.

Since the rise of the Nazi party in pre-Second World War Germany, all sorts of weird stories have existed about Hitler who, by the way, did his utmost to suppress his past or even eradicate it altogether. The most extreme example of this took place in 1938 when he razed the Austrian villages of Döllersheim and Strones, where his ancestors came from, to the ground in order to turn that region into a military training area. Although much material has been lost, his plan was not achieved entirely. Gossip about Hitler's life kept circulating until long after his death. For instance, the seemingly very convincing statements of Nazi lawyer Hans Frank about Hitler's alleged Jewish ancestry can be found in various forums on the internet, even though historians have long since proved Frank's unreliability as a source. In particular on this sensitive subject, the statements made should be substantiated by facts. The consequence of this myth of Hitler being a Jew is enormous, because if Hitler had been a Jew, the Jewish people would have been perpetrators as well as victims of the Holocaust and so they would have been burdened with a highly undesirable and undeserved load.

In early 2014, the spectacular story of an English soldier who had stood eye to eye with Hitler during the First World War made headlines for the umpteenth time. In an article entitled 'British soldier spares the life of an injured Hitler' on a Belgian website it was written that Hitler had been walking along, injured, on 28 September 1918 near Cambrai in northern France when he met this British soldier. Hitler lowered his weapon and the two looked in each other's eyes. Thereupon, the Tommy lowered his weapon as well and offered the German soldier – later on he discovered it must have been Adolf Hitler – a chance to escape. But what was really said in the book on which the article was based? The journalist who had written the article, had he actually read the book?

While many of the stories about Hitler keep coming back, I have attempted to repeat a number of much-discussed myths about Hitler in the run-up to the 75th anniversary of the day of his death. Furthermore, I came across a number of lesser-known myths, which are also dealt with in this book. Some myths are easy to unravel, others are more complex and require more attention as the history of their creation is more confusing. Stories that have been created in the years prior to Hitler's chancellorship were being retold in various forms in various periods. For instance, when early opponents of Hitler wrote that the NSDAP leader hadn't played such a glorious role in the First World War as claimed, the Nazis paraded various witnesses who could prove that Hitler had indeed been a hero. And so contradicting stories are created.

After 1933, these critical sounds disappeared and naturally only positive stories about Hitler were being told, which in turn were understandably shoved aside after the Second World War. Meanwhile though, numerous anecdotes have circulated that sought to prove whether Hitler was a coward or a hero. If in such a context, post-war historians disagree on the credibility of witnesses and sources, it sometimes becomes very trying to recover the truth.

The myths I have included differ in nature. Some were thought up by Hitler himself, others by his enemies. Some spring from prior to his death, a number from after that day as well. Some deal with objects with a connection to Hitler, others are about his dark soul and, of course, Hitler's corpse – allegedly disappeared – is dealt with extensively.

A number of myths are so absurd that there is no place for them even in this book. An example of this is the fabrication, eagerly distributed by neo-Nazis, that the corpses shown in photographs and films of the concentration camps are those of Germans killed during the Allied bombing of the city of Dresden in February 1945. I have ignored myths of this calibre as the mendacity of them is glaringly obvious. I did include, however, the missing order from the Führer about the extermination of the Jews.

The word 'myth' has numerous meanings. First of all, it is about the fantastic stories that are told about the origin of a population or religion. Those are often beautiful, tall stories in which the element of fantasy is more important than the historic truth. The second meaning of the word, that of an 'unfounded' story, is an extension of this. The word myth doesn't only point to a certain sort of story, it can also be used as a synonym for 'untruth'. While in the course of history facts have become more important than the sometimes wonderful stories, the meaning of the word has shifted as well.

The confusing thing when answering the question whether something is a substantiated story or an outright lie is that it has become a habit among conspiracy devotees to present all sorts of evidence to substantiate their stories. In other words, they do their utmost to prove that their story is no myth at all. This occurred for instance with the stories that emerged after the assassination of American president John F. Kennedy and the attack on the Twin Towers in New York. In various conspiracy theories, sometimes very convincing evidence was put up to 'prove' who the actual perpetrators of these attacks had been. This kind of 'convincing' argumentation plays a role in the various Hitler myths as well and that is exactly the reason why stories, which have largely been fabricated, are considered by some as the pure truth.

In each of the nineteen chapters, the birth of a Hitler myth is explained and whenever necessary put to rest. In principle, the chapters can also be read as separate stories. This book isn't a biography and although there is a certain chronological sequence, periods sometimes overlap each other because various stories take place in the same period. In the more extensive chapters, various other myths pop up sometimes. A large number of myths about Hitler are told and it is difficult to ascertain how many there are exactly.

The starting point of a chapter is at times something I found in the media or sometimes in sources that can be expected to make attempts at recovering the truth but appear to make a mistake somewhere. From that point onwards, the search begins through the works of historians such as Ian Kershaw, John Lukacs, Anton Joachimsthaler, Thomas Weber, Laurence Rees and journalist Ron Rosenbaum: authors who have long since put many of the Hitler myths to rest. It would be a sign of unbecoming arrogance to think that I, where many respected historians have failed, won't fail in completely unravelling all the Hitler myths in this book. But maybe this will be a modest direction post for those who want to know a little more about the various myths about Hitler and about the excellent work historians and researchers have done so far.

Chapter 1

Adolf Hitler, a Jew?

The mystery of his descent

'I have no idea about the history of my family. My knowledge of this is severely limited,' Hitler once said.[1] He had more than enough reasons for it. His father and mother were relatives and if the rumours were true, chances were that the most ardent Jew hater in history had a Jewish grandfather himself. It didn't end with just whispers. Long before Adolf Hitler rose to power in Germany, the press published stories about the vague descent of the 'so-called' Aryan Hitler. When later on fanatic party members attempted to recover information about his origin, he wasn't pleased at all. Hitler did everything in his power to hide his past. After the Anschluss of Austria and the German Empire, the entire Austrian village of Döllersheim, where Hitler and his family came from, was razed to the ground and turned into an army training area. The question arose if Hitler had ordered this because he had something to hide as it could be no coincidence that precisely at this location all traces of his parentage were being eradicated. Historians searched for answers to Hitler's descent until long after the war. The source of the mystery was common knowledge: there was a missing link in the family's pedigree. But was that the only reason for Hitler's conspicuous disinterest in his ancestors?

Adolf Hitler was the son of Alois Hitler and Klara Pölzl. Alois was a restless man who was often on the run and moved frequently. Prior to his marriage with Adolf's mother in 1885, he had been married twice already. He had children from one of these marriages but even before he got married, he had fathered a child.[2]

The doubt about Hitler's origin, which exists until this day, was caused, however, by obscurity about the identity of Alois' father, Adolf's grandfather. Alois was born out of wedlock and his mother, Maria Anna Schicklgruber,

---

1. Zdral, *De Hitlers, de onbekende familie van de Führer*. The quotation can be found on the back of his book.
2. Zdral, p. 17.

kept the name of the man secret who had impregnated her. Therefore that name wasn't entered into the official documents, drafted at his birth.[3] Alois was given the surname of his mother and so he wasn't named Alois Hitler but Alois Schicklgruber. That changed after Alois had reached adulthood. In 1876, in the presence of himself and his stepfather, the name of the father was entered into the open space on the certificate of baptism as well as on the birth certificate of the family lawyer. As official documents were involved, the date of the alteration was entered as well and so, years later, it could still be established that the name of Alois' father had been unknown once. And that establishment became the root of numerous wild speculations about the origin of Adolf Hitler.

A Jewish grandfather

When Adolf Hitler became better known in Bavaria, a discussion soon emerged about the question whether the name that was entered on the birth certificate actually was the name of Adolf's grandfather. Officially, the name of Georg Hiedler was entered but in particular later on, the name of his brother, Johann Nepomuk Hiedler, was mentioned as well. The most remarkable suggestion, however, pertained to Adolf Hitler's possible grandfather. It was suggested for instance that Adolf was a descendant from a Jewish family in Bucharest, and a Jewish baron named Rothschild was mentioned as well.[4] Information about these two possible ancestors, however, came from the Austrian secret police, which didn't like Adolf Hitler, and it wasn't based on truth.[5]

The most serious rumour about Hitler's Jewish grandfather, which still circulated after the war, was taken from the memoirs of Hans Frank, a well-known Nazi lawyer and governor-general of the part of Poland under German civil rule. These were drafted when Frank was imprisoned in Nuremberg after the Second World War awaiting his trial.[6] He brought an existing story about a third Jewish grandfather once more and convincingly into the world when he stated he had discovered, having been ordered to by Hitler, that Adolf's grandmother had been employed as a house maid by a Jewish family in Graz, Austria, called the Frankenbergers.[7] There she was

---

3. Kershaw, *Hoogmoed*, p. 32
4. Kershaw, *Hoogmoed*, p. 35
5. Kershaw, *Hoogmoed*, p. 35; Rosenbaum, p. 51
6. Kershaw, *Hoogmoed*, p. 35
7. Kershaw, *Hoogmoed*, p. 36

impregnated by 19-year-old Frankenberger junior. The father of the Jewish boy is supposed to have paid alimony to Alois's mother until his fourteenth birthday.[8] Frank's statement caused much discussion for a long time and popped up time and again long after the war.

Speculations about Hitler's origin

The obscurity as to the ancestry of the politician focused on racial purity was soon rich pickings for the critical press, which had more than enough opportunities in the 1920s to attack Hitler as he had not yet become the boss in Germany. The anti-Hitler campaign was fuelled by the socialist paper the *Münchener Post*, which published the sharpest criticism about Hitler in those years. It is said to have been the first newspaper to ridicule him but also the first that attempted to conduct serious research about him.[9]

The paper grabbed every opportunity to attack Hitler forcefully with both hands. In 1921, a polemic was published under the heading 'Adolf Hitler, a traitor'. The paper wondered whether he was of Jewish ancestry and if he maintained secret relations with the Jews. The polemic was fuelled, however, by material from Nazis who thought Hitler had behaved like a Jew when he grabbed dictatorial power over the party in 1921.[10] The paper itself wasn't anti-Semitic in nature but did not fail to use information from Nazis to hit his weak spot.

Less critical minds did research into Hitler ancestors as well. Before the war, as the Führer cult in Germany was in full swing, various Nazis and journalists conducted investigation in the region where Hitler's family originated. According to American journalist Ron Rosenbaum, who had conducted investigation into Hitler for ten years at the end of the previous century and who published his findings in his book *Why Hitler?* in 1998, messages about this kind of research caused Hitler to have violent tantrums and on occasion he would have said nobody was to know where he came from and who he was.[11] And yet, in the 1940s, Hitler himself had a secret investigation conducted into his pedigree. Although nothing remarkable emerged from this,[12] the sole fact that Hitler had this search conducted proved he knew very well there were obscurities about his ancestry and he

---

8. Kershaw, *Hoogmoed*, p. 36
9. Rosenbaum, p. 37
10. Rosenbaum, p. 89
11. Rosenbaum, p. 50
12. Kershaw, *Hoogmoed*, p. 36

was bothered about them. After all, the Führer had much to lose if it was found out one of his ancestors hadn't been racially pure.

A delicate previous history

It is ticklish to understand Hitler's ancestry. Apart from the vagueness surrounding Hitler's grandfather, it has also to do with the surname of Adolf's father, the various ways of spelling those names in the nineteenth century and the fact that Adolf's father and mother were related. The family had its roots in the Waldviertel in northern Austria, a rural region with small villages mainly inhabited by farmers. Chances are one would find a partner in one of these villages who was related in one way or another. That was the case with Adolf's parents as well.

So, the story begins with Adolf Hitler's grandmother, Maria Anna Schicklgruber. She was already 42 years of age and single when she gave birth to Alois, Adolf's future father.[13] In the Catholic villages of Strones, where she came from, her status as a single mother was a problem. It looks like her father and brother locked her out in this period but she was lucky enough to find shelter with a farmer from the village.[14] The name of Alois' father remained a secret, in any case in the official documents of the church and in the office of the lawyer.

Schicklgruber becomes Hitler

When little Alois was 5 years old, Maria Anna married the wandering mill worker Johann Georg Hiedler. Whether speculation existed at the time about Georg being the father isn't known, but it is likely that Georg and Maria Anna had had a relationship six years before. Evidence is lacking, however, and the five years between Alois' birth and the marriage is reason to suppose Georg was not the father of Alois. This view is strengthened by what happened to son Alois after the wedding. He did not grow up with his mother and her new husband Georg but in the family of Johann Nepomuk Hiedler, the brother of his mother's new husband. Nevertheless, within the Third Reich, Georg Hiedler was labelled the grandfather of Adolf Hitler, and that had everything to do with the official documents of Hitler's ancestors that had been preserved.

---

13. Zdral, p. 10
14. Jetzinger, p. 18. The story about the response of Maria Anna Schicklgruber's father cannot be found in the work of modern biographers such as Kershaw and Zdral.

Until 1876, Alois Schicklgruber retained the surname of his mother. That year he changed his name to Alois Hitler. At the time, Alois was 39 years of age but more remarkable was the fact that his mother had been dead for 29 years and her husband Georg had died 19 years before. Therefore, they couldn't be witness to an official alteration of names. And yet, on 6 June, Alois and 'stepfather' Nepomuk saw a lawyer in the small Austrian town of Weitra, where they had Alois named as the son of the demised Georg Hiedler.[15] The next day, they went to see the pastor of Döllersheim for the same purpose. The documents of the official alteration have been preserved. The surname of the brothers, Hiedler, was spelled as Hitler by the lawyer and the priest of Döllersheim replaced the words 'out of wedlock' by 'legitimate', crossed out the name of Schicklgruber and entered Georg Hitler in the empty space in the birth registry. The witnesses who were present said that George himself, when he was still alive, had asked to have his name added to the record.[16] So many years after the death of Georg and Maria Anna though, this change was weird and not really legitimate. Alois' father or mother should have made a declaration but that, of course, was no longer possible.[17]

Conspicuously, Alois was given the name Hitler instead of Hiedler. It isn't quite clear why this difference in spelling became his official surname but these variants were common practice in those days. In documents of the early and mid-1900s, names like 'Hietler', 'Hüttler', 'Hütler' and 'Hitler', are being used at random, all of them meaning small farmer,[18] according to Hitler's biographer Ian Kershaw. If there had been a conscious decision to change the spelling it can't be proved, but Adolf Hitler was pleased with it. He seems to have once told his friend from his youth, August Kubizek, that he was very pleased with his father's decision. He thought Schicklgruber too boorish and impractical. Then again, Hiedler sounded too weak. In his opinion, Hitler was a fine name and easy to remember.[19]

Kershaw stresses that changing the surname had nothing to do with the rejection by society of an illegitimate birth as at the time such children were no exception. After the change of names, Alois admitted this openly. According to Kershaw, the change must have had to do with something else, namely his inheritance.[20]

---

15. Kershaw, *Hoogmoed*, p. 32
16. Zdral, pp. 13–14
17. Zdral, p. 14
18. Kershaw, *Hoogmoed*, p. 35
19. Kubizek, p. 50
20. Kershaw, *Hoogmoed*, p. 32; Zdral, pp. 13–14

Whether Nepomuk himself wished to secure his inheritance by making Alois a Hitler or it was Alois' initiative isn't clear. It looks like Nepomuk intended to reserve his inheritance for the man he had raised. Widower Nepomuk had three daughters but no male offspring.[21] Although no documents are known showing how Nepomuk's inheritance had been arranged precisely, an indication exists that Alois benefitted most from the inheritance. Soon after Nepomuk's demise in 1888, he bought a farm in Wörnharts near Spital while in the previous period he had no money for this at all. The other children would receive nothing of the inheritance of Nepomuk Hiedler.[22]

Georg or Nepomuk?

Within the Third Reich, Georg Hiedler was the official grandfather of Adolf Hitler, while Alois' father grew up with Nepomuk Hiedler. Historians question Georg's fatherhood though because why didn't he recognise his son while he was still alive and why did he have him raised by his brother? The reason given that Maria Anna and Georg were so poor they couldn't afford to raise their child is questionable.[23] Furthermore, there is no evidence to prove that the mill worker had had a previous relationship with Maria Anna; after all, he married her five years after Alois was born. Prior to that time, Georg would have had no contact with Maria Anna.[24] Yet, the possibility remains that Georg actually was Adolf Hitler's grandfather. The fact that no evidence has been found to the effect that there had been an early relationship between Georg and Maria Anna doesn't mean this relationship had not existed. Georg lived in Spital, a village just 15½ miles from Strones where Maria Anna lived, and Ian Kershaw says Georg had been living with Maria Anna and her father for a while.[25] When this occurred isn't entirely clear but whether he lived with her or not, 15½ miles was easy to cover even at that time.

The Bavarian journalist Wolfgang Zdral, who has occupied himself intensively with the family of Adolf Hitler, suggests, along with various historians,[26] that Nepomuk was Alois' father. Nepomuk raised Alois and that leads to the question whether he would have done the same if Alois

---

21. Zdral, p. 14
22. Zdral, p. 15
23. Kershaw, *Hoogmoed*, p. 34
24. Zdral, p. 15
25. Kershaw, *Hoogmoed*, p. 31
26. Zdral, p. 16

had been the child of his brother. But if Nepomuk really was the father, it remains odd that at the official change of names, Georg was put forward as the father. Nepomuk's wife had already passed away at that time so he didn't have to keep anything from her anymore.

Apart from that, Alois may have had a reason of his own to put up Georg, his mother's husband, and not his educator Nepomuk as the father. In 1876, the year of the name change, Alois' cousin Klara Pölzl was employed as a maid in Alois' family and later on Klara became Alois' wife and the mother of Adolf Hitler. If Alois had a relationship with Klara or had feelings for her, it could have been a reason to have Georg officially named as the father. Nepomuk was actually Klara's grandfather and Georg was no more than the brother of Klara's grandfather. As Alois descended from the Hiedlers as well, he would blow his chances with Klara beforehand if he had Nepomuk named as his official father. His father would then be the official grandfather of his lover and Georg was, being the brother of her grandfather, just a little further down the family tree.

There is no conclusive evidence either for the relationship between Klara and Alois having started at an earlier date. In 1876, Alois was still married to Anna Glassi, whom he divorced in 1888. Subsequently he lived with another woman, Franziska Matzelberger, who – and maybe this is revealing – demanded that maid Klara leave the house. After Franziska had fallen ill, Klara returned to help in the household. As late as 1884, there was a question of an overt relationship between Alois and Klara after Alois' second wife had passed away. Therefore, it is unclear whether Alois busied himself with the consequences of accepting either Nepomuk or Georg as a father as early as 1876. But when Alois and Klara, Adolf Hitler's parents, wanted to get married nine years later, they needed to apply for dispensation from the Catholic Church as they were related. If it had been known that Klara's grandfather was Alois's father, permission to marry would probably never have been granted.

If Nepomuk had officially been labelled as Alois' father it would mean that in Adolf Hitler's direct ancestry a serious case of inbreeding would have occurred. Fortunately for Adolf Hitler, however, his father Alois had the name Georg Hitler entered into the documents. This then became the official view of the Nazis: Georg Hiedler was the grandfather of Adolf Hitler. This 'security' was, of course, of great importance. Inbreeding or a Jewish ancestor would severely blemish Adolf Hitler's reputation and the idea itself of someone ever finding out that the father of the Führer was the son of a man who had impregnated his niece would have been sufficient reason for Adolf Hitler to be cautious on the subject of his family tree.

Inbreeding

Was Adolf Hitler always aware of the Nepomuk problem? A remark in *Mein Kampf*, written in the 1920s, would not make one think so. In this book he writes that his father was the son of a poor small farmer.[27] As Georg had been a mill worker, he must have been talking about Nepomuk.[28] If Hitler had realised what consequence this would have, it is unlikely he would have included it in his book. In *Mein Kampf*, however, Hitler dealt with the facts of his past in a very arbitrary way, making it impossible to draw conclusions based on a loose remark about who was Hitler's grandfather.

As one of the Hiedlers married Maria Anna and the other raised her son, it is obvious that one of the brothers had been the father, certainly considering that Alois was eventually recognised officially as a descendant of the Hiedlers. Whoever was the father of Alois still being unclear,[29] it is imaginable that historians consider Nepomuk's fatherhood likely but it has not been proven. Therefore, the once open space on Alois' birth certificate keeps minds busy up until today.

A Jew from Graz

In a book about Hitler's youth from 1957, Austrian author Franz Jetzinger said the possibility of Hitler having a Jewish ancestor still existed. His source was the unreliable Hans Frank, sentenced for Nazi crimes mentioned earlier, whose work he quoted extensively. Therefore the story of Hitler's Jewish grandfather also found its way to the general public after the war. Although Jetzinger doesn't provide convincing and direct evidence, his assertion was initially taken for granted.[30] This eventually led to the fact that in serious literature about Hitler, even today, three possible grandfathers are discussed. Ian Kershaw enumerates them: Johann Georg Hiedler, Johann Nepomuk Hiedler and a Jewish man[31] named Frankenberger.

The story Frank dictated prior to his execution[32] deserves closer scrutiny, especially because it keeps popping up everywhere. Frank tells in his memoirs, published afterwards by his wife with the revealing title: *Im Angesicht des Galgens* – In view of the Gallows – that in 1930 he was ordered to investigate

---

27. Kershaw, *Hoogmoed*, p. 35; *Mein Kampf*, p. 2
28. Kershaw, *Hoogmoed*, p. 35
29. Kershaw, *Hoogmoed*, p. 31
30. Kershaw, *Hoogmoed*, p. 36
31. Kershaw, *Hoogmoed*, pp. 32–36
32. Rosenbaum, pp. 57–58

the threatening disclosure by William Patrick of the Jewish ancestry of his uncle, Adolf Hitler, at exactly the same moment when in various articles the suggestion was made once again that Hitler had Jewish blood.[33] Hitler received Frank in his apartment on Prinzregentenstrasse in Munich, where Hitler showed him a letter from his nephew, who was blackmailing him. The letter contained threats targeted at Hitler that some facts from the history of the Hitler family had better not be made public.

Frank investigated the case and found out that Adolf Hitler's grandmother, Maria Anna, had worked as a maid for a Jewish family in Graz named Frankenberger where she had been impregnated by Frankenberger junior. Hitler was aware of the story, Frank said, but Hitler told him he had learned from his father and grandmother that Alois wasn't the child of a Jewish man from Graz, but that his grandparents had blackmailed the Frankenbergers. They would have claimed that Frankenberger junior was Alois' father because in this way they were certain of financial support from the rich Frankenbergers for many years to come.[34]

Jetzinger already knew that at the time there was no family named Frankenberger living in Graz and that Jews were forbidden to settle in the province of Stiermarken, but he believed the story nonetheless.[35] Tangible evidence that Maria Anna had ever worked in Graz was missing, though. There were supposedly letters exchanged by Maria Anna and the Frankenbergers but they have never been discovered and Frank was Jetzinger's sole witness who could confirm the existence of this Jewish grandfather. Frank's unreliability and the obvious errors in his story[36] have caused most prominent historians in this field to attach no value whatsoever to the story of Hitler's Jewish grandfather. Even the notion Frank may have been in error of the name of the Jewish family has been looked into. That turned up nothing either.[37] Ian Kershaw therefore concludes: Whoever the grandfather may have been, he was no Jew from Graz.[38]

---

33. Kershaw, *Hoogmoed*, pp. 35–36; Rosenbaum, p. 66–67
34. Kershaw, *Hoogmoed*, pp. 35–36; Jetzinger, pp. 19–24
35. Jetzinger, p. 23
36. Kershaw, *Hoogmoed*, pp. 36–37. Kershaw states that the story about Hitler's grandfather is a fairy tale and that there are so many mistakes in Frank's memoirs that caution is required when quoting Frank, who was in a psychological crisis.
37. Kershaw, *Hoogmoed*, p. 36
38. Kershaw, *Hoogmoed*, p. 37

Hitler was no Jew

Suggestive stories about Hitler's Jewish grandfather keep popping up everywhere. They are often based on the untrue story by Hans Frank, but frequently they are also the result of serious misunderstanding or ignorance. In various messages, chosen at random on internet forums, one can read for instance that Adolf Hitler's grandmother is supposed to be a Jewess.[39] Outside the paper world of serious historians, the wildest stories still circulate in which suggestion is more important than argumentation. Like many conspiracy theories and other spectacular tales, the story about the Jew who exterminated his own people is obviously so intriguing it almost has to be handed down. Just because of that, it remains important to distinguish between fact and fiction about Hitler's ancestry.

As the only serious Jewish candidate for Hitler's grandfatherhood was a Jew from Graz, it can only be concluded, based on the presented evidence, that Hitler didn't have a Jewish grandfather.[40] The Jewish family that was named didn't even live in Graz at the time. To put it more strongly, almost no Jews could be found in the entire province of Stiermarken as they were officially banned from living there. Evidence proving that Hitler's grandmother, Maria Anna, had ever been in Graz is missing, just like the letters that would prove that the Jewish Frankenberger family was being blackmailed by Adolf Hitler's grandparents.[41]

Then what is the explanation for the conspicuous drive of Hitler and his followers to keep the family history of the Führer under wraps and possibly eradicate it altogether? First of all, it must be stressed that the speculations about Hitler's ancestry are not the only stories from Hitler's history the Nazis were so secretive about. Numerous sources of ticklish issues from Hitler's past were either destroyed[42] during the Nazi period or adapted to fit the ideology of National Socialism.[43] That is how the image of the Führer of Germany was kept as pure as possible.

Furthermore, it is unlikely that Hitler was completely ignorant about his family's history, as he suggested himself. If he hadn't known before that something in his family tree wasn't right, he would have read about it in

---
39. For instance on forum.scholieren.com en forums.hababam.nl
40. Lukacs, p. 179
41. Kershaw, *Hoogmoed*, p. 36
42. Hamann, HW, p. 197
43. Hamann, HW, pp. 206–207. When Hitler also rose to power in Austria, the house in Vienna in which he is supposed to have lived in 1909 was for instance adorned with wreaths and an honour guard of boys from the Hitler Youth, although he had never lived there.

the papers in the 1920s. What Hitler knew exactly, or thought he knew, is unknown. He probably entertained at least the same doubts as today's historians, who still can't say which of the two Hiedler brothers was Alois' father. A possible third father of Hitler couldn't be ruled out, which explains why he did his best to eradicate the history of the family as much as possible. The fact that it made quite a difference whether Hitler's mother had married the son of her grandfather Nepomuk or the son of her grandfather's brother Georg must have played a role as well.

The major cause of all the speculation about Hitler's ancestry was, of course, that the name of the father of Alois Hitler was initially omitted from the official documents. In combination with the silence of Alois' mother about who her partner had been and the illegal change of names when Georg, who had long since passed away, was named Alois' father, this became the basis for Hitler's silence about his own ancestry. Furthermore, the history of Alois, who had been born from a more or less incestuous relationship, had been married multiple times and had fathered children on three women, must also have been a reason for Hitler's silence on this subject.

Whatever the reason had been for grandmother Maria Anna and the Hiedler brothers to keep silent about the fatherhood of Alois, it remains shrouded in history. They didn't know, of course, that Nepomuk's granddaughter Klara would enter into a relationship with Alois, Nepomuk's possible son, so the Nepomuk problem wasn't relevant at the time. That Hitler's mother Klara was employed in Alois' home after he had been accepted as the son of Georg might have been the reason to have Georg officially labelled as the father can't be proven either.

Only when Hitler had become a well-known anti-Semite did the question of a possible Jewish grandfather arose. This initially made the suggestion implausible that Maria Anna Schicklgruber had long before kept quiet about the name of a Jewish lover. Of course, there were enough people who attached value to this spectacular story, if only for political purposes. But proof of Hitler's Jewish ancestry was missing then just as it is today, after many years of research without intervention by the Nazis. The involvement of the Hiedler brothers with Alois' fate and the registration of one of them as the father eventually formed the major indication that Hitler was just a descendant of one of the Hiedler brothers and not of a Jewish man from Graz. That is until 2009, when Belgian journalist Jean-Paul Mulders came up with a conspicuous report about his attempts to obtain DNA material from the American descendants of Hitler's father Alois in order to compare it to the material of the descendants of the Hitlers still living in Austria. If he could compare both groups it could be established whether Alois' descendants had Hitler's blood or not. If that were true, it would mean Alois was a real Hitler and therefore, Adolf as well. The prediction of the most serious historians of our time came true. There was a match between the material of Alois' grandchildren and that of the Hitlers still living in Austria. Since then, it has been an established fact that Adolf Hitler descended from one of the Hiedler brothers in the Waldviertel in Austria and not from a Jewish man in Graz.

Chapter 2

Did Hitler Live in Poverty?

The sad story of a poor wanderer

'Vienna only evokes bad memories of the saddest time of my life. The name of this fairy town means five years of starvation and misery for me.[1] *At the time, hunger was my closest companion, the only one that never left me,'*[2] *Adolf Hitler wrote in* Mein Kampf. *He called the chapter in which he wrote this 'Learning and suffering in Vienna' and in view of propaganda, it wasn't a bad move. Didn't every genius spend a time of adversity and privations? Or was what he wrote more than propaganda and had his time in Vienna really been that difficult? In the 1970s, historian Werner Maser claimed something different. He said Hitler had quite a lot of money at his disposal when he lived in Vienna.*

It isn't so strange that doubt exists about Hitler's poverty. Hitler himself had never been clear about it one way or the other. Initially, he wrote in *Mein Kampf* that he experienced hunger and misery in Vienna for five years but a little further down he writes: 'In 1909 and 1910, a change had occurred in my own situation, insofar as I didn't have to earn my daily living as a loose worker. At the time I was already employed as an illustrator and painter of watercolours'[3] Obviously, from 1909 onwards Hitler didn't suffer from starvation anymore. As late as the end of the twentieth century, a book entitled *Hitlers Wien* by German-Austrian historian Brigitte Hamann was published that definitely cleared up the issue.

The value of the Austrian Kron

At the time, Hitler lived in Vienna, the official Austrian currency was the Kron. In the 1950s, Franz Jetzinger asserted that some 1,000 Kron was

---

1. Combined quation from *Mein Kampf*, p. 20
2. *Mein Kampf*, p. 21
3. *Mein Kampf*, p. 34

sufficient for Hitler to sustain him for a year.[1] According to Werner Maser, a young teacher earned some 66 Kron a month and a lawyer about 70,[2] some 800 Kron a year. Brigitte Hamann put it more precisely. She stated that a student's scholarship amounted to some 800 Kron at the time but students had to make money on the side to make ends meet. The minimum sustenance level stood at 1,200 Kron. A bridge keeper made between 1,600 and 2,200, a teacher between 2,200 and 2,800 and a tax inspector between 2,800 and 3,600.[3] Therefore, 1,000 Kron would hardly be enough to make ends meet.

The difference in interpretation of how much one needed was the result of Jetzinger's wish, and especially Maser's, to prove that Hitler already had much money at his disposal in Vienna. Both writers wanted to show Hitler's poverty wasn't that bad and in order to claim this they twisted the facts accordingly.

A wealthy man

Before Hitler went to Vienna in 1908,[4] he had the money from the inheritance of his father at his disposal, Franz Jetzinger wrote. This initially amounted to 651 Kron. In 1910, he is supposed to have received a fair amount of money from an aunt out of an inheritance of 3,800 Kron, of which Hitler received a sizable part.[5] Maser overstated this a little. He claims Hitler didn't only have his father's part on the inheritance at his disposal but an orphans' allowance as well, together good for 108 Kron. In addition, he received a sizable amount of money from his aunt, Johanna Pölzl, after the demise of his mother. On top of that he received a sum that had originally belonged to his great-aunt Walburga Romedor. She had passed away in 1900, but at the time the money had been paid to his grandmother and through his mother part of it found its way to him. Hitler was, according to Maser, a wealthy man in Vienna.[6]

Very large sums?

Jetzinger's estimate of Hitler's wealth, on which Maser elaborated, probably matched the post-war mood in which many of Hitler's lies were unveiled but, whatever they said, only a little was right. Maser's theory about Hitler

---

1. Jetzinger, p. 139. Jetzinger asserts 2,000 Kron a year would be sufficient for two years.
2. Maser, AW1, p. 83
3. Hamann, HW, p. 148
4. Hitler had been in Vienna before but this time he settled for a longer period.
5. Hamann, HW, p. 65; Jetzinger, pp. 139–141
6. Maser, AW1, p. 83

having received a sizable inheritance from a great-aunt has no basis in fact. It is unknown how much money the woman possessed and so Maser was unable to mention sums. It has not been recorded anywhere what happened to this unknown amount after the demise of this great-aunt. If the money had been there, part of it could have gone to his mother through his grandmother. But even if it was a sizable amount, the question arises whether there was enough left of it when Hitler was old enough to inherit. The great-aunt passed away as early as 1900, Hitler's grandmother died in 1906 and his mother in 1907. Could this farmer's daughter and great-aunt of Hitler, Walburga Romedor, have been so wealthy that even after dividing the inheritance seven years later a sizable amount would have been left over?

That is debatable. It is more important, however, that any evidence of the existence of this inheritance is missing. Nonetheless, and without any argumentation, Maser takes it for granted that Hitler had received 'large amounts' of money from this inheritance, making him a distinctively wealthy man.[7]

Part of his father's inheritance was waiting for him but it could only be paid when Adolf had reached the age of 24. He received it in May 1913. The inheritance, including interest, amounted to 820 Kron.[8] According to Maser, he could sustain himself in Vienna for a year but he didn't stay there. In late May 1913, he moved to Munich with just an amount of money he could actually live on for a few months in his pocket.

Poverty

Maser's presentation of the matter wasn't correct after all but Hitler's own description of his time in Vienna, consisting of poverty and misery, is a myth for the most part as well. It had everything to do with the Führer and genius cults that were much more important in *Mein Kampf* than reality. A true genius who could help Germany get back on her feet had, of course, known hard times in the past and he would have had to have wrestled his way out of it.

The autobiographic fragments about Vienna in his book had been clearly written from a political point of view.[9] In Vienna, Hitler never had enough money to spend. From about the time he left the town of his puberty, Linz, for good and headed for Vienna, he was paid a monthly orphan's allowance

---

7. Hamann, HW, p. 65
8. Hamann, HW p. 65
9. Kershaw, HW, p. 65

of 25 Kron at least until 1911. His sister Paula received the same amount.[10] In addition, after the death of his mother in late 1907, he had inherited 1,000 Kron. He could sustain himself with it in Vienna for a while. He paid his landlady 10 Kron a month for rent.[11] The other 10 Kron for the room he had rented and shared with his friend August Kubizek would have been paid by the latter.

Hitler's elder half-sister Angela Raubal, by the way, thought he had to go and find a job so he could give his allowance to his sister, Paula.[12] Hitler had no plans in that direction though and he preferred to let his relationship with his family cool down rather than abstain from the money. He wasn't eager to go to work, and the story about him having worked as a builder in Vienna for a while has not been confirmed by a single witness. In August 1908, he did receive a loan of 924 Kron from his aunt, Johanna Pölzl, enough to hold out for a few more months[13] but from then on his financial situation deteriorated steadily. Two months after having received the loan, he left the student's room he shared. His friend August, who lived with him, was out of town at that time. Years later, they met each other again when Hitler had been Reich Chancellor of Germany for quite a while.

Subsequently, Hitler lived at another address in Vienna[14] until 20 August 1909 but, according to Brigitte Hamann, almost all information from that year is missing. It is very likely though that this period was, financially speaking, the hardest in Hitler's life. Rents in Vienna went through the roof and even people with a steady job could only afford them with difficulty.[15] Unemployment also increased and in winter the day care shelters in the city, rooms with a stove meant for homeless people, were overcrowded, even with entire families who lacked the money to heat their homes for the whole day.[16]

From late summer 1909 onwards, Hitler's financial situation was so bad he left the third room[17] he rented in Vienna as of 22 August within three weeks, probably because he couldn't afford the rent.[18]

During the next three months, Hitler was probably homeless. He could go to charity institutions like the Samaritan Sisters for a cup of soup. The

---

10. Bruppacher, p. 19
11. Hamann, HW, p. 67. The rent for the 'large' room in which they both lived amounted to a total of 20 Kron.
12. After Hitler's mother had passed away, Paula Hitler lived with Angela Raubal.
13. Hamann, HW, p. 147
14. He had moved from Stumpergasse 31 to Felberstrasse 22.
15. Hamann, HW, p. 153
16. Hamann, HW, p. 160
17. In a home on Sechshauerstrasse 58
18. Hamann, HW, p. 154

Did Hitler Live in Poverty? 17

autumn of 1909 and the subsequent period must have been harsh on Hitler. He lived like a tramp and would probably have spent his nights in reception centres or shelters.

After November 1909, Hitler ended up in a home for men in the suburb of Meidling and a few months on, in February 1910, he lived in a somewhat better home at Meldemannstrasse. Lodging in the safe and relatively tidy house wasn't free though and the majority of the tenants had a job and an income. Most acquaintances of Hitler in these homes for males were Jews, by the way. Together with a friend from the home, Hitler decided to set up a shop selling paintings. He painted and his companion sold them, often through small Jewish shop owners and sometimes after accepting an order from a Jew. But first Hitler needed painting material and without money that was impossible.

Consequently, Hitler decided to rekindle the relationship with his family, in particular with his aunt Johanna, who had helped him before. He sent her a letter, which earned him 50 Kron,[19] enough to buy painting material.

Hitler's harshest period was over, although he didn't make much money yet. He probably earned between 3 to 5 Kron per painting[20] and sometimes he earned a little more for a somewhat larger order. After a quarrel with his companion, he decided to sell his work himself; this meant he didn't have to share his profit with anyone else anymore, but still he wasn't the wealthy man he had been said to have been at the time, as claimed by Maser. The fact that he had an income of his own led in 1911 to him being sentenced by a judge to hand over his part of the orphan's allowance to his sister, Paula. This meant a serious loss of income; from that moment on, he had to make do with between 20 and 40 Kron monthly. With a maximum of 500 Kron a year, he lived way below the minimum sustenance level of 1200. But there was hope yet.

On 16 May 1913, he finally turned 24 and received the heritance of his father. Afterwards, he still had to paint to make a living but with 819 Kron and 98 Heller [unit of coinage] on him[21] he was finally able to do what he wanted: leave for Munich. A little over a week later, he left the city of Vienna where he had lived through such a hard time, as he said himself.

---

19. Hamann, HW, p. 169
20. Hamann, HW, p. 176
21. Hamann, HW, p. 423

Simon Denk Gasse

Many years later, in 1938, various papers in Austria published articles about a house in which Hitler was supposed to have rented a room while still living in Vienna. The front page of the *Neuigkeits-Welt-Blatt* showed a full-size picture of the house on the Simon Denk Gasse 11 with a large picture of Hitler over the front door.[22] Two members of the Hitler Youth are standing guard at the entrance. According to the article, this was the house in which Hitler is said to have lived but, strangely enough, in the article nothing is written about the other addresses and shelters where Hitler had lived.

If Hitler lived here, it must have been during the three months he was wandering around but this is implausible. The house is located in a better suburb that those where Hitler lived previously and it would have been crazy that between his cheap rooms and his stay in hostels, he should have rented a room that was far more expensive. Hamann pointed out that no written evidence exists that shows Hitler ever lived on the Simon Denk Gasse. In her opinion, it was a conscious deception, making research into Hitler's actual whereabouts in Vienna impossible.[23] The question is: why was this necessary? Hitler usually did not want too much digging into his past but it was weird that for some reason his poverty had to be veiled in view of the statements he made about it in *Mein Kampf*. We will probably never find out what was behind this publication.

Exaggeration

Hitler was far from being rich when he lived in Vienna. The suggestion he had been hungry and had lived in bitter poverty for five years was equally untrue, however. Both Maser and Hitler had overstated things: Hitler with the clear political goal in mind to present himself as the genius who had known hard times, Maser with the intention to catch Hitler on a lie. It was true, Hitler lived a sober life in Vienna and that he had a hard time as a homeless person, in particular in the years 1909–10. But afterwards, he swung into action. With his paintings and his father's inheritance, he could choose another direction. And that direction was Munich, the location of the new starting point from where Hitler would build his Nazi empire.

---

22. Hamann, HW, p. 155
23. Hamann, HW, p. 155

Chapter 3

Adolf Hitler, a Hero?

His role as a soldier in The First World War

'Hitler distinguished himself in battle as one of the most courageous soldiers. His comrades from that time later said they had often wondered why Hitler hadn't been struck by a bullet much earlier. As he was so courageous and so dependable, he was appointed as courier. He was to run under enemy rifle fire to take messages from one officer to another. This was extremely dangerous but Hitler always did his duty with courage and imperturbability. For this, the Emperor first awarded him with the Eisernes Kreuz 2 and later on even with the EK 1 for which only the most courageous soldiers were eligible,'[1] *according to the children's book* Die Geschichte von Adolf Hitler den Deutschen Kindern erzählt *(The history of Adolf Hitler as told to German children) published in 1941.*

A better summary of the myths about Hitler's military past during the First World War is hardly imaginable: Hitler was very brave; his job was a very dangerous one and in particular his decorations and the statements of his comrades in arms emphasize this. And yet, uncertainty about these 'facts from the Nazi period' has existed for so long that well-known Hitler's biographers hardly make statements about his experiences during the First World War.

An enthusiastic start

The war of 1914 was something the whole nation longed for,[2] Hitler wrote in *Mein Kampf*. One of the best-known examples of proof of the enthusiasm to which Hitler referred is a picture taken by future court photographer

---

1. Quote from the aforementioned children's book of 1941 about Hitler, as translated in Weber's *Adolf Hitler en de Eerste Wereldoorlog*, p. 106
2. *Mein Kampf*, p. 180. The quote reads verbatim: 'That war of 1914 was probably not pressed upon the masses but it was something the entire population longed for.'

Heinrich Hoffmann at the Odeonplatz in Munich. The picture shows a cheering crowd, one day after the German declaration of war.[3] After the war, Hitler saw this picture and told him he had been in the square as well. Hoffmann made an enlargement and discovered Hitler standing among the people in the centre of the picture. It was often published with a circle or square around Hitler's head.[4] It was good propaganda. In 1936 for instance, it was published in the *Illustrierte Beobachter*, a picture magazine that was sold all over Germany.[5] It is striking that the Hitler of 1914 already sported the characteristic thin moustache for which he became so well-known later on. In a review of Hitler portraits in the same magazine we see him as late as 1921 with the same famous moustache[6] but in other pictures of between 1914 and 1928 he always wears a normal, bushy moustache. A meaningless detail or is more going on?

Hoffmann has probably edited the picture. This isn't certain as the negative no longer exists and there are, of course, other explanations for the difference of the size of the moustache.[7] But it is conspicuous that Fritz Wiedemann, Hitler's direct superior during the First World War, only knew him with a large moustache. When he met him again after the war, the external change immediately struck him; Hitler had trimmed his moustache.[8] A picture that had been tampered with would perfectly match the way the Nazis manipulated Hitler's military past.

The Langemarck myth

One of the first myths about the First World War that became known all over Germany and was referred to by Hitler in *Mein Kampf* was the so-called *Langemarck-Mythos*.[9] This myth arose on 11 November 1914 when,

---

3. Herz, p. 29
4. Kershaw, *Hoogmoed*, p. 137, 157
5. *Illustrierter Beobachter*, pp. 12–13. The picture is next to a similar picture from the winter of 1919–20 at the Wittelsbachrer Brunnen in Munich. It shows Hitler, again in the front ranks, listening to a man protesting against the 'dictate of Versailles' imposed on Germany after the war. But this second picture is much more blurred and it is doubtful whether it really is Hitler.
6. *Illustrierter Beobachter*, pp. 42–43
7. The rumour goes that Hitler possibly trimmed his moustache in connection with wearing a gas mask.
8. Wiedemann, *Der Spiegel* nr. 47/1964
9. Unruh, p. 10. The name of the village of Langemark is spelled without the c. In Germany, however, it was written with a c to make it look more German. Actually, the base of the myth must have been west of Langemark near the village of Bixschote.

in a report of the German military leadership, there was an entry about young soldiers who stormed the enemy west of Langemarck loudly singing *Deutschland, Deutschland über alles*. Entire regiments, pupils and students are said to have sacrificed their youth for the fatherland. Soon, Langemarck became the symbol of youthful enthusiasm and self-sacrificing.

In *Mein Kampf*, Hitler also described his own baptism of fire in the spirit of this Langemarck myth. Although Hitler's regiment didn't fight in the direct vicinity of Langemarck, Hitler's description contains the same elements. The young soldiers in his regiment responded to the first shelling with a loud hooray and sang *Deutschland, Deutschland über alles* at the top of their voices while going straight to their death. After four days of battle, the 17-year-old youngsters who had survived looked like old men, according to Hitler.[10]

It looks very much as if Hitler had contributed to the creation of the Langemarck myth with his description. In reports about the battles in the region, the same elements appear and they may be an indication that they are probably founded on incorrect assumptions. Thus, Hitler's version was a myth but the original story of Langemarck itself was a myth as well. For instance, in the report of 11 November 1914, the claim that most soldiers were very young doesn't match with the statistics of the age structure of the various regiments;[11] the number of volunteers being large is questionable[12] as well, and there is even uncertainty about the singing of the *Deutschlandlied*.[13]

It also happens that soldiers had been ordered to shout hooray as soon as they stormed the enemy positions, so that yell was more than just an expression of enthusiasm. Would Hitler have replaced reality with the myth of Langemarck? When one reads the long letter about his first battle he sent to an acquaintance in Munich[14] and compares it to the corresponding fragment in *Mein Kampf*, it does look like it. In this letter of 5 February 1915, nothing is said about the shouting of hooray. As to singing, Hitler writes, the soldiers did just that – many for the last time – in Lille before they went to the front. And as to the *Deutschlandlied*, nothing is said in the letter either. Hitler used the Langemarck myth as the source for his own biography. That way, Langemarck eventually became part of the cult of the Third Reich.[15]

---

10. *Mein Kampf*, p. 184
11. Unruh, p. 63
12. Unruh, pp. 64–68
13. Unruh, pp. 14–15; Weber, pp. 53–54
14. A letter to Ernst Hepp, included in Maser, *Hitlers brieven en notities*. The letter can also be read in Maser`s *Adolf Hitler, Legende, Mythos, Wirklichkeit*, pp. 130–136
15. Consequently, the Langemarckhalle was built in the grounds of the Berlin Olympic stadium in 1936. An opening in the stands offered a view on the tower that was erected

Hitler as a hero

Although Hitler seems to deal extensively with the First World War in a number of chapters in *Mein Kampf*, he actually tells almost nothing about his own service in that war. For instance, he keeps silent about the fact he had only been a foot soldier for eleven days or so. He arrived in Flanders in late October 1914 and on 9 November 1914 he found himself appointed as staff courier.[16] This function has always been the source of discussion as far as Hitler's status as a hero is concerned. What did he actually do after 9 November? Loiter at some headquarters far behind the front lines? Or had he been a courier with the extremely dangerous task of taking messages to and from the forward lines?

As Hitler gained fame, the Nazis went out of their way to reconstruct the past of their Führer in as fitting a way as possible. In *Mein Kampf*, Hitler made such an attempt but in particular during the 1930s much was published about his military past. Old cronies from his regiment such as Balthasar Brandmayer, Hans Mend and Adolf Meyer, wrote books about Hitler's experiences, a history of the List regiment,[17] of which Hitler had been a member, was published and the press published all sorts of articles about his military past. Critical minds also made themselves heard and claimed Hitler hadn't been so heroic after all. After the seizure of power in 1938, there obviously was only room for non-critical publications and, particularly in books for the young, Hitler's role in the First World War was glorified.

Solleder and Meyer

The history of *Hitler's Reserve-Infanterie-Regiment 16 List* by archivist and member of the regiment Dr Fridolin Solleder was published in 1932 and didn't contain a single trace of Hitler glorification. In the 500-page book, former warriors, commanders and even a British soldier describe the history of the regiment. It mainly deals with personal experiences of soldiers that, in addition to the more objective descriptions by Solleder himself, lend the book the necessary drama. Apart from some references and in a picture, Hitler doesn't appear in it. In the introduction, reference is immediately made to the Langemarck myth. The List regiment, so Solleder writes, sang

---

    on top of this memorial building.
16. Weber, p. 63
17. Adolf Hitler served in the Bavarian 16. Reserve Infanterie Regiment. The regiment was named after its first commander, Julius List who was killed in action during the battle of Geluveld as early as 1914.

the anthem *Wacht am Rhein* near the village of Geluveld before it went to war, fourteen days before the battle of Langemarck began.

In the book *Mit Adolf Hitler im Bayerischen Reserve-Infanterie-Regiment 16 List* by Adolf Meyer, published in 1934, one year after the seizure of power by the Nazis, the author does deal extensively with Hitler's military past. It contains an introduction by fanatic National Socialist Julius Streicher, in which it becomes immediately clear that the book was written to fend off the assertion that Hitler had been a cowardly soldier. But even though Meyer attempts to attribute a prominent role to Hitler, his own experiences seem to be far more important than his rare meetings with Hitler.[18]

The first time Meyer met courier Hitler was at the end of June 1915. Meyer and another subaltern officer were at an assembly point of the army near the French village of Fromelles. Both men wanted to have a picture taken of themselves and were looking for someone who could do so. By chance, they saw Adolf Hitler who was, and that was mentioned explicitly, between the front line and the Starnberg base[19] on his way to Fromelles. Hitler was asked to take the picture and, of course, it was included in the book in evidence. Meyer indicates he would certainly have forgotten the meeting if he hadn't met Hitler more frequently later on.[20] Here, it is indicated that Hitler moved between the front line and the location of the regimental staff. An important fact as this event continues to play a role until today.

The second meeting between Hitler and Meyer took place at roughly the same location. Meyer was tasked with keeping horse-drawn carriages away from the front to spare the valuable animals. One night, Meyer stopped a coach on its way to the so-called Rote Bänke. A battalion commander was in the coach and he was obviously not overly pleased that he and his adjutant had been stopped. They got off anyway and Meyer went to look for someone who could take them to the Rote Bänke on foot. After some searching, Meyer met Adolf Hitler, who took the two men along.[21] Hitler appeared to be the only one to have helped Meyer out; he also was one of the few who knew the way to Rote Bänke, a location just behind the forward line.

Meyer also deals with one of the occasions when Hitler was injured near the Somme and had to leave the battlefield. He stresses that Hitler returned to his old regiment as soon as he had recuperated and this, he says, weakens

---

18. Here, only the meetings with Hitler are being discussed.
19. The Germans gave German names to all sorts of locations in the vicinity.
20. Meyer, pp. 32–33
21. Meyer, pp. 35–36

the criticism of Hitler's political opponents that as soldier he didn't amount to much.

Later on in the war, the regiment was deployed near Roeux. In a chaotic afternoon, Meyer was escorted by Hitler from the regimental command post to the front line. When they were subjected to heavy fire, Meyer's first reaction as a soldier was to seek cover until the shelling stopped. Hitler, on the other hand, attempted to escape from the cauldron as soon as possible, using the natural cover the terrain offered. Meyer just had to go along. The return trip proceeded in more or less the same way and both soldiers came through unscathed. Meyer made it clear that he always had the feeling that on this kind of mission he was in less danger because of Hitler coming along.[22]

A final story Meyer tells about his former crony Hitler, who had meanwhile risen to *Reichskanzler* at the time the book was published, having entered a room one day where Meyer and a number of others were being instructed by a usually less complimentary commander. Hitler handed a message to the major and left. After he had gone, the major is supposed to have said that when he gave this courier an order, he could be sure of it being carried out the way his best officers would have done.[23]

Meyer's book makes it clear that Hitler was a first rate courier who was known for his drive but the only story that resembles a hero's story was the mutual trip when Hitler skilfully slipped across hazardous terrain.

The rider on the grey horse

Regimental crony Hans Mend, who became known as the 'wild hunter of the List regiment' also wrote a book in the 1930s about Hitler during the First World War,[24] in which he portrayed Hitler as an eminent soldier. He says: 'Hitler was courageous, fearless and excellent.'[25] The Nazi press praised the book as a Christmas present for every Hitler follower and a year later it was used in the failed presidential election campaign.[26] At the time, Mend was a follower of the NSDAP and considered it his duty to tell the real story about Adolf Hitler. 'Anyone who knew him at the front will have to admit he was an exemplary front soldier who as battle courier in the trench warfare has made superhuman achievements at his dangerous and responsible

---

22. Meyer, pp. 65–66
23. Meyer, p. 78
24. Entitled *Adolf Hitler im Felde*
25. Weber, p. 107
26. Weber, p. 304

post.'²⁷ It is doubtful whether Hitler himself was pleased with the book as it also contains funny stories in which he appears to be somewhat clumsy, for instance when he was charging rats with his sabre in the middle of the night.²⁸ But in the end, this book also tells a positive story about Hitler's role in the war. Mend had, in his own words, the opportunity to frequently observe Hitler's courage and at the time got to know his exemplary nature in battle.²⁹

Other friends of Hitler

In 1915, Balthasar Brandmayer was a new member of the group of couriers and became Hitler's inseparable comrade.³⁰ He also wrote a book about him in the early 1930s when, publication wise, this was so important for Hitler. Brandmayer recalls a trip between Fromelles and Aubers in northern France when shells rained down all around them. Hitler wouldn't stop and dragged Brandmayer on each time. Once having returned safely, Hitler was on the alert again, waiting for a new assignment when Brandmayer, extremely exhausted as he was, took a nap.³¹

Fritz Wiedemann, regimental adjutant and as such in charge of the couriers, was pleased with the Austrian soldier. Hitler was one of the most reliable couriers he had and he kept that image alive until well after he Second World War, even when he published a book about Hitler in the mid-1960s entitled *Der Mann der Feldherr werden wollte*. He managed to recall that Hitler got injured during a shelling of the regimental headquarters. Despite his injuries, Hitler wanted to stay with the regiment.³²

Whether that should show his heroism remains a question. Probably Hitler wanted to stay with the regiment rather than end up in an insecure situation, either at home or at the front. But Wiedemann was positive about Hitler's commitment. Although the couriers, like the regimental staff, led a relatively cozy life when it was quiet at the front, sometimes they had to make their way to the front line under enemy fire.³³Max Amann was another comrade who was Hitler's superior during the First World War. After 1945, Amann still praised Hitler's role in the war. Whenever Amann

---

27. Machtan, *Hitlers intieme kring*, p. 74
28. Machtan, p. 75
29. Maser, HMK, p. 141
30. Russell, p. 88
31. Russell, pp. 88–89
32. *Der Spiegel*, nr. 47/1964 & Joachimsthaler, p. 165
33. Joachimsthaler, p. 127

needed a courier at night, Hitler was always ready to do the job. When Hitler was once again the one to stand up to do his duty, Amann said once: 'Always you!' Hitler is supposed to have said that Amann should let the others sleep.[34]

Brandmayer, Wiedemann, Amann and Mend[35] all said that it was hard to find fault with the courier Hitler. But these comrades in arms were also followers of Hitler who joined the NSDAP. Their judgment of Hitler was, of course, far from objective. Brandmayer was known for being Hitler's friend and that helped him to obtain various roles. Until 1939, Wiedemann was employed as Hitler's personal adjutant and Amann was named *Reichsleiter* NSDAP and manager of the Nazi publishing firm of Eher. As to Mend's judgment, is it also difficult to say whether it was objective but that was for quite different reasons.

Propaganda and the rise of myths

In October 1934, a group of Nazis organised a reunion for the Regiment List in Munich. Although the magazine *Der Illustrierte Beobachter* covered it extensively, the reunion ended in failure. Many members of the regiment failed to show up and the pictures that were taken mostly showed walk-ons. Mainly followers of Hitler from the old regiment attended. Hitler wasn't present either. Historian Thomas Weber assumes Hitler wasn't there because he knew many members of his former regiment didn't think too kindly about him. For the magazine, this was no problem at all: it just used an old picture of Hitler for its report about the reunion.[36] This fitted Hitler's strategy in the first period of his leadership like a glove. On the one hand, he vehemently attacked his opponents, on the other, much propaganda was made for the virtues of Nazism, in which the fabricated wartime experiences of the Führer also played a role. They were even deemed so important that they were included in history lessons.[37]

In order to imbue the youth with the importance of the Führer, Hitler appeared in all sorts of publications. In 1939 for instance, a special edition of a newspaper entitled *Adolf Hitler im Weltkrieg* targeted at the *Hitler Jugend* was published containing Hitler's experiences in the First World War. And apart from maths books with drawings of swastikas, pictures

---

34. Russell, p. 89
35. Mend would soon change his view on this.
36. Weber, pp. 317–318
37. Weber, pp. 319

and songbooks for the youngest with lyrics like: *'Wir hören die Musik, Wir hören die Trommel. Wir hören: Sieg Heil! Sieg Heil! Sieg Heil!'* (We hear the music, we hear the drums, we hear: Sieg Heil! Sieg Heil! Sieg Heil! – Hail to the Chief), booklets about the heroic acts of the Führer during the war were published as well. A famous story that schoolchildren were told was an action in which the Führer overwhelmed twelve Frenchmen all by himself. This story, which also existed in a version with British soldiers, was loosely based on reality but had nothing to do with Hitler himself.[38] In another book, the author had noticed that in *Mein Kampf* almost nothing was said about Hitler's own experiences during the war but he explained it away by saying that Hitler had always been modest about his achievements. The book emphasizes, however, that Hitler had been the best courier, that the trenches had been his home and that for months on end, he didn't have his own bed at his disposal.[39]

An event that must certainly have occurred and for which Hitler was even decorated took place in the so-called Bayernwald near the village of Wijtschate in Belgium. There, the Germans had been involved in heavy combat against the French for days when regimental commander Philipp Engelhardt, along with the couriers Anton Bachmann and Adolf Hitler, went to take a look at the edge of the forest in which the Germans were hiding. When Engelhardt proceeded outside the cover of the woods he was immediately subjected to fire and both couriers didn't hesitate a second. They threw themselves at their commander and dragged him into a ditch. After the loss of his predecessor Julius List they couldn't bear losing a commander again.[40] Hitler was to receive the *Eisernes Kreuz 2* for this. But this version of the story is from 1932, while the version recorded in 1915 was quite different. That year, there had been four couriers protecting Engelhardt, who wasn't under fire.

It is most conspicuous that Bachmann is portrayed as the hero in 1915 and not Hitler. Bachmann had climbed out of the trench to rescue an injured soldier. It goes without saying that the 1932 version was part of the pro-Hitler propaganda while the 1915 version, when Hitler was still completely unknown, hadn't yet been infected with it.[41] Bachmann was unable to protest as he was killed during the First World War.

---

38. Weber, pp. 242–243
39. Beier-Lindhardt, pp. 34–38
40. Van Capelle & Van de Bovenkamp, pp. 74–75
41. Weber, pp. 63–64

Henry Tandey

The massive glorification of Hitler as a war hero was mainly the work of his fanatic followers but Hitler may have played a part in it as well. In 1937, through his war comrade adjutant Wiedemann, he obtained a painting showing a scene from the First World War. Hitler must have said at a certain moment that he recognised the brave English soldier in the painting. At the end of the day, and based on that remark, a story was born that would haunt English soldier Henry Tandey for years. The story goes that on 28 September 1918, at the front in the French village of Marcoing, the Englishman is supposed to have spared the life of a German soldier at whom he had pointed his rifle. As the soldier was injured, he had let him go. This German soldier is supposed to have been Hitler, another proof that he had been active in the forward lines. Tandey would be known as the 'man who saved Hitler' until his death.[42]

This event also hadn't taken place in this way. On said date, Hitler wasn't even in Marcoing. He had just returned from leave and was stationed in the vicinity of Wervicq, over 62 miles from Marcoing. How would he have covered this sizable distance, all alone and have returned as a wounded man? In 2012, a thin booklet about Tandey, entitled *The Man Who Didn't Shoot Hitler*, was published, resulting in a minor internet hype. The spectacular story about two soldiers standing eye to eye popped up everywhere, without mentioning, by the way, that the story, in particular in the last chapter of the booklet, is completely being blown to pieces. In that way (heroic) stories about Hitler, reliable or not, are being sucked dry well into our time.

Why was it necessary to portray Hitler as a hero anyway? In order to answer that question, we must go back to the 1930s. Although Hitler had been wise enough to leave his role in the war more or less open in *Mein Kampf*, during these years he was under frequent attacks by his political opponents. In his book *Adolf Hitler im Ersten Weltkrieg*, Thomas Weber states that two things occurred in reaction to each other: political opponents who wanted to prove that Hitler was a liar were looking for discrepancies being told about him and simultaneously the Nazis tried to keep the Hitler myth alive. When Hitler ran for president in 1932, the attacks on him became even more violent.[43] In order to fend off these attacks, numerous war stories about him were published, especially in the early 1930s.

---

42. Johnson, from p. 143
43. Weber, p. 312

Hitler was a coward

The attempts to portray Hitler as a coward aren't something from after the Second World War. The first expressions of doubt about his heroism stem from the time when he rose to become the leader of the National Socialists. In March 1923, the *Münchener Post* wrote in an article about Hitler that he hadn't been at the front line for a long time but in a safer zone behind it. The injuries he is supposed to have sustained wouldn't have amounted to much either.[44]

Hitler as a soldier had only seen fighting for ten days or so. On 9 November 1914, right after his first battle, he was named courier on the regimental staff. He sustained his first injury in that capacity. But this didn't happen in combat, his opponents claimed, but because a stray shell came down in the very garden where he was sunbathing. He would have received his military decorations mainly for the work he had done far behind the front.[45] Speculation like that kept haunting Hitler until just prior to the elections in 1933. Papers such as the *Münchener Post, Frankfurter Zeitung, Berliner Tageblatt* and the political paper *Der gerade Weg* published articles criticising Hitler. After 1933, these papers were either banned or brought into line.

Der gerade Weg

A famous incident, in which former member of the regiment, Hans Mend, played an important role, illustrates what was said about Hitler's role as hero in the early 1930s. On 9 October 1932, Mend, who had expressed himself positively about Hitler in a book, took back what he had written. As the former comrade failed to enter the circle around Hitler, although the NSDAP had seen to it that the book was on sale everywhere, he became so angry he had a letter published in the paper *Der gerade Weg*. He wrote he wanted to have nothing to do with Hitler and his party anymore and that Hitler wouldn't have been portrayed as a hero in his book if he had said everything he had suppressed previously. Hitler, so Mend said, had never been a soldier of Mend's calibre. But what really bothered him became clear at the end of the short letter: at a certain moment, Hitler refused to shake hands with Mend because he felt too good for him. Obviously, a personal grudge played a role but Mend did distance himself from the contents of his

---

44. Russell, p. 116
45. Russell, p. 115

book and said Hitler had never been a good soldier and certainly not a hero. What exactly he had suppressed can only be guessed at.

On 1 December 1932, *Der gerade Weg* published a second letter by Mend. He responded point by point to the reaction to the first letter that had been published in other papers. He indicated he hadn't been forced to write positively about Hitler in his book but that the publisher had edited the original manuscript. In addition, he wrote that he knew Hitler wasn't overly pleased with his book but that he had always supported Hitler and that Hitler even had declared his friendship in a letter. In Mend's opinion, Hitler gradually became too arrogant to pay attention to his old friends. In short, Mend still criticised Hitler as a person but he didn't repeat his criticism of Hitler as a soldier.

After January 1933, little was heard about Mend any more. He was arrested but released by the grace of Hitler; later on Mend was even willing to revoke his first letter. Even though Hitler was against it, Mend's book was reprinted, earning him a lot of money.[46]

When Mend turned to selling paintings and drawings by Hitler he drew attention to himself once more. The Gestapo took his book out of circulation and he was charged with abuse of children, a charge that probably had no basis in fact.[47] After being imprisoned in two concentration camps, he was released in late 1938.

The Mend protocol

A year later, Mend made contact with a resistance group and he told them what he had apparently suppressed until then: Hitler was a homosexual. When the regimental couriers had been quartered in a brewery in 1915 and slept in a hay stack, they caught Hitler, who was 'busy' with his friend Ernst Schmidt.[48] The report, containing Mend's statements, became known as the Mend protocol later on and, although it has been much discussed, its value is questionable. Decades later, Lothar Machtan referred to it in the book *Hitler's intieme kring* (Hitler's intimate circle), in which he also claimed Hitler was a covert homosexual.

In the course of time, Mend made various statements about Hitler and his role as a soldier. His inconsistencies may well have had to do with the pressure of the press or of the Gestapo, but he changed his opinion so frequently

---

46. Machtan, pp. 78–79
47. Machtan, pp. 80–81
48. Weber, p. 155

that his testimonies are considered unreliable by many historians. Moreover, prior to 1933, Mend had been sentenced ten times for fraud and the forging of documents and many of his statements turned out to be incorrect.[49]

Echo der Woche

Mend wasn't the only one who criticised Hitler's so-called impeccable military past. As early as 29 February 1932, prior to Mend's publications, the Hamburg paper *Echo der Woche* published an article claiming that Hitler hadn't been a hero and that he had made up various things during his time in the army. He had never been a front-line soldier; he had never fired a shot and he actually owed his Iron Cross to good relations with the officer responsible for the decorations. The article had been published anonymously but was written by a comrade from the regiment and company commander Korbinian Rutz.[50]

The article was published less than five months after the suicide of Geli Raubal, Hitler's niece, in which he is supposed to have played a dubious role. At that time, it was less than a year before Hitler would seize power. Hitler could do without another scandal; that's why he did what he often did: he sued the paper. He won his case but not because it had been established that he had been a hero.

He won because his lawyer stated that the anonymous officer who had allegedly written the article didn't exist. Furthermore, the article read that Hitler had been an Austrian deserter and that was demonstrably incorrect. Only one officer broke the code of honour prevalent among members of the regiment by testifying against Hitler. But the testimonials of various other witnesses who spoke favourably of Hitler far outweighed this single testimony.[51]

Hitler's comrade in arms, Adolf Meyer, also wrote about the case in his book *Adolf Hitler im Regiment List*. He emphasized in particular that a non-suspect socialist witness, former regimental comrade Michael Schleehuber, despite his totally different political ideas, had never said anything detrimental about Hitler and that he was surprised to read negative matters about his military past in other newspapers. The socialist still held his wartime crony

---

49. According to Mend, during the battle of Geluveld, Hitler would have been one of the most courageous couriers, while this battle was the first and only one in which Hitler wasn't a courier yet. By the way, Mend claimed he would have talked to regimental commander List at a time when List had been dead for a long time. Weber, p. 156
50. Rees, p. 72; Weber, p. 312; Joachimsthaler, p. 125
51. Weber, pp. 312–313

in high esteem.⁵² Meyer's book containing the aforementioned anecdotes from which it would appear that Hitler had been at the front frequently was clearly Hitler propaganda. And that, of course, wasn't uncommon for a book published in 1934.

The *Volksfreund*

Another local newspaper, *Der Trierische Volksfreund*, also published a critical article by a regimental comrade of Hitler long before Mend's public letters.⁵³ This time it was a soldier named Josef Stettner who wrote that Hitler, compared with soldiers in the trenches, led a kind of luxury life with a warm bunk and later on, when he was billeted in a small village 6.2 miles from the front, even with a room for himself. 'We would have given a tooth to change places with Hitler', Stettner wrote.

He stated that Hitler's experiences at the front mostly consisted of 'consuming makeshift honey and tea rather than participating in combat'. He got more to the point when he wrote that Hitler was a regimental courier and those didn't come to the most forward lines at all.

Company couriers, on the contrary, did the dangerous work, taking messages all the way to the front.⁵⁴ What Hitler had written in his letters about his function being the most dangerous in the regiment⁵⁵ was fiction, according to Stettner. His was quite a different presentation of facts to those in the thin booklet of 1939 for the *Hitler Jugend*, in which courier Hitler was under fire continuously, sprinting through hails of bullets without cover.⁵⁶

Decorations

Adolf Hitler received various military awards during the war. Apart from the Bavarian Military Medal 3rd class, meant for soldiers serving in a Bavarian regiment, and the Cross for Military Merit, awarded to soldiers who had been injured, Hitler was awarded with two conspicuous decorations that were to prove his fearlessness: the *Eisernes Kreuz 2* and the *Eisernes Kreuz 1*.

In December 1914, Hitler and four others were awarded the *EK 2* for their achievements in the Bayernwald.⁵⁷ In a letter to Ernst Hepp, he told he had

---

52. Meyer, p. 15
53. In March 1932
54. Weber, pp. 113–114. The quotations in this paragraph can be found on p. 114.
55. Joachimsthaler, p. 125; Weber, p. 105
56. Beier-Lindhardt, pp. 34–35
57. Protection of regimental commander Phillipp Engelhardt as described before.

been awarded the *EK 2*. Meanwhile, he went on, he had been promoted to courier and, compared with the filthy trenches, this was a change for the better but at the same time the job had become more dangerous.[58] He wrote to Joseph Pop, his former landlord in Munich, that 2 December, the day of the investiture, was the happiest day of his life.[59] It has been mentioned before that the events in the Bayernwald had become part of the Hitler propaganda and that the really heroic act that took place there had been mistakenly attributed to Hitler but that he had actually been there seems to be correct.

The *EK 1* awarded to Hitler in August 1918 is the subject of much discussion. The argument that this is the highest award for a soldier and that Hitler had to have been courageous or have done something important probably makes no sense. The available testimonials are predominantly Nazi propaganda. This doesn't necessarily mean, however, that Hitler achieved nothing at all during the war. Werner Maser states that the rumours that Hitler received the award incorrectly emerged among other things through the actions of regimental comrade Georg Schnell. He declared he had lodged a complaint with Sergeant Major Max Amann and the major of the company, Rudolf Hess, because Amann himself had entered Hitler's name and his own in the recommendation without the company knowing about it. In Schnell's view, Hitler didn't deserve the *EK 1*.[60] Whether this is correct isn't clear but Maser says it is. Whatever the case, Hess wasn't a major at all in the List regiment at the time.

According to the Nazi propaganda from 1932, Hitler was awarded the *EK 1* after he had cornered an entire group of Englishmen with the only weapon he had, a pistol, and taken them to the regimental staff.[61] In other versions of the story, it concerns twelve to fifteen prisoners who may well have been French. Prior to Weber, other historians have always claimed this was propaganda but Weber found out something similar had indeed taken place near the French village of Vézaponin. On 4 August 1918, the commander of the List regiment wrote in a letter that he had twelve Frenchmen, arrested by him, repair a bridge and further that in the previous period *Leutnant* Gutmann personally took some prisoners and had written an important intelligence report.[62] About Hitler, nothing was mentioned in the letter but it seems that Weber had discovered the origin of the myth. The regimental

---

58. Maser, HMK, p. 135
59. Maser, HMK, p. 139
60. Maser, HMK, p. 140; Joachimsthaler, p. 173
61. Weber, pp. 242–243
62. Weber, p. 243

staff had been involved in the occupation of the bridge all right and Hitler had been part of it. Whether or not Hitler took part in this action isn't clear. On the same day the letter was written, Hitler did receive his *EK 1*. A 'mistake' could easily have been made.

Hans Mend also helped to spread the myth. According to Maser, he said that Hitler was awarded this decoration as he had arrested a group of French soldiers[63] and the story popped up again in the regional Nazi paper *Die Volksgemeinschaft* of 7 March 1937.[64] It appeared from the letter of the regimental commander, however, that Hitler was no hero but that his superior, Gutmann, was honoured. And precisely that name is essential in regard to Hitler being awarded the *EK 1*. It had been the very same Gutmann who had recommended Hitler for this decoration,[65] and that was a nasty issue for the Nazis because Gutmann was a Jew. Gutmann's name being obscured and the role of hero being attributed to Hitler can't be a coincidence. The Nazis wanted to prevent it becoming common knowledge that Hitler had been recommended for this decoration by a Jewish regimental adjutant.

Hitler's decoration would have had to do with something else. Werner Maser says he was awarded the decoration for having taken a message to a German artillery battery under trying circumstances[66] and that may well be right. One of the most meticulous sources is a short letter from 1918 containing the recommendation for a decoration for Hitler. In this letter, deputy regimental commander Freiherr von Godin outlines why Hitler deserves the *EK 1*. This isn't about some act of great heroism that Hitler performed but it is a recommendation, stating that Hitler had been with the regiment since the beginning of the war, that he was a cold-blooded courier and that he, after telephone communication had broken down, delivered messages in life and death situations, thanks to his tireless drive and self-sacrifice.[67]

It seems that Gutmann had promised the couriers an Iron Cross if they managed to deliver messages in difficult situations to the correct location. But it took Gutmann a few weeks before he persuaded the divisional commander as this achievement wasn't so spectacular after all.[68] Probably Freiherr von Godin understood this as well and he began his recommendation by stating

---

63. Maser, HMK, p. 141; Williams, pp. 190–191
64. Weber, p. 242, 437
65. Weber, p. 242, Maser, HMK, p. 144
66. Maser, HMK, p. 144
67. Joachimsthaler, KB, pp. 175–176 A picture of the document of Freiherr von Godin is included in Russell, p. 142 and Kershaw, p. 144
68. Kershaw, *Hoogmoed*, p. 144

that Hitler had performed his duties in the regiment in an excellent way since 1914. This matched seamlessly with what his future adjutant Wiedemann said about him: Hitler was a brave courier who deserved his *EK 1*. He always did his duty quietly and calmly.[69]

Wiedemann's characterisation could well have been the reason for Hitler's decoration. This was also mentioned first in Freiherr von Godin's recommendation. Hitler was awarded the decoration for duty done during the entire war, the actual occasion being the delivery of a message to the correct location and, of course, Gutmann's promise. Historian Anton Joachimsthaler also concludes that Hitler was probably a dependable soldier and that he deserved his *EK 1*, but he did add emphatically: not for the arrest of fifteen French soldiers.[70] Thomas Weber stresses in his recent book that mainly members of the staff were awarded some decoration or other but not the common soldier in the trenches. Weber states in so many words that Hitler's *EK 1* wasn't so much a symbol of courage but the result of the fact that he had served for years at regimental headquarters.[71]

Why was Hitler never promoted?

If Hitler had been a hero, it would have been obvious he should have been promoted. It never came to that though. That was strange as during the First World War so many soldiers had died that it would have been logical that Hitler, an experienced soldier, would have risen through the ranks. Max Amann, a sergeant in Hitler's regiment, has said that Hitler was to be promoted at some time. When Amann summoned him to tell him he would be promoted, Hitler was startled and he asked Amann immediately to cancel it for he would have less authority with decorations than without. According to Amann, Hitler never gave the real reason for his refusal.[72]

Historians have searched their minds for possible reasons. For instance, if he had been promoted, the chances were that Hitler would have been transferred to another regiment[73] and he wanted to avoid that at any cost. Hitler had no contact with his family any more (his parents had passed away) and hardly with his old friends from Munich. That is the reason why he had come to see his regiment as some sort of replacement family.[74] This

---

69. Joachimsthaler, KB, p. 156
70. Joachimsthaler, KB, p. 173
71. Weber, pp. 240–241
72. Joachimsthaler, KB, p. 160
73. Joachimsthaler, KB, p. 159; Kershaw, *Hoogmoed*, p. 139
74. Weber, p. 159

argument is open to challenge. Thomas Weber, for instance, mentions two soldiers from Hitler's regiment, Alexander Moritz Frey and well-known Adolf Meyer, who stayed in the regiment despite their promotion. They were not the only ones. Weber himself presumed Hitler was too eccentric and too obstinate and he lacked qualities of leadership.[75] During the so-called Wilhelmstrasse trial in Nuremberg after the Second World War,[76] Wiedemann testified that he and his colleagues couldn't perceive any qualities of leadership in Hitler.[77] He said Hitler didn't have them at the time. His superiors could have granted him the honour of a promotion but as he didn't want it himself, they abstained.[78]

After the Second World War

It is conspicuous that until well after the Second World War relatively little attention was paid to Hitler's service during the first. Almost all sources are suspect, coloured politically or written in hindsight, and that makes it hard to judge them correctly. In his biography of Hitler from 1953, Alan Bullock only devotes a few pages to the First World War but he does deal, for instance, with the contradicting testimonials about Hitler and the improbability of him taking fifteen Frenchmen prisoner all by himself. Yet he wrote, 'Despite the fact Hitler wasn't in the trenches themselves, his work was undoubtedly dangerous and for almost four years he stayed at the front or not far behind it.'[79]

At the end of the twentieth century, and many biographies later, a new and exhaustive standard work about Hitler by Ian Kershaw was published. In this book as well, attention to Hitler's experiences during the First World War remained limited to a few pages. Kershaw didn't want to butt heads with the tricky sources from that period either. Although he did mention possible reasons for Hitler's refusal to be promoted, he didn't pass judgment. He did presume, however, that Hitler didn't say anything about his function

---

75. Weber, pp. 160–161. Nor was Hitler's social background a reason to reject his promotion. In addition, Weber calls the idea brought forward by Amann that there was no vacant position ridiculous.
76. In Nuremberg, various trials took place after the war. The best known were those against the most famous surviving Nazi big wigs including Albert Speer and Hermann Göring. The so-called Wilhelmstrase trials were those against various ministerial departments including the department of Foreign Affairs. Many of these departments were located at the Wilhelmstrass in Berlin.
77. *Der Spiegel*, nr. 47/1964
78. Joachimsthaler, KB, p. 160
79. Bullock, p. 30

of courier in *Mein Kampf* as he wanted it to look like he had spent four years in the trenches. Almost in contradiction to the aforementioned, Kershaw did state couriers ran great risks and that the group of couriers suffered relatively many casualties. Kershaw may have banned the story about Hitler overwhelming the French soldiers to the empire of fairy tales,[80] but he did write: 'Everything points to it that Hitler not only carried out his orders dutifully but also showed commitment and no lack of physical courage.'[81]

In between the publication of these two books, of course, many books appeared in which Hitler's role during the First World War was discussed. *Korrektur einer Biografie* from 1989 by Anton Joachimsthaler was probably the most important of them all. The work is a correction on everything that has been published about Hitler's life between 1908 and 1920 and it contains a lengthy chapter about his period as a soldier. For instance, Joachimsthaler strongly criticises the book by Werner Maser, the man who claimed, among other things that Hitler had fathered a son during the war. According to Joachimsthaler, the reason why Hitler said nothing about his function of courier in *Mein Kampf* was actually unknown but after the Second World War it was assumed that the simple function of courier didn't agree with his status as Führer.[82] Furthermore, he stressed that many of Hitler's war cronies owed all sorts of functions to him, and he called Hans Mend an outright psychopath.[83] In his view, Hitler was a fine soldier after all and somebody who liked to be one.

Even after Joachimsthaler's critical corrections, books on the same subject continued to appear but were not always based on thorough research. All too often, unfounded fabrications were copied verbatim from propagandist sources from the 1930s. For instance, in a book from 2003, it says that the function of a courier was no less dangerous than that of a front-line soldier and that during the war Hitler had learned how to kill people with a bayonet and a hand grenade.[84] The latter must certainly have been part of his military training but in all probability, Hitler killed no one during the war.

In 2005 a book about the Regiment List, *Corporal Hitler and the Great War*, was published. In the introduction, the author says there is no doubt about Hitler's courage during the Great War and, moreover, he admits Hitler took messages from headquarters to the front.[85] A conspicuous appearance

---

80. Kershaw, *Hoogmoed*, p. 144
81. Kershaw, *Hoogmoed*, p. 139. Other quotes by Kershaw can be found here as well.
82. Joachimsthaler, KB, p. 129
83. Joachimsthaler, KB, p. 143
84. In the book *Hitler, ein Sohn des Krieges by* Koch-Hillebrecht, p. 15
85. Williams, p. 2, 203

in a series of picture books about the Nazi period entitled *Frontsoldat Hitler*, published in 2006, contains an interview with author Stuart Russell with the son of one of Hitler's regimental cronies, who said his father had told him Hitler had always reported voluntarily for the most hazardous assignments, nor had he shied away from routes across dangerous terrain.[86]

All the more conspicuous was the publication of *Adolf Hitler im Ersten Weltkrieg* by Thomas Weber, in which all doubts about the old sources and Hitler's heroic role pass review once again. Weber may well have been the first author after Joachimsthaler who looked into Hitler's performance during the war seriously and he concluded that even the cautious presentation of historians might well have been too positive. He also had to make do with the known witnesses with the difference that he not only put the statements of these witnesses under the microscope but he also checked whether all the assumptions corresponded with the usual chain of events in a war. Furthermore, he discovered some new sources.

Weber advances the thesis – which has meanwhile been included in popular books[87] – that Hitler didn't come to the forward lines frequently at all and that, logically speaking, he rarely went there in connection with his function. Regimental couriers took messages to the rear areas and from there they were taken to the front lines by other couriers. Hitler was no battalion courier who had to take messages to the forward lines but a regimental courier. Members of the regimental staff were sometimes called *Etappenschweine* by front-line troops. In this case, the word *Etappe* is used in the sense of a supply depot for troops in transit, located behind the front where life was a lot easier than in the trenches on the front line. So, it is imaginable that front-line troops held those in contempt who could spend the night in such a location. Hitler led a rather quiet life as courier of the regimental staff. Weber says that the task of a courier was very dangerous but it wasn't the most dangerous task in the regiment, as Hitler sometimes claimed in his letters.[88] Stories about Hitler distributing messages amidst hails of bullets and having the most dangerous job in the army, kept popping up, however, in books about the First World War, but in reality, Hitler was usually in places were fighting didn't take place.[89] Weber says Hitler lived in relatively good conditions and, unlike soldiers in the trenches, he didn't have to bear the stench of decaying corpses.[90] Furthermore, according to Weber,

---

86. Russell, p. 83
87. For instance in Van Capelle & Van de Bovenkamp, *op. cit.*
88. Weber, p. 105
89. It may be significant that a number of houses where Hitler had been billeted still exist, while almost everything in the front line at the time had been pounded to ruins.
90. Weber, p. 104

the closer one was involved with headquarters, the greater the chance of being awarded important decorations like Hitler's *EK 1*. Real combat troops would have been very frustrated over this.[91]

The myth is over

All sources about Hitler's experiences in the First World War must be approached with suspicion: Hitler's letters, recollections of his wartime friends, articles by his enemies and many of the retellings and interpretations after the Second World War. Apart from a few letters by Hitler himself, hardly anything was written about him during the First World War. And why should it? At the time he was a complete unknown. Only when he became active politically did writings about his experiences at the front emerge. Eventually, distinction could be made between two sides: the anti-Hitler camp of journalists and critics and the pro-Hitler camp that by means of court cases, responses to publications and especially in the 1930s in the form of biographies, attempted to make clear that Hitler had been a courageous soldier. During the Nazi era, Hitler eventually became a hero who had arrested fifteen French or twelve British soldiers all by himself in a trench as an ultimate act of heroism.

After the Second World War the image became even more blurred, because who of Hitler's cronies from the regiment could be taken seriously and who couldn't? All those who had joined Hitler's party were under suspicion but also those who had been more critical of Hitler obviously hadn't always used reliable information in their publications.[92] The lack of dependable information may well be the reason that until long after 1945 very little information about this period found its way into biographies of Hitler.

When establishing whether Hitler was a hero or not, the question of his two Iron Crosses is important. There are clearly stories about both and the heroic acts that are supposed to be behind them appear to have had nothing to do with Hitler. It is almost certain, however, that Hitler was awarded the *EK 1* for his years of loyal service, his courage and his delivery of messages under trying circumstances. Definitely not for a spectacular act of heroism.[93]

---

91. Weber, p. 111
92. Joachimsthaler, KB, pp. 152–154. For instance, Korbinian Rutz who admitted in 1945 that part of his criticism of Hitler, including the story that Hitler had been injured when sunbathing, was incorrect.
93. Weber, p. 111. While considering Hitler's heroism, it must be borne in mind that, according to Weber, decorations were not always presented to the most courageous soldiers but often to those with the best relations with the leadership.

How much risk did Hitler run every day? If a courier's job really was the most dangerous job in the army, as Hitler had written in a letter and as sometimes claimed in Nazi propaganda, then he would have been a true war hero. However, he was on the regimental staff and thus he was a regimental courier. The regiment was divided in battalions and those were subdivided in companies, each with their own couriers. Regimental couriers hardly ever appeared in the foremost trenches; that was the place for battalion or company couriers. Consequently, Hitler ran less risk than the other couriers and obviously even less than the soldiers in the trenches. Out of a picture from 1915, showing Hitler with seven other couriers, seven were still alive after the First World War. One had passed away but not at the Western Front. He died after being transferred to Romania.[94] In short, Hitler didn't play a hero's role.

On the other hand, unlike a postman whose only enemies are stray dogs, Hitler did his job in a war situation. There are few stories suggesting he was a coward or lazy. On the contrary, the war lasted for some fifty-one months, of which Hitler had spent forty-two at the front: according to Weber, that was well above average.[95] The story about him sustaining his first injury while sunbathing has proved to be no more than gossip and was probably an example of the cynical soldier's humour about the despised *Etappenschweine*. It is striking that the 'heroic tales' of Hitler's wartime cronies contain little about true heroism. Among Meyer's anecdotes, there really is only one manly story about Hitler. According to Meyer, he was a courier who manoeuvred very deftly across terrain under fire, something Brandmayer admitted as well. Furthermore, Hitler pops up somewhere between the forward lines and regimental headquarters in a rather unimportant fragment that was probably added to prove that he did more than lie in the sun behind the front lines. Another anecdote indicates that Hitler knew the way to the front very well. So it doesn't surprise anyone that the Nazis had to fabricate stories in order to portray Hitler as a true war hero.

Hitler has never been a hero who appealed to the imagination. According to many of his former comrades, he was always keen on delivering messages, even at night, and he did his job well. This was also the conclusion drawn by historians such as Anton Joachimsthaler and Ian Kershaw. Even when Weber found reasons to further differentiate a number of facts hitherto taken for the truth, it justifies the conclusion that not much is left of the myth of Hitler being a war hero.

---

94. Weber, p. 249
95. Weber, p. 248

Chapter 4

Did Hitler Have a Son?

The consequences of an affair during The First World War

One day during the First World War, French girl Charlotte Lobjoie was making hay when she and other women working in the field saw a German soldier approaching. He had a sketchbook with him and it looked like he was drawing something. The girl, who showed interest in the soldier, made a little small talk and not long after an affair grew between the two. During an evening with a little too much alcohol and affection, the girl became pregnant. In 1918 she gave birth to a boy she named Jean-Marie. His father is supposed to have been Adolf Hitler.

Almost a century later, the website of the Dutch newspaper *Algemeen Dagblad* published an article with the blaring headline 'New evidence: Hitler had a son who fought against him during the Second World War'.[1] It was based on an article in the French magazine *Le Point*, in which new evidence was presented. 'It appears from documents in the archives of the German armed forces that during the Second World War, envelopes containing money were delivered to Mrs Lobjoie. Mr Loret found paintings, signed by Hitler, in the attic of his mother's home. A portrait by Hitler of a female was found in Germany that showed many similarities with the French woman,' so the website read.

Could something actually be true after all of the assumptions Werner Maser made in the 1970s about the son of Hitler he supposedly discovered? Or was it merely a question of a recurring old myth about Hitler resurfacing once again?

---

1. *Algemeen Dagblad*, 17 February 2012

Adolf Hitler: father of a son

During the time Hitler gained a name in Europe, many inhabitants of the region in northern France where the Lobjoie girl had lived are supposed to have known that he was the one who had fathered a child in their neighbourhood. They had probably recognised him as the soldier who had been strolling around there during the First World War but the story didn't end there, however. Even before Hitler gained a name as a politician on the rise, some Germans claimed he had a child. They would have learned it from Hitler himself and they also knew he had drawn a picture of the child's mother that would still exist.

When Hitler was roaming through Belgium and northern France in 1940, among other things to rekindle war memories, he obviously couldn't fail to visit those places where he had spent a lot of time with his girlfriend Charlotte, so people said. As he knew from 1918 onwards that he had a son somewhere, during one of his trips through Flanders, he took an interesting detour past the farm of Joseph Goethals where Hitler had been billeted for some time and where he regularly had met his girlfriend. He talked to Goethals in 1940, who was an important witness, of course. What the discussion was all about remains in the dark, however, although his adjutant, Heinz Linge, was able to tell it had something to do with a secret from the past.

A courting corporal

Charlotte and Adolf are supposed to have been close friends in 1916–17, a period interrupted by Hitler's mandatory departure to Germany in connection with an injury he had sustained. In particular, during the months of May until and including July 1917, when Hitler was stationed in western Flanders, he met Charlotte quite often. After Hitler had gone on leave in September 1917, the two never saw each other again. The girl had become pregnant in the meantime. In March 1918, she gave birth to a boy she named Jean-Marie. For some reason, she placed him with her parents and after they had died Jean-Marie ended up in a boarding school. Later on, he was adopted.

The boy heard nothing from his mother for a long time. Because he had fought against the Germans in the French army during the Second World War, he was assaulted in his home town of St Quentin in 1940 by the SD. They took him to Paris for interrogation and he was released again without explanation. As a physical examination had been carried out as well, it was assumed it had been for research into his origins. Jean-Marie Loret[2] found his mother, who had meanwhile become an alcoholic, in Paris. When she was already mortally ill, she told him of his father, Adolf Hitler. That was in 1948 and Hitler had been dead for three years.

Werner Maser searches for evidence

In 1976, Werner Maser received a letter from Jean-Marie in which he claimed he was Hitler's son. Maser decided to investigate and spoke to various witnesses, who confirmed Loret's story. Strangely enough, in pictures of Jean-Marie's mother, she even looked like the woman in one of the drawings Hitler had made during the First World War of a woman wearing a headscarf. In a lengthy article in the magazine *Zeitgeschichte* of 1977,[3] Maser enumerated all witnesses and scraps of evidence he had been able to find.

The evidence proved to be shaky though. In the article, Maser almost exclusively presented witnesses who testified in 1977 about events that had taken place sixty years before. In addition, these were all indirect witnesses who said that they had known someone who had told them they had recognised Hitler as the one who had had a relationship with someone from the region. There was, for instance, an official who had learned from the Mayor of Seboncourt that the French press had reported as early as 1934 about the existence of a son of Hitler. Maser's witnesses from Germany were also indirect witnesses. They claimed to have learned from Hitler himself or from some high-ranking Nazi that the Führer had a son in France. One of Goebbels' associates said he had learned from his boss himself that Hitler had fathered a son during the First World War. Apparently, all of the direct witnesses had passed away.

Other historians

Naturally, the brothers in the trade responded to Maser's article. Historian Anton Joachimsthaler, for instance, usually very conscientious, doubted Maser's assertion that during the war a young girl could have followed a soldier for one and a half years and he wondered how it could be that a

---

2. He had taken the surname Loret from his mother's husband, who wanted to recognise him but didn't want him around.
3. Maser, Adolf Hitler: 'Vater eines Sohnes', 1977

theory, based only on assumptions, could gain so much attention.[4] Hitler's wartime friends knew nothing about a relationship between him and a French girl, and even her sister said that Charlotte had never been in touch with Hitler, although she had associated herself with a German sub-lieutenant. According to the British newspaper the *Sunday Times*, the genetic research Maser had ordered didn't reveal anything conclusive either.[5] In the first part of his biography of Hitler, Ian Kershaw disclaimed the issue and only dealt with it in a footnote, even emphasizing the implausibility of the story.[6] In his extensive work about Hitler in the First World War, author Thomas Weber was curt about it as well. He wrote: 'The story, told often that Hitler had fathered a son during the war is indeed incorrect.'[7]

Maser's most interesting witness was Heinz Linge, Hitler's adjutant, whose recollections and service record would be published by Maser after Linge's death. Linge managed to tell Maser that Himmler and Hitler had a private discussion in 1940. In the course of it, Hitler is supposed to have ordered Himmler to track down his son. How Linge could have known this, as neither he nor someone else had been present, remains unanswered. In his memoirs, Linge was far from certain about this conversation. He said he couldn't be certain about what it had been about. He only assumed the conversation was about a woman and her son.[8] Furthermore, in Linge's memoirs one can only read that Hitler had been in Ardooie on 29 May 1940 at the farm of Josef Goethals,[9] where Hitler had been billeted during the First World War. Linge couldn't have heard, however, what Hitler and Goethals had been talking about.[10] Maser did use the visit to Ardooie though to prove the relationship between Hitler and Charlotte Lobjoie. During the First World War, Charlotte is supposed to have visited her friend Adolf there regularly. The address and pictures of the Goethals' farm kept popping up everywhere, even though at this address there was no farm at all anymore. There were houses now that couldn't have had anything to do whatsoever with the Goethals' farm. Some of the pictures of Hitler, supposedly taken near the homestead of Goethals, had certainly been taken

---

4. Joachimsthaler, KB, p. 161
5. Joachimsthaler, KB, p. 163
6. Kershaw, p. 159 (footnote 116)
7. Weber, p. 139
8. Linge, p. 116
9. In Stuart Russells' book *Zeitgeschichte in Bildern* from the series entitled *Frontsoldat Hitler* there is a picture of the house on Markt 18. It obviously isn't a farmhouse and it doesn't look like the house had been there as early as 1917. Yet the caption reads that Hitler had been billeted there in 1917.
10. Linge, p. 115

in Fournes, another Belgian village where Hitler had been billeted during the First World War and which he had visited on his tour through Belgium and northern France. Pictures in which both Goethals and Hitler are talking near the farm actually do not exist at all.

And yet, Maser used Hitler's visit to the farm of Goethals as evidence for the relationship between Charlotte and Adolf. If Hitler had been there in 1940, he must have had a good reason for it and, according to Maser, Charlotte and the child Hitler had fathered were exactly that. In the story about the visit that appears in Linge's posthumous memoirs, many details are incorrect. For instance, the route Hitler is supposed to have taken didn't even take him close to Ardooie. In order to get there, Hitler and his entourage would have had to make a wide detour, possible of course, but not likely. In his desire to prove that Loret was Hitler's son, Maser had hurt himself badly. He had put all kinds of things into Linge's mouth and because Linge had passed away in the meantime, he couldn't contradict him anymore. The date of the visit was also incorrect. On 29 May, Hitler was actually in his Führer headquarters, the *Felsennest* in Germany – and there is ample evidence to prove it.

The trips Hitler made through Belgium and northern France took place in early June and the trips described by Linge, with Hitler's wartime friends Max Amann and Ernst Schmidt, at the end of June.[11] Linge could, of course, have been in error as to the date but his story in which Hitler had been almost festively received in Ardooie didn't sound too convincing either. Keeping in mind that the village church, which also stood on the Markt (Market square) where the farm is supposed to have been, was severely damaged during the fighting in 1940, it is hard to imagine that many people would be out to treat Hitler to a joyous reception.[12] Among the pictures that were frequently taken during Hitler's trips that did take place in 1940, not a single one was taken in Ardooie. Maser probably made himself guilty of falsification of history deliberately.[13]

Dewitte

The way the story about Hitler's visit to Ardooie came about had already been investigated by Erik Dewitte,[14] an inhabitant of the Ardooie region. His information offers a fine inside view of Maser's argumentation. According

---

11. On 25 and 26 June 25 1940.
12. Debaeke, p. 164
13. Debaeke, pp. 163–165
14. The following story is mainly a retelling of the story of Dewitte's unpublished article: 'Was Adolf Hitler in Ardooie in June 1940?' Siegfried Debaeke, an inhabitant of the Ardooie region, confirms Dewitte's analysis in an email of 2012.

to Dewitte, the birth of the Ardooie myth had everything to do with the municipal secretary of Ardooie at the time, Lucien van Acker. He wrote about the story, which gained fame in the 1970s in a yearbook published in 2006.[15] It looks like the secretary brought a self-convincing fairy tale into the world.

In 1977, the year when Maser's story about Hitler's son was published, Dewitte took a pair of German reporters of a well-known magazine[16] to the home of Walter Duyck. Dewitte said the Germans were looking for the painting by Hitler that Duyck would have in his possession. It was the painting of the girl wearing a veil that should depict Hitler's girlfriend, Charlotte Lobjoie. The reporters also visited secretary van Acker, who could tell them, of course, that during the First World War Hitler had been billeted in the farm of Goethals. The story of Hitler having returned there in 1940 was, according to Dewitte, a lie that had either been concocted by van Acker or by farmer Goethals himself. It was supposedly retold by van Acker to the two reporters in the village. In his own search for the truth about Jean-Marie Loret, Werner Maser contacted van Acker, who knew the story as well and told him about it. Various details in the story proved to be wrong in the version as told by Goethals and van Acker as well as in Heinz Linge's version, which ended up in his memoirs. And for this, Maser was responsible.

It had been Linge who had recalled the address of the farm. This was a remarkable feat of recollection since he had completely forgotten the date of Hitler's visit to Ardooie. The address of farmer Joseph Goethals, Markt 18 in Ardooie, was correct but this was his address in 1970. In 1940, he had lived at a very different address, Markt A 317. The numbers of the Markt in Ardooie were entirely different at the time, so Linge could never have remembered Markt 18 as Goethals didn't live there yet! Consequently, the number came from Maser himself. The secretary had told him about Joseph Goethals and when Maser published Linge's memoirs, he must have included the 1970 address in addition to the story of the mysterious conversation between Hitler and Goethals.

The story continues

Maser should have known better. A first glance at the 'modern' house on the Markt should have made him realise this couldn't be Goethals' farm.[17]

---

15. The article by Dewitte mentions exactly where, namely in a contribution to the Year book 2 of the Regional Geographic Society Ardooie-Koolskamp from 2006.
16. Dewitte did recall there was a logo of a well-known German magazine on the car of one of the journalists but he couldn't remember whether it was *Bild* or *Stern*.
17. There are various pictures on the internet of the house, which looks far too modern for a building of 1940, let alone 1917. In the book *Frontsoldat Hitler* by Stuart Russell there is a picture on p. 108 of a house that doesn't look like a farmhouse at all.

Further, as a historian he never should have satisfied himself with some indirect witnesses as proof of the relationship between Charlotte and Adolf – for which he couldn't find a single witness from the First World War. Despite Maser's weak argumentation though, the French magazine *Le Point* reprinted the spectacular story in 2012, resulting in the old fabrications popping up all over the world again, in particular on the internet.

Of course, there actually were some interesting new things to tell. Hitler and Loret, for instance, had the same blood type and then there was the painting, signed by Hitler, of the French girl with a veil who resembled Charlotte Lobjoie. Also new would be the envelopes containing money that had been delivered, on the basis of documents from the archives of the German armed forces, to Charlotte Lobjoie during the Second World War.[18]

Furthermore, in pictures Loret shows a certain physical resemblance to Adolf Hitler and the resemblance between Charlotte Lobjoie and Paula Hitler, his sister, is also striking but obviously that doesn't mean they are genetically connected. If Adolf's sister looked like his so-called girlfriend, Charlotte's son could look like Adolf as well, even if he wasn't his son. Based on that kind of evidence, all sorts of assertions are possible. One could even presume that Jean-Marie's mother Charlotte was Hitler's sister because Paula Hitler did look like her. But in order not to create a new Hitler myth I most strongly stress that such wasn't the case ....

The search for Hitler's DNA

It is weird that when presenting the new evidence from 2012, the press completely ignored the work of Belgian journalist Jean-Paul Mulders, who in 2009 revealed in an accessible, thin but convincing booklet that Loret was no relative of Hitler at all.

Like so many who were intrigued by this issue, Mulders looked for evidence for or against the story about Jean-Marie Loret. The only way to be certain whether Loret and Hitler were related was a DNA test, so Loret attempted to obtain a DNA sample from Hitler's family. Adolf Hitler's remaining DNA is stored in Moscow, however, where his entire lower jaw, parts of his upper jaw and possible traces of his blood are preserved. And those are hard to come by.

Mulders did manage to get a sample of the deceased Jean-Marie Loret from the back of a stamp on a letter he had sent. To be certain, he compared this DNA with samples from the adhesive strips of four different letters from the

---

18. 'Hitler aurait eu un fils avec une Française', in *Le Point*, February 2012

man.[19] Next he proceeded to search for the DNA of Hitler's Austrian family. After a few relatives had refused to co-operate, Andreas Hüttler, a farmer from the region the Hitler family originated from, was willing to provide a DNA sample. Mulders also covertly took a few cigarette ends from Walter Hüttler, who lived a couple of streets away and who had left them in the ashtray on a bench in front of his house. The names of the men being Hüttler and not Hitler is a result of the many variations in spelling that had occurred often in the past when registering those names. The Hüttlers are not direct descendants of Adolf Hitler's father but are certainly related to the Hitlers.

Mulders also went searching for the DNA of Hitler's relatives living in America. Those were the children of Adolf Hitler's cousin, William Patrick Hitler. He was the son of Adolf Hitler's half-brother, Alois. After the war he retired to Long Island near New York, where three of his sons are still living under the surname Stuart-Houston. One of the four has already passed away. The brothers were unapproachable but he managed to obtain two napkins on which the DNA of one of the brothers could be found.[20]

Consanguinity of the male branch of a family can be shown by comparing the Y-chromosomes. It turned out that this Y-chromosome of Andreas and Walter Hüttler, both members of the Hitler family, matched that of the American relative Alex Adolf Stuart-Houston. That isn't only relevant to the question of whether Jean-Marie was Hitler's son, it also proves that historians like Ian Kershaw had been right in assuming that Hitler's father didn't have a Jewish father but was the child of either Johann Georg Hiedler or Nepomuk Hiedler.[21] Furthermore, the DNA that was found could possibly be used to prove that the blood on the couch on which Hitler committed suicide and the blood in his preserved jaws was his after all.[22]

It was Mulders' intention, however, to establish whether Loret was Hitler's son. The comparison of both DNA samples provides irrefutable proof that Jean-Marie Loret wasn't related to Adolf Hitler.[23] Whether it will stop the speculation about the children Hitler is supposed to have fathered on a former nun named Pia[24] or on Eva Hitler in Argentina[25] is unlikely. Maybe these myths will be thoroughly investigated as well one day. Until now, they are so implausible nobody should waste too much time on them.

---

19. Mulders, p. 23. These were similar.
20. Mulders, p. 73
21. See chapter 'Was Adolf Hitler a Jew?'
22. See chapter 'Did Hitler actually commit suicide?'
23. Mulders, p. 87
24. Der Spiegel 46/1977
25. Basti & Van Helsing, pp. 397–398

Chapter 5

Hitler the Socialist?

The obscurity about his 'opportunistic' political choice

For Adolf Hitler, the First World War ended in a military hospital in Pasewalk north of Berlin. There he learned on 10 November 1918 that Germany was no longer a monarchy, that hostilities had been terminated and that a revolution had broken out in the country. Hitler considered this a thrust with a dagger in the army's back. When he heard about it, he cried so much he could hardly see anything, possibly a belated result of the temporary blindness caused by gas he had sustained in northern France. Hitler's emotional experience was an important fragment in Mein Kampf *but the book was also the only source in which the story appeared. The result of Hitler's considerations, lasting days, about the importance of events in that period would be catastrophic for the entire world as Hitler ended them with one of his most famous quotes: 'But I decided to become a politician.'*[1]

Hitler suggested literally that from that moment on he wished to apply his anti-Marxist and anti-Semitic views to political practice, but later historians saw right through this self-propaganda. Why for instance, did he dwell for such a short time on the period after his release from Pasewalk in the part of *Mein Kampf* that followed right after this statement? It was a very remarkable period in the history of Munich. After recuperating, Hitler had returned to the city where socialists and communists took over power, while Hitler was still part of his regiment. Did he, as a soldier, support the socialists and Marxists he hated so much? Or was he a socialist in this period himself and was his eventual choice of anti-Semitic, right-wing politics the result of opportunism?

---

1. *Mein Kampf*, p. 233

Hitler's biography corrected

After the First World War, Hitler was a soldier under a socialist and even communist government but the confusion surrounding the question of Hitler's political awakening and his possible socialistic leanings starts, like so many other Hitler myths, with his own reticence about this part of his life. He allegedly knew nothing about his family's history anymore but in *Mein Kampf* he devoted no more than a single page to the first chaotic six months after the First World War in Munich. It was a period in which a sequence of rulers tripped over each other, the assassination of Bavarian president Kurt Eisner and a reign of short duration, dominated by communists. Apparently, this omission didn't strike famous historians such as Bullock, Fest and Maser that much, but things changed when Anton Joachimsthaler published his correction of Adolf Hitler's biography. He dwelled extensively on the period of revolution right after the First World War.

Joachimsthaler reasoned that Hitler had, after all, not decided in Pasewalk to become a politician but that because of the revolution politics came to him in the barracks in Munich,[2] a view Ian Kershaw shared. Joachimsthaler deemed it suspicious Hitler had written so little in *Mein Kampf* about the period of revolution, lasting from November 1918 until May 1919, and so he distrusted Hitler's statement that he had decided to become a politician before he came to Munich.

Hitler didn't have a profession and, just like many other soldiers, he reacted with resignation to the socialist and Marxist revolution. He made no counter-revolutionary attempts, although he later said that the soldiers' councils were a tool of Bolshevism. Even when troops arrived to relieve the city, Hitler did nothing. What is more, he became deputy representative of the battalion and so he had a function under the extreme left-wing rule. During that period Hitler had left Munich for a few months but even in the camp for French and Russian prisoners of war in Traunstein where he was put to work, soldiers' councils were in power that were subordinate to the government.

When Hitler returned to Munich from Traunstein on 16 February 1919 – not in March as he had most probably written in *Mein Kampf* on purpose – he participated in a demonstration of the left-radicals on the Theresienwiese and a few days later he was made part of a guard detail in Munich central station. This can be ascertained from a picture in which Hitler is seen in a room somewhere in the station. Joachimsthaler pointed out that these

---

2. Joachimsthaler, KB, p. 184

guards behaved themselves quite badly sometimes. While at work, they were involved in theft and all sorts of other misdemeanours. It wouldn't be known whether Hitler took part in this.

Joachimsthaler left unanswered how deep socialism was rooted in Hitler. The fact that he stayed in the army during that period was also a form of survival. But he did take on various duties during the socialist rule and, in any case, he did actually have socialist leanings he wanted to cover up in *Mein Kampf* later on. Therefore, he kept quiet about his role during the November revolution.

Ian Kershaw agrees

In his voluminous biography of Hitler, published in 2001, Ian Kershaw follows Joachimsthaler's argumentation almost completely. He also stressed Hitler expressed himself in a very negative sense, especially later on, about the Raden Republic, which he saw as a temporary Jewish rule.[3] Kershaw also assumed Hitler wished to cover up something and he also mentions Hitler's function as a station guard. In February 1919, according to Kershaw, Hitler became the trusted representative of his company and in that capacity he had to see to it that material from the department of propaganda of the socialist government found its way to the troops. Thus, the only conclusion could be that Hitler was employed by the leftist parties that were in power at the time and it remained that way during the short 'red dictatorship', when Hitler was even elected deputy representative of the battalion.[4] Kershaw concludes that Hitler's support of the socialists wasn't so strange after all in the chaotic times of the revolution but that this support was 'difficult to match with his hatred of social democracy'. In Kershaw's opinion, Hitler was no devoted socialist but acted out of pure opportunism.[5]

Weber's analysis

The book by Thomas Weber about Hitler during the First World War, published in 2001, also contains a chapter about the period right after the conflict. Weber's image of the time is roughly comparable to that of Joachimsthaler and Kershaw. After recuperating from his injuries sustained at the end of the war and being released from the military hospital in

---

3. Kershaw, Hoogmoed, p. 166
4. Kershaw, Hoogmoed, p. 174
5. Kershaw, Hoogmoed, p. 175

Pasewalk at the end of November 1918, Hitler returned to Munich as he had to rejoin his regiment. The socialist revolution had, meanwhile, led to the abolition of the monarchy. Kurt Eisner, leader of the Independent Social Democratic Party (USPD), a spin-off of the more moderate socialists of the SPD, had seized power. Two weeks after his arrival, Hitler, along with his wartime friend Ernst Schmidt, was posted to prison camp Traunstein outside Munich, where French and Russian prisoners of war were still housed. At the end of January or early February, the two returned to Munich.

After his work in Traunstein, Hitler also had, according to Weber as mentioned earlier, a job as guard of the railway station in Munich from 20 February 1919 onwards. In both functions, he served the socialist revolution but it doesn't automatically mean that he was a fanatic socialist himself.[6] Most of the members of the regiment were of moderate political conviction and during the nationwide elections of 19 January 1919 they voted for moderate parties. Weber says there is no evidence that the majority of Hitler's regiment had become radical, 'neither to the right nor to the left'.[7] But the majority did support the Weimar coalition, consisting of Catholics, left-liberals and social democrats. And exactly this Weimar Republic that counts as the first German democracy was completely rejected later by Hitler.

Following the assassination of Kurt Eisner, the chance of a peaceful future was lost. A Red Army was founded and the Bavarian Soviet Republic was proclaimed. Even if Hitler wouldn't have had any communist leanings, the call of the elected government to fight against the communists was ignored by him, according to Weber.

Yet Weber also concludes that Hitler sympathised with the extreme leftist rule[8] and in his book it even looks like he claims Hitler was a socialist. His arguments are known, meanwhile. Firstly, he was elected in the socialist Raden council in the barracks he lived in and, secondly, he walked in the funeral cortège of the murdered socialist Kurt Eisner, meaning he was a follower of the left socialists he hated so much later on. However, Weber's argumentation is rather shaky. He points to a movie fragment of the funeral cortège and to a picture taken by Heinrich Hoffmann, Hitler's court photographer, of the same event. In the picture, Hitler is supposed to have worn the red armband of the revolution. The picture is rather blurred, though, and Hitler can't be recognised instantly. The movie fragments are not sufficient evidence. They appear in a very subjective part of a documentary

---

6. Weber, p. 255
7. Weber, p. 266
8. Weber, p. 278

by journalist, author and producer Guido Knopp. After zooming in on a man with a thin moustache, who can hardly be established as being Hitler, the image turns red; the colour of the communist revolution.[9]

Weber climbs out on a limb here in his usually often thorough study because, based on such vague black-and-white material, not a single conclusion can be drawn, in particular not about the colour of an armband. Weber also uses Hitler's appointment to deputy representative of his regiment as proof of his flirt with socialism, and in that capacity he would have had to maintain contact with the new communist 'government'.

According to Weber, Hitler supported the incumbent government in the end and he was certainly not yet an ultranationalist and anti-socialist. Hitler's views hadn't crystallised yet, he said. So Hitler had been lying in *Mein Kampf* about his political awakening in Pasewalk. Weber's most conspicuous conclusion though is this: 'We can't arrange the evidence from this period about him that has been preserved in such a way that it matches the image of him as a socialist or that of the ultra-nationalistic, pan-German anti-Semite he would become later on. There is one simple reason for that: he was neither. Hitler was confused and his life could still go either way.'[10]

Plöckinger crushes the rest of the evidence

In 2013, a book by Othmar Plöckinger was published that closed the gap between the publications about the period right after the First World War. Conscientious researcher Plöckinger first points out that no information is available about Hitler's political activities during the revolution, nor is there, in his view, any ground for Joachimsthaler's assertion that Hitler had been present at the socialist manifestation on the Theresienwiese of 16 February 1919. According to Plöckinger, an ordinance exists in which Hitler's entire regiment was ordered to attend this event but that doesn't mean that the members of the regiment, whether they had obeyed the order or not, would be devoted socialists or communists. Within the barracks there was much discussion about the order and there must have been soldiers who refused. There is no certainty whatsoever about Hitler's participation. The fact that Hitler had been a soldier in Munich and in Traunstein in barracks that were subordinate to socialist or communist rule also says hardly anything about his actual political conviction.

---

9. Hitler, Eine Bilanz, volume 1
10. Weber, p. 180

Plöckinger also bans the story about Hitler's work as a station guard to the realm of fairy tales. The picture, in fact the only piece of evidence for the assumption that Hitler was a station guard, should depict him with the other guards. The man in the centre of the picture seems to be Hitler indeed, but the origin of the picture is extremely uncertain. First of all, the date of the picture of the eight men grouped around a table isn't correct and the persons in the picture have not been identified yet. It could just as well be a picture taken before 1918 when Hitler was still in Belgium or northern France. That assumption isn't so strange as it seems: a French paper is actually lying on the table. From the picture published in Joachimsthaler's book, it can't be ascertained which paper it is but the quality of the one in Plöckinger's book is much better. It turns out to be the French paper *Le Journal* and according to Plöckinger it is striking, to say the least, that a French paper is on the table of the guards in the railway station of Munich.[11] As this picture is the only piece of evidence for Hitler being a station guard and an active subject of the socialist government, it can calmly be said this is another Hitler myth.

Hitler's role as a trusted representative in February 1919 also doesn't automatically mean he entertained all sorts of socialist ideas. In this capacity, Hitler would have had to co-operate with the department of propaganda of the socialists but it hardly entailed a political function and, moreover, it was a temporary one. The only point that remains is Hitler being elected as representative of the soldiers in the soldiers' council after the communists had seized power.

On 15 April 1919, Hitler was elected as one of those representatives and if he had actually co-operated with the communists, for the future Hitler this obviously was something to keep secret. But there is actually no evidence for his active co-operation with the regime. The political situation in Munich was very complex at the time and from the barracks, whether under communist rule or not, information about the military and political situation in the city found its way to the imperial troops who had to expel the communists from the city.[12] Hitler's regiment refused to support the Red Army in its struggle against these troops and declared itself neutral on 26 April 1919, in fact a form of passive resistance.

---

11. Plöckinger, US, pp. 38–41
12. Plöckinger, US, p. 51

Insufficient proof

If it is true that Hitler first 'joined' the socialists in order to become their most fanatic foe in the future, it does fuel the opinion that his political choices were mainly prompted by opportunism. In the beginning of his career he may not have meant what he said at all but he just wanted to succeed as a politician on the rise. And if hatred of Jews, anti-socialism, anti-communism and tirades against the Treaty of Versailles could be of any help, he would surely have deployed those elements. There is possibly other evidence for his opportunism but his work for the socialists, mentioned in many sources, can't be part of it anymore. As unsatisfying as it may be, based on existing sources it is impossible to make definite statements about his political conviction in the period until March 1919.[13] During the next period, nothing can be said either about his political sympathies, opportunistic or not. Even when he was elected as soldiers' representative in the communist Raden republic, he didn't actively support the regime, nor did he lift a finger to help expel them. Pictures and movie fragments that are supposed to show Hitler was rubbing elbows with the socialists, were either dated incorrectly or too vague to draw definite conclusions from. At the end of the day, there isn't sufficient evidence for the idea that Hitler was very active during the era of the Raden republic or that he had previously supported the socialist government.

---

13. Plöckinger, US, p. 41, translated by author

Chapter 6

Where is the Blutfahne?

The myth of a lost Nazi relic

It was 9 November 1923 and a train of NSDAP men, attempting to stage a coup d'état, was marching through the streets of Munich. Adolf Hitler was preceded by a number of standard bearers and armed men. At the end of a narrow street near the Feldherrnhalle in the city centre, the police were waiting for them. In the ensuing firefight, fourteen coup perpetrators and four police officers were killed. One of the bearers managed to escape but his flag was soaked with the blood of various rebels who had been killed. The flag was to become one of the most important relics of the Nazis. After the war, the flag vanished without a trace.

The mystical Nazi flag was shown in television series, movies and books but what happened to it at the end of the war is unclear. Hitler's biographers did mention the flag sometimes but hardly occupied themselves with the question of where it was. A search through various sources provides a series of possibilities but the reliability of them is often hard to check. As the flag is a unique object about which the tallest stories circulate, definite statements of its fate should be approached with a healthy distrust.

A number of possibilities

It could well be that the flag, which was kept at party headquarters of the NSDAP, the so-called *Braune Haus* in Munich, had been lost during a bombardment. A second possibility suggested is that the flag fell into Soviet hands. A third option suggested is that the flag is in the possession of a collector in northern Germany. There is also discussion about the question of when the flag was last on public display. Some sources claim it was on 17 April 1944 on the occasion of the funeral of *Gauleiter* Adolf Wagner, while other sources mention 18 April, one day later. At that date, the flag would have been used in the presence of Heinrich Himmler at a ceremony in Berlin of the *Volkssturm*, a people's militia consisting of grown-up men considered unfit for regular military service and young boys.

It was Heinrich Wilhelm Trambauer who had carried the flag during the Hitler putsch of 1923. During the firefight, Trambauer is said to have fallen to the ground with his flag, after which it got soaked with the blood of three men.[1] He escaped with the flag into a house,[2] draped it around his waist, subsequently went to his own house and hid it there.[3] A few months later, he gave the flag to Karl Eggers, one of the other perpetrators of the failed putsch, who returned it to Hitler in 1924. The flag was to become a sacred Nazi relic and was used at all sorts of meetings. The official start of this tradition was the NSDAP Party rally in Weimar on 4 July 1926. After a speech about the enormous importance of the SA, Hitler handed the blood flag to an SS man. Thereafter, 500 standard bearers paraded past.[4] Joseph Goebbels named the meeting 'profound and mystical', almost like a religion.[5] The flag was stored in the 'capital of the movement', Munich in the various offices of the NSDAP. In the party main office on Schellingstrasse, a hall of fame had been created in which the flag was on display and after the party had moved into the new head office in the far larger *Braune Haus* the flag hung in the so-called *Fahnenhalle*. Until the end of the war, this became the permanent quarters of the flag.

History

From 1933 onwards, the flag was taken out on 9 November each year for the memorial march of the Hitler putsch. From the start point of the original route, the *Bürgerbräukeller*, a train of veterans and Nazis including Hitler marched to the *Feldherrnhalle* and from there to the *Königplatz*, where the victims of the putsch had been reburied. The train was always preceded by the *Blutfahne* of the NSDAP. At other official gatherings of the Nazis as well, such as the Party rallies in Nuremberg, the flag was frequently

---

1. The Bavarian Historic Lexicon states that the blood of Andreas Bauriedl, Anton Hechenberger and Lorenz Ritter von Stransky-Griffenfeld ended up on the flag. How it was ascertained that the blood came from these three men isn't clarified.
2. Theatiner Strasse 30 (Bavarian Historic Lexicon)
3. In another version of the story, the Munich police is supposed to have taken the flag but returned it to the NSDAP in 1925.
4. Kirsten, p. 29
5. Kershaw, Hoogmoed, p. 366

present. Usually, it was carried along by Trambauer but after his death Jakob Grimminger, another veteran of the putsch, took over.

Where is the flag?

It is hard to determine where the flag was shown in public for the last time. It must have been on 17 April 1944, at the funeral of *Gauleiter* Adolf Wagner in Munich or on 18 April at a gathering of the *Volkssturm* in Berlin in the presence of Heinrich Himmler. The flag is supposed to have been taken back to the *Braune Haus*. In 1945, the building was severely damaged during a bombardment. If the flag had actually been there, it must have been all but impossible to extricate the correct one from among the debris of the building.

Pictures of the *Fahnenhalle* prove, however, there were lots of flags in the building. It is unlikely the Soviets obtained the flag, provided it was in Munich at the time of the bombardment. As it was, the Soviets captured Berlin while the Americans took Bavaria and Munich. That the flag was last seen in Berlin doesn't mean much though. The said gathering took place in April 1944, almost a year before the end of the war. The flag was habitually stored in Munich, so it is logical it had been returned there after the gathering in Berlin.

The myth

The blood flag was and still is a mythical flag among modern admirers of National Socialism. Extreme right dreamers, for instance, think that the flag is waiting in South America for the rebirth of the *Viertes Reich*. Other than that, other than in a rare instalment of a television series, the flag doesn't get that much attention anymore as it is too much of a detail in history. If it is true that a collector in northern Germany is in possession of the flag, something could be said about its authenticity, based on thorough research. As of today, however, its whereabouts are unknown and that also places the alleged fate of the *Blutfahne* in the category of unproven Hitler myths.

Chapter 7

Was Mein Kampf Hitler's Own Work?

The myths about Hitler's unread book

Mein Kampf is one of the most talked about but less read books ever in the world. At the same time it isn't surprising it is still widely discussed because of its controversial contents. Hitler and his book are still frequently used as argument in all sorts of discussions. As soon as someone goes off the rails by comparing a political scenario with that of the NSDAP or by saying a book shows similarities with Mein Kampf, *the press and public come down hard and the original subject of the discussion soon gets lost. A comparison with* Mein Kampf *will usually hold no water. It does show though that Hitler's book, even unread, is still a sensitive subject.*

Whether after so many years, *Mein Kampf* should be freely available is the subject of a frequently recurring discussion. Champions seem to see proof of the ultimate democracy in it when it is freely available. In a society in which everything can be said and every book read, *Mein Kampf* can't count as an exception. And yet, forbidding the 'most unread book' in the world seems rather senseless, if only because many don't take the trouble to read the book from beginning to end because of its many recurring charges and sidesteps. What kind of book was *Mein Kampf* anyway and, as often claimed, was it read in the past just as rarely as today? Who did contribute to it?

A forbidden book

After the collapse of the Third Reich, the Allies prevented the book from being sold in Germany, but even after their departure the book did not appear on the market. The rights of the book had fallen into the hands of the Free State of Bavaria, which stopped a new printing. There was no question of actual prohibition though. A similar situation arose in the neighbouring Netherlands. There, too, the state claimed to be the owner of the rights, so a ban was not necessary there either. All the more striking was the ruling in 1987 by the *Hoge Raad* – the highest court in the Netherlands – that it was irrelevant who owned the rights as the book was forbidden after all. Only a reference edition for academics was allowed, but that has never been published.

Of course, it was possible to clarify history with quotes from Hitler's book in other books or articles. The German historian Christian Zentner, for example, made use of this loophole in a publication of commented fragments from *Mein Kampf*. When the rights to the book finally expired after seventy years, the very extensive critical edition of the *Institut für Zeitgeschichte* in Germany was published in 2016. It was an immediate bestseller and translations were published in several countries, even though these were two thick volumes in large format.

During Hitler's time as *Reichskanzler* of Germany, the book had already been translated and published in many countries, including the United States, Great Britain and various countries on the European continent; in some of those it was also reprinted after 1945. Nevertheless, the discussion about the book continued. In 2007 a debate was held in the *Tweede Kamer* in the Netherlands, comparable with for instance the House of Commons (UK) or Congress (USA), about a reprint of *Mein Kampf* (or *Mijn Kamp*). A majority voted against. In 2015, the Scottish Labour MP Thomas Docherty called for a national debate on whether *Mein Kampf* should be banned in Great Britain. The book will probably add little to democracy but the question remains how many members have taken the opportunity to read this banned book before passing judgement.[1]

The history of the book[2]

Much is unclear about the origin of *Mein Kampf* but Hitler began seriously putting his thoughts on paper during his imprisonment in Landsberg, when he wrote a plea he would use in the trial against him. The text, over sixty pages long, partly resembles what he wrote in *Mein Kampf* about his time in Vienna, the social problems of that time, his supposed racial problem and Marxism.

An article by Hitler, published in April 1924 in the nationalist magazine *Deutschlands Erwachen*, contains much material that was to be included in

---

1. Zentner, p. 7; Maser (HMK), p. 7; *The Guardian*, 26 January 2015
2. This and the following two paragraphs have mainly been taken from the work (GB) of Plöckinger from 2006.

Mein Kampf,[3] such as remarks about the negative aspects of German trade policy and German politics prior to the First World War, which can all be found in the chapter entitled Munich. The idea to write a book must have originated in the same year. Proof of this is a letter Hitler wrote to Siegfried Wagner, the son of composer Richard Wagner, in May 1924. In it, he said he was writing an account. Its element can easily be found in the first clumsy idea about the title of the book: *4.5 Jahre Kampf gegen Lügen, Dummheiten und Feigheit, eine Abrechnung* – 4.5 years fighting against lies, stupidity and cowardice, an account. The 4.5 years mentioned in the title initially stood for the period prior to the First World War. Later on, this shifted to the *Kampfzeit*, the period of struggle of the NSDAP between 1919 and January 1933. Initially, the lies, stupidity and cowardice also stood for the lies of those who had thrown in the towel at the end of the First World War and later on for the characteristics Hitler attributed to the leaders of the Weimer Republic.

The account, the starting point of the book, was extended gradually and the connection with previously written chapters was cut. Hitler now also appeared as the hero of his own life and the book partly turned into a biography.[4] In the course of time, the title was also shortened until only *Mein Kampf* was left.

The process of writing the book was characterised by chaos. Chapters were shuffled around; biographical chapters were added and the book was split in two parts so an epilogue for the first part had to be written. The date of publication was constantly postponed as well. In November 1924, a public announcement was made to the effect that a book by Adolf Hitler was about to be published but it was moved forward time and again. This was probably caused by financial problems, the question of Hitler's citizenship and a threatened extradition to Austria. Hitler may have fought in the German army but officially, he wasn't a German. To publish a book brimming with criticism of the political leaders at the time was therefore very unwise. The first part of the book was first on sale as late as 18 June 1925.

On the *Obersalzberg* in Bavaria where Hitler later had his famous villa the *Berghof* built, and in the village of Berchtesgaden at the foot of the mountain, Hitler continued working on the second part. It was published on 11 December 1926. In addition to *Mein Kampf* he wrote a second book, which was published as late as fifteen years after his death.

---

3. Plöckinger, GB, p. 23
4. Ryback, p. 86

Contributors

One of the many myths about *Mein Kampf* is that it was hardly Hitler's own work. Many of his associates are supposed to have contributed to it. Othmar Plöckinger,[5] who conducted a meticulous investigation into the period in which the book originated, states, however, that the book really was Hitler's own work for the most part. Thereby he also doubts the assumption, often taken for a fact, that he dictated the contents of the book while in Landsberg prison to the future second man in the Third Reich, Rudolf Hess, or to his driver, Emile Maurice. Both Hess, who is often mentioned as co-author, and Maurice were not in Landsberg prison at the time he prepared the plea for his trial. They arrived later and so they couldn't have contributed to that part. In the past the most unusual names of co-authors were mentioned such as his niece Geli Raubal, who was still at school in the period the book was written. Adolf Müller, the hard-of-hearing printer from Munich, would also have taken the dictation.

Actually, two people contributed to stylistic corrections in *Mein Kampf* as late as the spring of 1925. They were the rather unknown Josef Stolzing-Cerny and the future wife of Rudolf Hess, Ilse Pröhl. Stolzing-Cerny was an anti-Semitic folk writer who worked for the Nazi paper the *Völkische Beobachter* from 1922 onwards. As editor, he mainly applied corrections and changes in style. He did help to adapt the structure of the book though but there is no evidence of massive contributions as regards content. The exact contribution of Ilse Pröhl as to content is unknown.

The role of her future husband, Rudolf Hess, is usually overestimated. He is supposed to have written the first and second part together with Hitler in both Landsberg and Berchtesgaden, or to have rewritten large parts of it. But Hess could only help when Hitler had already made substantial progress. His contribution to the first part can therefore only have been rather limited. He did edit the second part of the book though. Yet Plöckinger calls the large role of Hess in the writing of *Mein Kampf* a legend that has taken root in historical literature.

It is striking that stylistic and small changes as to content continued to be made up to 1939. Most of them must have been of a stylistic nature. Whoever applied them isn't known exactly.

The success of the book

The first print of part one, almost 10,000 books, sold out in 1925. A second printing, again 10,000, was published in December of that year. Sales of the

---
5. Plöckinger, GB, p. 121

first part didn't progress too well and the second part didn't do well either. In the following years sales dropped further. In 1928 both parts together sold a little over 3,000 copies. In 1930, even before the seizure of power, sales increased again. Both parts were merged into a popular edition and of those over 50,000 were sold.

The temporary climax, over a million sold, was reached in 1933, the year in which Hitler rose to power. In the years after, sales dropped again to between 400,000 and 600,000.

After 1933, *Mein Kampf* was used at inaugural ceremonies of party officials and the book was promoted by the army leadership. Libraries also had numerous copies in stock. In addition, the book was being given as a wedding present. This attributed to the reputation of the book as such a mandatory present that it would probably not be read often. At schools, the book was hardly used either, maybe because it was considered too difficult. The contents of *Mein Kampf* occupied a prominent position though. Subjects were often discussed in class, and in all kinds of school books Hitler's thinking took an important place.

The increase of the number of printed copies in 1939, at the beginning of the war is remarkable, just like in 1943 and 1944 when the tide of war turned against Germany. The reason for this last increase was probably the attempt to boost the Nazi morale in these hard times. The last copies of *Mein Kampf* were printed in the autumn of 1944.

Eventually, some 12,450,000 copies of the book were sold in Hitler's lifetime. During the war, 65 per cent of those were printed against only 35 per cent before. Between 1942 and 1944 only 40 per cent of the anticipated sales had been realised. It is hard to find out what people thought about the book. After 1933, it was part of a totalitarian system. Statements by Germans from right after the war aren't always reliable. Someone who admitted having read the book recognised in some way that he was aware of the ideas even before the massive excesses of the system actually took place. The image that is presented of the book being unreadable and unread was helpful in denying involvement or advance knowledge.

Hitler's style

Hitler's way of writing is often considered chaotic. His style is associative and therefore he takes all sorts of detours in *Mein Kampf*, which distract from the main line. This is particularly remarkable in the biographic part at the beginning of the book. The history of his life is interrupted all the time by various political lectures. As soon as Hitler's birthplace, Braunau on the border between Germany and Austria is mentioned, he turns to bombastic statements about destiny having seen to it that he was born precisely on the border between two countries that really belonged to each other. This kind of distracting remarks makes it perfectly clear that his biography is entirely subordinate to the political goal of the book.

Mein Kampf is also a confusing book as it tracks back over entire sentences and paragraphs to statements that have yet to be finished. Added to this is a vast number of paraphrases and redundant repetitions of one and the same point of view that count like the only substantiation of it. Those repetitions suggest a logical structure but on closer inspection this is no more than an argument being worked towards a climax in which, for instance, a shortcoming evolves from a charge to an outright insult.

Furthermore, Hitler likes to evade discussions as to content by discrediting opponents or to establish beforehand that an argument can't be right. The lack of evidence for his own points of view is also striking. Usually he doesn't get beyond a confirmation of its importance: his views are important and sensible and, having said that, that's the end of the argument.

All this seems to be the direct result of Hitler's talent as an orator. The style elements used, like the climax and the repetition, fit much better in a speech than in a book where fragments can be read over and over. This also fuels the idea that the book has supposedly been dictated for a large part. Therefore, it is most striking that in the first print, contrary to an earlier proof, a total of 4,000 day-to-day words like *nun* and *aber* have been included. Thus, the manner of speaking has been purposely inserted later.[6] The reason for this can only be guessed at. Hitler possibly hoped to make the book more accessible to the reader.

Hitler's train of thought

In a study of the book in 2009 by Barbara Zehnpfennig, she states Hitler's thinking did have a systematic nature, despite the criticism. The structure of the book may well be described as chaotic, this is in part due to the frequent interruptions of the writing process and from the many adaptations of the text because of political developments at the time.[7]

The 'system' in Hitler's thinking has to do with his willingness to recognise the ultimate consequence of his argumentation: if the army was not the cause of the defeat in the First World War, then there would have been a question

---

6. Plöckinger, GB, p. 72
7. Plöckinger, GB, p. 29 e.v.

of treason, so there must have been a traitor among the Germans. And that traitor was the Jew, because it couldn't have been a German, as proven by the Austrian history in which the German element had always been the connecting factor. In view of the fact that the patriarch of communism, Karl Marx, was a German Jew who was honoured especially in the Soviet Union and Hitler had already noticed in Vienna that many Jews from the east were entering German territory,[8] for Hitler the knife cut both ways: Germany was under threat from an internal as well as an external enemy.

The German Jew had not only rooted himself in the press and in politics, he also exerted an influence on the ideas of non-Jews. And that is maybe an unconscious masterstroke. Hitler could label all ideas he didn't like as influenced by Jews, even if they came from an Aryan. The only way to get the German people back on their feet was to eradicate this influence from the German populace; the ultimate consequence being Auschwitz.

Another conspicuous element in Hitler's argumentation is that there is often only one cause of a problem. There is no room for nuance or discussion, alternatives are hardly ever mentioned and real proof of a thesis is usually lacking. Hitler's movement was a people's movement that seemed to benefit the man in the street in particular. And it goes without saying that only one cause and one solution to the German problem appeals to the population much more than a complex problem with numerous solutions.

Hitler used Biblical phrases and quotes quite frequently, especially when he attempted to work towards a climax. One of his better-known speeches ended with a variation on Our Father and the last word was 'Amen'. And in *Mein Kampf*, a fragment about the right to own foreign property is followed by an intriguing mix of his own thinking and of the Bible when he says: 'Then swords will turn into plows and the daily bread for the descendants sprout from the tears of war.' Hitler seems to see in the war the necessary foundation on which the descendants can build their future. So, it is the base of his idea of *Lebensraum*, the notion that Germany needed more space to feed its population.

That kind of reference to the Bible appears in many different places, but the opposite to the exalted Biblical language also appears: the slanging match. In moments of excitement, Hitler sometimes goes all the way in his book, especially when Jews are involved, and he doesn't shy away from saying Jews carry diseases and comparing them to animals and bacteria.

In *Mein Kampf*, sources aren't mentioned. It appears from the works by, for instance Brigitte Hamann and Tymothy Ryback, that there was an

---

8. Hamann, HW, p. 467 e.v.

abundance of them. From the works of other biographers of Hitler also, an image appears of a man who vents few ideas that are entirely his own in *Mein Kampf*. Hitler, however, wanted to present an image of somebody who had all his ideas neatly arranged at a young age and who knew what he wanted to achieve. Omitting these sources actually helped to confirm that image.

'*Mein Kampf* is, in its chaotic platitude and dependence on daily political reality, the mirror image of the development of Hitler's ideology,' according to Plöckinger.[9] And this ideology, and so *Mein Kampf* itself, has been effectively summarised by that renowned biographer of Hitler, Ian Kershaw: 'In the early twenties, Hitler got the strong notion he had a "national mission" – Messianic attitude as remarked ironically by someone at the time. That mission can be condensed as follows: mould the masses into a nation; take over the state; destroy the enemy in our midst – the November criminals, that is to say Jews, Marxists, in Hitler's eyes all of the same breed – build up your defence; see to expansion of territory "by means of the sword" in order to secure Germany's future by putting the *Raumnot* (lack of space) right and obtaining new territories in eastern Europe.'[10]

The dagger thrust legend

The dagger trust legend is a theory that explains why the German army had not actually lost the First World War, saying it had been politics that had stabbed the army in the back, as it were. Hitler's version of this could be heard in his speeches but he also dealt with it in his book. 'Now, in the autumn of 1918, we are standing on the terrain for the third time onto which we stormed in 1914. The villages of Comines, where we came to rest in the past, had now turned into a battlefield. But although the terrain remained the same, the people had changed: now the soldiers were also involved in politics. Like anywhere else, the poison from the fatherland began to have an effect here also,'[11] as Hitler described the reason in *Mein Kampf* why Germany, in his opinion, had lost the First World War.

Hitler's reasoning was the extreme right-wing version of the dagger trust legend that went around in army circles. Hitler thought that when in November 1918 a revolution erupted in Germany, Jews, socialists and democrats had stabbed the almost victorious German army in the back with

---

9. Plöckinger, GB, p. 29
10. Kershaw, HDH, p. 364
11. *Mein Kampf*, p. 227

a dagger, forcing it to stop fighting.[12] He made little distinction between these groups of 'traitors'. The original dagger trust legend, however, was a conspiracy theory about the defeatist influence of the *Heimat*, for which the civilians and the politicians were responsible in the first place, not necessarily the Jews.

Hitler's vision on the end of the First World War had little to do with reality though. While the battle was still raging at full force, there were various reasons that made the outcome of the war insecure for Germany. The army had to fight a vastly superior opponent, many mistakes were made in waging the war and the battle weariness of the soldiers increased. Although the army leadership already knew in the summer of 1918 that the war at the front might well end in failure, it kept saying that the Germans would win the war. Events proved otherwise. The German Emperor was dethroned; left-radicals established workers, councils in order to exert influence; in Munich, the socialist republic was proclaimed; soldiers revolted and a socialist *Reichskanzler* took charge of the country.

The dagger trust legend gained even more popularity due to these chaotic developments, and more than likely it became one of Hitler's favourite subjects. He took it out fanatically on the 'November criminals', those who had been responsible for the capitulation in November 1918. In *Mein Kampf* he continued: 'So, everything had been in vain ... And two million men had died for nothing ... Did all this really happen so now a group of miserable criminals would put their hands to the fatherland?' But the dagger trust legend was a legend and not for nothing. The suggestion that the army could have won the war was a false one. The army suffered its largest losses during the last phase of the conflict and the morale of the troops dropped steadily. And of course, the German population had also long lost its stomach for war. The chance of losing the war was more than even, and if that happened, the way for an invasion of the German Empire lay wide open. Negotiations for peace seemed to be the only sensible option.

These negotiations, though, had burdened the nation with the Weimar Republic and the Treaty of Versailles, causing Germany to lose territory, forcing her to make repair payments and to disarm. What the alternative – continued fighting – would have achieved couldn't be foreseen, especially by the common citizen. That just didn't happen. And so, Hitler could vent conspiracy theories like the dagger trust legend for years on end. Yet, in the light of history it can be established what could have happened if the fighting had continued until the end. Although the end of the First World

---

12. Weber, p. 298

War wouldn't have progressed precisely the way it did, Hitler's second war did clearly show the result of this 'fighting to the bitter end'.

Unreadable

The inaccessible style of Hitler's writing is one of the reasons why the book was hardly read. The earliest critics of the Nazi movement were pleased to know that Hitler's followers had rarely read the book and that they couldn't take it seriously. Even among the Nazi big wigs, the book would have been rarely read or not at all. Otto Strasser, an early member of the NSDAP who belonged to the left wing of the party and opposed Hitler later on despite his anti-Semitism and nationalism, told a remarkable story in a book, published in 1940, about a speech in which he had quoted from *Mein Kampf*. Consequently, he was asked in astonishment whether he had actually read the book. After some questioning it turned out that a large group of prominent Nazis, including Joseph Goebbels, hadn't read the book.[13] Although Strasser often repeated this story, each time with other prominent Nazis, he stuck to his statement that the book was the best sold but the worst read book ever.

Hatred of Jews

The question of where Hitler's anti-Semitism came from has been the subject of exhaustive discussions since the war. Vienna's anti-Semitism is often mentioned but Munich, where Hitler embarked on his political career, could be decisive here. In *Mein Kampf*, Hitler says himself he became an anti-Semite in Vienna. It is questionable though whether this is credible.

When Hitler was living in Vienna as a young adult, anti-Semitism was already all around. The rediscovered swastika, the Führer cult and the hatred of Jews were well-known elements in Viennese politics. Hitler's essential elements of his world view, such as the myth of pure German blood; the international enemies of the Teutons: the Catholic Church, the Jews and the Freemasons; the imminent global war in which the Aryan race would retake its original rights; a German state that not only consisted of Germans but also of English, Dutch and Scandinavians and the myth of the Force from above, the Germanic folk leader ruling like a God, always right and

---

13. Ryback, p. 97: Ryback points out that Goebbels had nothing but praise for *Mein Kampf* in his diary (date 14 October 1925).

infallible; this can all be found in the writings of anti-Semite and Viennese author Guido von List (1848–1919), apart from the rediscovered swastika.[14]

It seems likely Hitler copied these elements, including anti-Semitism, from this or some other Viennese author or politician. At the same time though, he had various Jewish acquaintances and there were also many Jews among the buyers of his paintings. The Jewish doctor of the Hitler family, Dr Bloch, treated Hitler's mother in Linz and stood by her on her deathbed, to Hitler's full satisfaction. Years later, the doctor was still so much honoured by Hitler that he is supposed to have said: 'He is an *Edeljude*. If all Jews were like that, there would be no anti-Semitism.'[15] When Hitler had long left Vienna, another Jew played an important role in his life during the First World War when he was awarded a decoration through a Jewish officer. This kind of example makes it hard to believe that in Vienna Hitler was already the Jew hater he was to become in later years.

Most of the statements in *Mein Kampf* about Hitler's political awakening are doubtful. It was to his advantage to exploit his political conviction as early as possible, especially in regard to the Führer cult in which a genius had to seize the reins. At birth, you are a genius already, you can't learn to be a genius. Hitler's alleged statements during the First World War from which it would appear he had been convinced of the relation between Marxism and Jewry at an early age have never been confirmed by witnesses either.

Despite these nuances, Hitler must have acquainted himself with the vast supply of anti-Jewish pamphlets and papers in Vienna and he held Viennese nationalist politician Georg Schönerer in high esteem for turning against foreign Jewish elements.[16] In any case, Hitler took these ideas about Jews, which weren't practically useful for him, to Munich with him as memories and when he returned, frustrated, from the First World War he began using them in politics after the communist revolution. When he joined a small political party he could combine his aversion towards Bolshevism, which had become common practice in Munich after the revolution, with the anti-Semitism he knew from Vienna. From that moment on he started lumping Jews and communists together more and more.[17] The fact that he was successful in his speeches in which he presented this mixture could be called the beginning of what was to evolve into his extreme hatred of Jews. The process by which anti-Jewish sloganeering led to purposeful anti-Jewish

---

14. Haidinger, pp. 38–39
15. Hamann, HE, p. 261 and cover
16. Hamann, HW, p. 34
17. Kershaw, HDH, p. 364

measures and the ultimate attempt at destroying the Jewish population was a gradual one afterwards. Although anti-Jewish measures were soon brought into effect after the seizure of power in 1933, it took until the 1940s before there was talk about extermination camps where killing of Jews was a goal in itself. It is all the more conspicuous that Hitler talks about the killing of the Jews from the 1920s onwards, already using terms like 'gas' and 'concentration camps'.[18]

It is said that Hitler's hatred of the Jews was more important to him than his foreign policy and that he had their extermination on his mind as early as 1919. That is difficult to prove, however, as his words could only be turned into action after 1933. As already said, the extermination of Jews really gained momentum in the 1940s when it became clear that Germany was not going to win the war in the Soviet Union. This was according to the prediction Hitler had thought up and developed himself that the Jews would suffer the consequences when they plunged the world into a war again.

Written by himself

Large parts of *Mein Kampf* were written by Hitler himself but that doesn't mean his ideas were original. He found them everywhere, only he didn't mention where. It is certain that others tampered with the text but the role Rudolf Hess was supposed to have played in this is still overstated. Hitler in turn kept his silence about who had helped him and who were responsible for all the changes in subsequent editions. And that fits neatly into the image of the great leader and the genius he wanted to present in his book, as such a man obviously neither needs sources nor assistance from others.[19] *Mein Kampf* was a popular book but sales were mandatory for a part and it is hard to establish whether the book has actually been read. For those who have read it, more often than not, the book will have been a confusing mixture of weak and repeated arguments for disturbing theories that are being fired at the reader in a narcotic manner and partly styled spoken language.

---

18. Fontaine, 1992
19. In other chapters, including 'Was Hitler an artistic genius', the genius cult around Hitler is dealt with more extensively.

Chapter 8

Hitler's Second Book

The myth of a secret manuscript never published

It was considered one of the most important discoveries on the subject of Hitler after the war: the diaries of the Führer from which quotes were published in the German magazine Stern *in 1983. It soon turned out to be an outright forgery. The historical facts mentioned in the diaries weren't correct, Hitler's use of language seemed different than usual, the handwriting wasn't Hitler's and the paper and ink used were post-war. Konrad Kujau, who had sold the material to the weekly, admitted he had forged it. He was sentenced to a long prison term. The question arose whether this was the only falsification of Hitler's work that had been published. For instance, how about Hitler's second book that was never published. Could that be a forgery as well?*

Many things about the manuscript of Hitler's second book were still unclear after the war and the fact that it was found in America long after was a complicating factor. How did it end up there and was it still possible to determine what kind of manuscript it was? Gerhard L. Weinberg, who found the material, was a German-Jewish historian who had fled Germany as a little boy with his family and had ended up in America at the end of the 1940s. After the stories about the falsifications of Hitler's diaries and during the later publication of the English translations, he was to provide more clarity about the authenticity of the document. The main question was: if Hitler had taken the trouble to write a second book, then why was it never published in his lifetime?

The secret manuscript

At the end of the war, many official documents of Hitler and other high-ranking Nazis were destroyed. On the *Obersalzberg* for instance, Hitler's adjutant, Julius Schaub, burned large stacks of papers, letters and other documents of Hitler. Other material was hidden and it even seemed as if all sorts of documents were left behind on the wet floor of the bunker in Berlin. Other objects were shipped to the various Allied countries that took over power in Germany. In that tangle of destroyed, hidden, relocated and fortunately sometimes categorised and well-preserved documents, it was difficult to search for the manuscript that Hitler had wanted to publish as a book in the second half of the 1920s. It took until 1949 before a reference to the manuscript appeared in a book by the French officer Albert Zoller. He had spoken to Hermann Göring and one of Hitler's secretaries and had written a book about it. He kept the name of the secretary who had provided him with such important information to himself. The woman, who turned out to have been Hitler's long-time secretary Christa Schröder, told him that Hitler had started on a book about foreign policy in 1925.[1] Nobody had seen the manuscript, she said, but Rudolf Hess was the only one who knew more about it.[2] Based on this single reference, Weinberg decided to search for the document.[3]

Meanwhile, the usual Hitlerian secrecy about the manuscript had arisen, in particular because of Zoller keeping silent about the identity of the secretary. Her remark that Hitler had briefed only Hess about the contents of the book could have meant that it concerned a mysterious text describing who knows what kind of secret plan. The so-called fact that hardly anyone knew about it was simultaneously confirmed and denied by a high-ranking German official and head of Hitler's *Kanzlei* for years, Otto Meisner. He stated that the manuscript, with the intriguing title *Mein Bundnis mit England* – my relation to England – was only known to Julius Schaub. So, he confirmed that there were only a few people who knew the manuscript but he did mention a name other than Schröder's. And that meant that after the war at least four people would have known of the existence of the book: Christa Schröder, Rudolf Hess, Otto Meisner and Julius Schaub. There was hardly any question anymore about it being a truly secret manuscript and further investigation revealed that many more people were aware of Hitler's writing activities after *Mein Kampf*.[4]

Discovery of the manuscript

In 1951, it turned out that, indeed, more people knew something about the existence of the second book. A man named Erich Lauer had seen

---

1. The year was not right. Schröder must have been mistaken.
2. Plöckinger, GB, p. 161
3. Weinberg, p. xi
4. Plöckinger, GB, p. 161: On p. 162, Plöckinger mentions another two contemporaries who knew Hitler was writing a second book: Rudolff Buttmann and Winifred Wagner.

the manuscript of a book by Hitler at his and Hitler's publisher Eher. The employee who had showed it to him once told him there were two copies of the document: one in the safe of the publisher and the other kept at the *Obersalzberg*. After the war, this information ended up in the Institution of Modern History in Munich and that meant that, apart from Weinberg, the institute was searching for the manuscript as well.

Weinberg was the first to discover the material, in 1958 in an archive in Alexandria, Virginia, USA. There it had been assumed, without a proper analysis of the document, that it was a part of *Mein Kampf* and it had been categorised accordingly. A memo attached to the manuscript revealed that an American officer had found the document in a publishing firm in Munich. The original had been sent to America with a copy to Great Britain. In 1961 the document was published for the first time, in German, and the reactions were diverse. Baldur von Schirach, the former leader of the *Hitler Jugend*, and Rudolf Hess, Hitler's former second man, both imprisoned in Nuremberg, thought it was a forgery. Albert Speer, however, remembered that Hitler had once said something about an unpublished book he had written. Hess also knew about its existence, as already indicated by secretary Schröder. A letter by Hess from 1928 was found in which he wrote that Hitler was busy writing a book. As in 1928 both parts of *Mein Kampf* had long since been completed, Hess must have meant the manuscript of Hitler's second book. The content of the book, which had meanwhile been returned to Germany, does reveal that the text concerned must have been written around 1928.

The 'mysterious' dictation

The content of the book was dictated to Max Amann, publisher and brother in arms of Adolf Hitler; at any rate, that is what Weinberg assumed. According to Othmar Plöckinger, who in connection with *Mein Kampf* had already discovered that there were many fairy tales about the dictation of Adolf Hitler, there is no evidence for that assumption. Apart from the assumption that Amann also took the dictation of *Mein Kampf*, which was doubted by Plöckinger, there is nothing to be found about it. Therefore it is more likely that the manuscript of Hitler's second book had been dictated to a secretary of the publisher.[5]

The most important new subject of the book is the issue of South Tyrol. At the end of the First World War the Austrian province was ceded to Italy, causing great unrest among the German-speaking population. Mussolini

---

5. Plöckinger, GB, pp. 163–164

was after all a Nationalist and under Italian rule, the German culture of the majority of the population in the region was suppressed. Moreover, massive immigration of Italians took place. Obviously, Austrian and Bavarian Nationalists weren't pleased and, going by the vision that all Germans had to live within the German empire, this should also have applied to Hitler. But he was of the opinion that his claim on South Tyrol should be waived in favour of an alliance with Italy.[6] Because of this, Hitler found himself in a position in which he was under attack from both left and right. Therefore, the issue was very important for him. And although he had already written about it in the second part of *Mein Kampf* and the parts of the book about South Tyrol had already been published in the form of pamphlets, in 1928 Hitler felt the need to make his views known once more in his new book. In 1939, Hitler and Mussolini entered into an agreement about the region, at the expense of the population, but ten years earlier it had not come to that yet.

Apart from the issue concerning South Tyrol, the rest of the manuscript contained few innovative ideas and no big revelations at all. The usual theories about race and *Lebensraum* were dealt with once more and Hitler stressed even now that Germany had lost the First World War by a dagger trust in the back of the army by the politicians. Of course, Hitler's anti-Semitism played an important role again. Although the text is of interest to historians, Ian Kershaw rightly points out that nothing much new is to be found in the book. To believers in conspiracies and to those who hoped to discover the great secret of Hitler's thinking, this second book must have been a disappointment as to its content.

Never published

After the text had been dictated, there had been no more alterations and corrections, Weinberger said. If the book had been close to publication, this would have been the thing to do – in *Mein Kampf*, such changes were indeed made.[7] It follows from the simple fact that no more attention was paid to the manuscript, that it was eventually considered less important or less suitable for publication. Kershaw roughly mentions two reasons for this: money and the lack of actual value of the manuscript.[8] The issue of South Tyrol became less important by the day and sales of *Mein Kampf* in 1928

---

6. Kershaw, Hoogmoed, p. 379
7. Weinberg, p. xxiii
8. Kershaw, Hoogmoed, p. 379

were far from satisfactory. That year, just 3,015 copies of the book were sold.[9] Weinberg assumes that publisher Amann must have understood that Hitler would become his own rival on the market with his new book. Yet, until May 1929 there was still public discussion about Hitler's new book. Then it fell silent. In 1929, sales of *Mein Kampf* did double[10] but even if that would have meant there was a market for the second book, it was too late to publish the unedited manuscript. In that year, the political situation changed too quickly and in order to remain up to date, the text would have required radical changes.[11]

No secret

Hitler's untitled second book was a repetition of his first in many ways. It contained an additional chapter about South Tyrol but the theme was largely the same: Germany needed *Lebensraum* and the Jews got the short end of the stick again. Furthermore, it was no secret that Hitler was working on a book once more. Various people from his entourage knew about it, including Winifred Wagner, daughter-in-law of composer Richard Wagner and a close friend of Hitler. The manuscript turned out not to be a forgery. It was an original text by Hitler that was completed after *Mein Kampf* and never published, partly because to do so would not have been lucrative and partly because the content was already outdated before the book could be printed.

---

9. Weinberg, p. xxiv; Plöckinger, GB, p. 181
10. Plöckinger, GB, p. 182. In that year, a total of 7,664 copies of *Mein Kampf* (part I and II) had been sold, to be exact.
11. The Young plan, which demanded recovery payments from Germany until 1988, was vehemently opposed by the NSDAP in that year and was not mentioned in the script of Hitler's second book.

Chapter 9

Did Hitler Believe in the Protocols of the Wise Men of Zion?

Hitler's belief in a forged document

One of the most famous forgeries in world history is a document with the intriguing title The Protocols of the Wise Men of Zion. *It is a compilation of twenty-four protocols, from which it would appear the Jews are striving towards world dominance. Exactly how this forgery came about isn't known, but that the Protocols are based on various fictitious texts is hardly a point for discussion. Hitler knew the manuscript, he even referred to it in* Mein Kampf, *but did he really believe in the authenticity of the manuscript or did he simply use it for his own anti-Semitic goals?*

The *Protocols* already existed before Hitler took power and they were no brainchild of the Nazis. The first version is from 1903 and was published in Russia. Whether the Nazis knew it was a forgery or not, it goes without saying that they didn't stop the distribution of a document that damaged the Jews so efficiently. The indestructible myth of the *Protocols of the Wise Men of Zion* was, according to Joseph Goebbels, very useful for propaganda.

Contents of the *Protocols*

The *Protocols of the Wise Men of Zion* is a text that was drafted by twelve, thirteen or 900 wise men at a special and secret Jewish congress.[1] During this meeting it was discussed how the Jews could achieve world dominance. This was explained in twenty-four protocols. It is not so strange that it still is unclear which congress it was, who attended it and who wrote the *Protocols*, keeping in mind that it is a forgery, but there are still those who believe in

---
1. Hagenmeister, p. 89

the authenticity of the document. In reality, however, it is a compilation of various fictitious texts that were presented as an authentic document.[2]

In these *Protocols*, various issues pass review, such as international politics and the economic conspiracy of the Jews, the propaganda to be conducted, the press, the destruction of religion as a herald of the rise of the Jewish God and the future Jewish ruler. Names and dates are not mentioned in the text, and the issues being discussed are so common that it does not appear strange that the document still enjoys a vast popularity among the believers in conspiracies.

The history of the document

The history of the origin of the *Protocols of the Wise Men of Zion* is very complex but it seems that the French satirist and lawyer Maurice Joly unwittingly provided the basis for it. In 1864, he published a book[3] in which Machiavelli and Montesquieu, sitting in hell, were discussing the policies of French Emperor Napoleon III. Joly's book is supposed to have been prohibited in France but it is said that the text was smuggled to Russia, where parts of it were used in drafting the *Protocols*. Another part of the document was copied from a book by journalist-author Sir John Retcliff, alias Hermann Goedsche. He was an anti-Semite author of historic novels during Romanticism in Germany. His book entitled *Biarritz* was based on Joly's but he added a story to the political dialogue about a secret meeting of representatives of the twelve tribes of Israel that took place after midnight in a cemetery somewhere in Prague. At the end of the book, a rabbi took the floor, voicing the wish that the Jews would dominate the world in a hundred years. This part in particular was published time and again in Nazi Germany.

It has also been said that the work originated during a Zionist congress in Basle but substantial evidence does not exist for this. Following the first publication of the *Protocols* in Russia, the document was translated into various languages and distributed around the world. The first German edition was published in 1920, a few years before Hitler started writing *Mein Kampf*.

The *Protocols* are still being distributed today. They can be found on the internet in various languages. Many websites indicate it is a forgery but,

---

2. Hagenmeister, p. 94
3. Entitled: Dialogue in hell between Machiavelli and Montesquieu about power of the state and democracy.

particularly in the Arabian world, they are still considered authentic: the Hamas manual, for instance, refers to the *Protocols*. A few years ago, Klaas Smelik of Gent University published a book about the Protocols entitled *The Seven Lives of the Protocols of the Wise Men of Zion*. About the falsified text popping up time and again he says: 'Each time one thinks the falsification is exposed once and for all, it starts a new life within a new historical framework. Extremely frustrating.'[4]

The *Protocols* and the Nazis

After the first German edition of the document, Alfred Rosenberg, the Estonian party ideologist of the Nazis, published a commentary on the document in 1923. Thereafter, the *Protocols* were reprinted several times. Adolf Hitler also referred to the *Protocols* in the first part of *Mein Kampf*. He wrote: 'How firmly the entire existence of this population is based on a continuous lie is established in the "*Wise Men of Zion*" in a unique way. It is a document which fosters a glowing hatred against anything Jewish. "It is a forgery," the *Frankfurter Zeitung* groans time and again and that is the best proof of the authenticity of it. Whichever Jewish brain has proclaimed these revelations doesn't matter at all, the fact is they reveal the nature and the goals of the Jewish people in an almost appalling manner, explaining the internal connection as well as the highest goal.'[5] It didn't matter to Hitler whether it was a forgery or not, as long as it described the true nature of the Jew: an almost medieval way of dealing with sources.

The *Protocols* kept popping up, even after 1933. It was expected of German students to know the text and Nazi papers such as the *Völkische Beobachter* and *Der Stürmer* often referred to the anti-Semitic *Protocols*. Minister of Propaganda Joseph Goebbels had read the book once but deemed it unsuitable for propaganda, but in May 1943 he corrected this[6] when he remarked in his diary that the *Protocols* were just as actual as on the day of the first publication.[7] It is likely his reassessment had been influenced by a discussion he had with Hitler on 12 May. Goebbels wrote that Hitler had

---

4. *Reformatorisch Dagblad*, 31 January 2011
5. *Mein Kampf*, pp. 358–359
6. Goebbels' diary, pp. 1932–1933. Goebbels usually wrote a day later about what he had been through or had discussed. He entered his remarks about the Protocols on 13 May 1943. He would have studied them on 12 May or earlier. His discussion with Hitler took place on 12 May.
7. Goebbels, 13 May, pp. 1932–1933

said that the *Protocols* could lay claim to absolute authenticity.[8] But what does that mean? Did Hitler not doubt the authenticity of the document for a moment or does the careful repetition of his words indicate that he actually left the authenticity of it unanswered? It is hard to say because by saying the *Protocols* could lay claim to authenticity, Goebbels left unanswered whether Hitler really thought they were genuine.

Hitler did not alter his views on the *Protocols* over the course of many years. In his view, Jews all over the world were equal, and whether living in a ghetto in the east or on Wall Street, their goal was the same everywhere.[9] That goal was described in the *Protocols* and it made no difference really whether they were authentic, laid claim to it or were a forgery.

To Hitler, Russia was a sterling example of a country completely dominated by the Jews and their ideas. The *Protocols* being first printed in Russia matched Hitler's idea perfectly that communism and Zionism were one and the same thing. Ian Kershaw states that the *Protocols* influenced the origin of this vision.[10]

Hitler's belief in a myth

Whether Hitler did or didn't believe in the authenticity of the *Protocols of the Wise Men of Zion* isn't clear. He knew there were doubts about the genuineness of the text and therefore he probably didn't give a clear opinion on it. His total agreement with the anti-Semitic tenor of the text is no point for discussion either. Hitler himself was quite clear about that. Apart from its authenticity, the material was more than suitable to substantiate Hitler's truth about the Jews: the Jews were striving for world dominance and thereby engaged in a mysterious battle with the Aryan people, among others. More than a century after the first publication of the *Protocols* and over seventy-five years after the death of Hitler, the myth still survives in some sense because 'you don't convince real anti-Semites'.[11] But there is no doubt whatsoever about the content of the document being entirely fictitious.

---

8. Goebbels, p. 1933. It says verbatim (in German): 'Der Führer vertritt den Standpunkt, dass die Zionistische Protokolle absolute Echtheit beanspruchen könnten.' 'The Führer is of the opinion that the Zionist Protocols can lay claim to absolute authenticity.' Obviously, this is formulated very cautiously politically. It does not say that Hitler thinks they are authentic but they may well be. Ian Kershaw, (volume 2, p. 783) used the same diary as a source but he concludes Hitler really did think these Protocols were 'absolutely authentic'. If Goebbels is the only source, this is an uncertain assumption. (By the way, it was not Kershaw's intention to prove that Hitler thought these Protocols were authentic, he only wanted to show in what way Hitler spoke about the Jews in 1943.)
9. Goebbels, 13 May 1943, pp. 1932–1933
10. Kershaw, Hoogmoed, p. 214
11. A statement by author Klaas Smelik in the *Reformatorisch Dagblad*, 31 January 2011

Chapter 10

Did Hitler Create an Economic Miracle?

His role in rebuilding Germany

Hitler was the inventor of the German Autobahn – highway. With its construction, he managed to stimulate the economy to such an extent that unemployment in the country had evaporated overnight. From 1933 onwards, prosperity increased to such a level that it had become an economic miracle and, according to the Nazis, Hitler's genius was mainly behind it, naturally. Probably because the situation in Germany actually improved after he had risen to power, after the war people kept saying that the economic rebuilding of Germany in the 1930s was the only good thing Hitler had been responsible for.

For the Germans, life in the 1930s was far better than in the previous years but the question remains whether or not in Hitler's Germany there was a sound economic policy that could have held out for long. According to Dutch historian Willem Melching, there 'was no question about any sound funding of his economic wonder. In fact, from 1937 onwards, Hitler steered Germany inevitably towards the economic abyss.'[1] So, many critical observations can be added to the persistent myth of Hitler's fantastic economic policy, something historians and economists have known for a long time.

Ancient ideals

After Hitler rose to power, surprisingly little was achieved of the stereotype image of the National Socialist economic policy. For instance, Hitler had written in *Mein Kampf* that the National Socialist state didn't know any classes,[2] but a society without them has never materialised in Germany. Other old National Socialist ideas were the nationalisation of large

---

1. Melching, p. 15
2. *Mein Kampf*, p. 702

companies and the redistribution of property ownership, but that didn't amount to much either.[3] Furthermore, Hitler had promised he would nationalise warehouses, enabling small businesses to survive, but apart from the elimination of the competition by Jewish shopkeepers, Hitler did nothing that looked like it.[4] Romantic ideas about guilds and agriculture that were to become the foundation of the 'new' Germany came from a radical side of the party that Hitler didn't like too much. Based on this ideal, the agricultural sector was heavily protected by, for instance, imposing minimum prices, but economically speaking that yielded very little as well. Instead of a return to the countryside the process of urbanisation also continued in the Nazi period.[5] German farms were too small and too old-fashioned to be able to compete against foreign farmers and, besides, wages in the war industry were relatively high, causing the young to migrate to the cities. The sector could only survive by extensive protection.[6]

Unemployment

An idea that did gain immediate and full attention after 1933 was solving the massive unemployment in Germany. In 1933, the country numbered 5.7 million unemployed; at the beginning of 1938, this figure had dropped to just 200,000.[7] Right at the beginning of his chancellorship, Hitler had declared in a speech on radio[8] that unemployment would be solved within four years and that it was given absolute priority. But, as with so many things, Hitler had not thought up the ideas for the provision of labour himself but had copied them from his predecessors. He hardly came up with new ideas. By constructing roads, building houses and countering dual incomes and deploying jobless citizens in agriculture,[9] but in particular because the international economy was rising, he succeeded in quickly reducing unemployment. At the same time, the wages of those who already had a job were frozen, which could only be achieved by the abolition of free trade unions. In *Mein Kampf*, Hitler had stated that trade unions were

---

3. Sijthoff, p. 20
4. Melching, p. 90
5. Sijthoff, p. 21
6. Melching, p. 91
7. Sijthoff, p. 16. It is difficult to say whether those numbers are reliable but they do give a clear indication.
8. Ullrich (AH), pp. 5–55. During his speech on 1 February 1933.
9. Ullrich (AH), p. 455. It is often unclear what the precise effect of the various projects was. There are, for instance, hardly any statistics about the effect of countering dual incomes.

necessary but that 'all necessary organs of this state should come from the (National Socialist) movement itself'.[10] The trade unions should therefore be National Socialistic and that prevented protests against the freezing of wages. However, all these policies aimed at solving unemployment could only lead to an increase in the national deficit.[11] Freezing wages could make little difference to that.

Economic policy

A *Wirtschaftswunder* – economic miracle – such as the one that supposedly existed in Germany should have been based on a well thought out economic plan, one would think. Whether in the 1930s in Germany there was such a plan or real economic policy, is doubtful.[12] Ian Kershaw was quite clear about it. Organs including contractor *Organisation Todt*, the *Hitler Jugend* and the Four Year Plans 'were suspended somewhere between the party and the state' and were 'mutually competing and sometimes overlapping bureaucracies which in turn led to endless discussions about authorisations'.[13] The Nazi policy was more ad hoc than improvising,[14] more pragmatic than based on a well-defined idea. 'Many decisions were taken and revoked, various organisations and institutions were created and ended up on a dead-end track in the long run, many officials enjoyed power and prestige and eventually faded into total oblivion.'[15]

Hitler did have ideas of his own but they were actually aimed more towards great ideals than economic reality. He thought, for instance, that the German population could only have a future if Germany became a world power.[16] That position could only be achieved by creating much more *Lebensraum* in territories where useful raw materials were available. His promise that the National Socialist worker would benefit materially from the growth of the national society[17] may have sounded fine but in *Mein Kampf* he had written long before that he was striving for territorial expansion and in the long run, that inevitably meant war. What material gain this yielded for the common man became clear at the end of the war.

---

10. *Mein Kampf*, pp. 699–700
11. Sijthoff, p. 28
12. Sijthoff, p. 18
13. Kershaw, Hoogmoed, p. 702
14. Sijthoff, p. 19
15. Sijthoff, p. 19
16. *Mein Kampf*, pp. 755–756
17. *Mein Kampf*, p. 703

In order to reduce unemployment, rearmament and the creation of *Lebensraum*, Hitler especially used the existing 'capitalist-industrial culture' and he never instigated a social economic revolution.[18] The construction of the *Autobahnen*, the rebuilding of cities, the building of the largest holiday resort in the world – the never-finished *Seebad Prora* on the island of Rügen – and stimulating the automobile industry may well have suggested something else but Hitler's policy was often first and foremost a continuation of existing policy. Hitler further appeased various groups in society through financial means, according to historian Willem Melching, such as the army, farmers, the industry and the working class, for which employment was as good as guaranteed. How these expenditures were to be funded was completely unknown. According to historian Götz Aly, Hitler immediately assumed he would rob Europe dry during a war in order to finance this German *Wirtschaftswunder*.[19] Whether Hitler was purposefully preparing for this as early as 1933 is an open question but in *Mein Kampf* he had already voiced the need for *Lebensraum*. As a result of rocketing state expenditure, in any case the notion of *Lebensraum* at least became a self-fulfilling prophecy.

The Autobahn myth

Many of the ideas for renovation or change were not original Nazi ideas at all. The best example is the construction of a network of highways. The idea still exists that Hitler was the inventor of the modern network of highways in Germany but the plans had actually been made long before he rose to power. Although Hitler did stimulate the construction, it was not his idea.

The first highway in Europe was the *Automobil-Verkehrs- und Übungs-Strasse* (AVUS) near Berlin, which could also be used as a race track. Anyone who enters Berlin today on the E 51 uses the old highway annex race track. Hitler had nothing to do with its construction, though. Building began as early as 1913, the year in which Hitler, still an unknown draughtsman, moved from Vienna to Munich. Construction was delayed by the First World War and was only completed in 1921. Another stretch of highway, constructed in the early 1930s before Hitler came to power, was between Cologne and Bonn. Because in Nazi propaganda it should be Hitler who was behind the new German *Autobahn*, this highway was downgraded to a normal provincial road, after which Hitler could symbolically scoop up the

---

18. Sijthoff, p. 22
19. Melching, pp. 81–82

first earth for the construction of the highway between Frankfurt am Main and Darmstadt on 23 September 1933.[20]

Constructing highways enabled Hitler to reduce unemployment. He said in the future 2,485 miles of highway would be constructed but in reality, fewer than 621 were completed. That was a lot but not as much as planned, and the project also had less effect than previously thought.[21] In terms of publicity, the new highways in Germany were a success, Willem Melching says, but in economic terms they were of marginal importance.[22]

The image of *Projekt Autobahn* was so positive, however, that the German press still wrote about the construction of the highways long after it was cancelled because of the high cost of the war. As Hitler appeared less and less in public during the war, journalists started using positive images from the past with which the negative consequences of the war could be obscured. That was the reason pictures of Hitler opening new highways remained popular. It is likely that the image the Nazis presented in the press over and over again somehow lingered on in the rest of Europe after the war.

Economic problems

The president of the *Reichsbank*, Hjalmar Schacht, was no more of a great reformer of the German economy than Hitler was. He was more of a liberal than a Nazi economist and, being the man he was, he continued the policy of his predecessors: taxes that had been raised in the past remained, the repayment of foreign debts that had been delayed or suspended were terminated much more easily, and under Schacht as well everything was aimed at preventing the devaluation of the German *Reichsmark*.[23] As Hitler had promised to reduce unemployment, Schacht was to set aside large funds, but that was a continuation of existing policy as well.

The sharp decrease in unemployment may have looked fabulous at first sight but the investments needed led to a huge deficit in the state. There was a considerable risk of inflation and the freezing of wages that was in force caused tension as well. Employees who wanted better wages could not just

---

20. Ulrich (AH), p. 456. In the 1920s more sections of highway were constructed in Germany, apart from those near Cologne and Berlin.
21. At the peak of the construction some 120,000 men were employed. A large number, but as there were nearly 6 million unemployed in 1933 it was nowhere near enough to solve the problem.
22. Melching, p. 90
23. Sijthoff, pp. 24–25

switch to another. Nonetheless, there was the question of rising wages in the form of paid overtime or holiday arrangements.[24]

In connection with increasing production, the country could not continue looking inwards but had to export. Therefore, Schacht subsidised the exports in such a way that the prices of German products abroad could remain low. With the money that was made in this way, the country was able to obtain the necessary goods and raw materials from other countries. There was, however, still no question of 'cohesive and unequivocal economic planning'.[25] Kershaw points out that there was the question about a slight relief following the annexation of Austria and the Sudetenland,[26] but nonetheless, Joseph Goebbels called the financial situation of the country 'extremely critical' and in his diary even 'disastrous'.[27]

In 1936, when the income of the country rose slightly, maybe something could have been done to redress this disastrous situation, but in 1939 the national deficit had shot up to no less than 60 billion Reichsmark within six years, a vast sum of money for the time.[28] In 1939, twelve days after the management of the *Reichsbank* had sent a memo to Hitler requesting a stronger financial policy to avert inflation, Schacht was sacked.[29]

Yet the state did manage to wrest 8 billion RM from the Jewish community. Earlier on, Jews who left the country were obliged to pay a so-called emigration tax while their homes and possessions were sold below market value, but now Jews possessing over 5,000 RM were required to buy state bonds.[30] These measures didn't really help either. In 1939, German bankruptcy seemed inevitable unless a drastic turn was made towards the expansion of territory.

Hitler's predictions seemed to come true. In *Mein Kampf* he had said that Germany was too small and possessed insufficient raw materials to turn the country into a world power. Hitler, though, had created the financial-economic problems himself. It is an open question whether the war that was soon to come was the result of Hitler's old ideas from the 1920s he carried out knowingly or the result of a chaotic policy that in the end forced the country to apply his ideas about *Lebensraum*. Therefore, it is interesting to see to what extent the German economy in the 1930s was a war economy.

---

24. Sijthoff, p. 30
25. Kershaw, Vergelding, pp. 250–251
26. Important for the mining of iron ore, brown coal, tungsten and uranium ore.
27. Kershaw, Vergelding, pp. 250–251
28. Sijthoff, p. 29
29. Kershaw, Vergelding, p. 251
30. Historia, 'De weg uit de crisis', p. 57

Rearmament: the myth of the war economy

Outside Germany it was thought that the economic progress in the 1930s kept up with the establishment of a war economy in the country. This myth suited Hitler very well. During the 1930s, the country came across as a mighty opponent in a possible war. But the reality was a little different. Although sizable investments were made in the armed forces in the early 1930s, there was no question yet of a war economy. Initially, the French armed forces were still stronger than the German.

Melching says, however, that Hitler's economic policy only had one goal: rearmament.[31] He is undoubtedly right. Before the war, investments in the armaments industry rose to no less than 17 per cent of the national income. In comparison: in 1980, during the Cold War, the Netherlands spent 3 per cent of her national income on defence[32] and in 2013, 3.8 per cent of the US national income was spent on it. In 1938 this percentage was 1 in America and 8 in Great Britain. The 17 per cent Germany spent in 1938 could only mean one thing: war.

The investments in Germany were only sufficient for a fast war and not for an extended conflict, or *Totaler Krieg* as Goebbels later called it. American reports from 1945 indicated, surprisingly, that until 1943 Germany had not prepared itself at all for such an all-out war, although it had been expected. The strength of the Third Reich appeared to be *Blitzkrieg*, not the war of attrition it would become later on. In 1939, these expenditures had been sufficient to establish a strong and modern army with a new fleet and a state-of-the-art air force but its armed forces were still smaller than the French. In addition, Germany had too few raw materials at its disposal to embark on a well-prepared, lengthy war. After the war in Poland, for instance, the ammunition had all but run out. In order to continue the war in 1940, production of ammunition had to be increased sharply but was decreased again following the quick victory over France.[33] War expenditures in Germany became really extreme after 1943.

An overview of the percentages of the gross national product spent on the military in Germany, Great Britain and the United States[34] supports

---

31. Melching, p. 90
32. Volkskrant, 19 August 2014. In 2013 it was 1.3 per cent.
33. Sijthoff, p. 33
34. Sijthoff, p. 34. In this overview, the remark must be made that, certainly with the gigantic percentages mentioned in the 1940s, criticisms can be made that the author of the article admits. The percentages per country, probably composed in another way, are used here as an indication, not to suggest an airtight argumentation.

the notion that Germany spent a lot. The difference between the period up to 1939 and later showed that investments in the military and industry were far below the level required for a long battle of attrition. For instance, when Hitler took office, the percentage rose immediately from 1 per cent in 1932 to 3 in 1933. Subsequently, it quickly rose to 8 in 1935 and 17 in 1938. At that moment, Great Britain still lagged far behind Germany but the knowledge that Germany was diligently rearming would soon change that.

The image of the expenditures after 1940 is surprising though. The percentage of Great Britain's national income spent on the war industry between 1940 and 1943 was much higher than in Germany, with the absolute peak at 84 per cent in 1942. In Germany, expenditures increased dramatically as well; the peak being 61 in 1943, relatively far lower than British spending.

This series of numbers, although there is room for argument, indicates that from 1935 onwards, Germany was heavily investing in the armed forces. Hjalmar Schacht commented: 'I supported rearmament in so far as it was necessary to guarantee the security of Germany. I grew increasingly suspicious though when he (Hitler) attempted to use the entire funds of the country to equip the armed forces.'[35] Historian Vollker Ullrich concludes that the 'strongest impulses' for the economic resurrection of Germany and the decrease of unemployment was based on rearming the Reich in the long run.[36]

Hitler's self-fulfilling prophecy

The economic progress of the Germans in the 1930s cannot only be attributed to the investments in the armed forces and the armaments industry. In foreign countries, economies were on the rise as well and labour projects did indeed contribute to people getting jobs. Improvement and construction of public works like highways provided employment, although the number of people working on them was far lower than expected. In addition, much money was spent in supporting farmers and vast sums were spent on the ever-expanding apparatus of the state, which became more corrupt by the day.

The problem in investing in armament, road building and construction of houses is, according to Melching, that they did cause growth in production and employment but contributed little to exports.[37] After all, Germany had

---

35. Gilbert, p. 21
36. Ullrich (AH), p. 456
37. Melching, p. 94

no intention to export its arms but to use them. The notion that in the 1930s Germany was prepared for war as it was waged in the 1940s is an illusion. And yet, a secret note by Hitler in the Four Year Plan of 1936[38] reveals he was already aiming for war. The investments may not have been aimed at total war but the army and industry had to be ready for war within four years. Kershaw summarises it as follows: the notion of dominance over Europe and achieving *Lebensraum* in the East seemed unrealistic in the early 1930s but once 'the economy was back on its feet, rearmament made good progress and the regime scored one diplomatic victory after the other', things started to look like Hitler would eventually get the job done.[39] With that, one of his predictions in *Mein Kampf* came true.

---

38. Melching, p. 94
39. Kershaw, Vergelding, p. 35

Chapter 11

Hitler, an Artistic Genius?

The myth of an artist

'How can anyone, who is the personification of evil, produce so many beautiful things? He was an artistic genius and has even created masterpieces. Auction rooms are still interested in Hitler's works and his works of art hang over the fireplace of many a rich family,'[1] *so the social network site Plazilla reads. Responses to the message are serious but rather uncritical. A few clicks further away opens a review of a recent book about Hitler's artisanship in which the opposite is voiced. 'In the world of art, everyone unanimously agrees that Hitler didn't do too well. His watercolours are dry and scholastic, his nudes are lifeless, his city views lack the correct perspective and any vivacity.'*[2]

These contradicting views[3] on two random websites more or less reveal the standard train of thought about Hitler's artisanship. The last, negative vision expresses in particular how Hitler's art was rated after the Second World War. The first shows there are people, not necessarily admirers of Hitler, who still think he produced fabulous works of art or that he was even an artistic genius. Is this just the result of a limited view of art or maybe did something of the Nazi propaganda about Hitler's artistry linger on?

So, Hitler's works of art are rated very differently, partly as a result of propaganda during the years of the Third Reich. Naturally, Hitler's followers were of the opinion that the art Hitler had produced in his early years showed a great gift for painting. The leader of the *Hitler Jugend* wrote in a book about Hitler's paintings: 'They unveil to you the artistic personality of a man who has become the prototype of the creative genius

---

1. See plazilla.com: Adolf Hitler's works of art.
2. It is about a review of a book by Lambert Giebels, entitled *Hitler as an Artist*, written by Frans van den Muijssenberg on the STIWOT website tracesofwar.nl
3. The first 'vision' contains at least four assumptions or myths that cannot be proved, apart from that the text is full of mistakes in spelling and grammar. In the second, the alleged unanimity of the rejection of Hitler's art is slightly exaggerated but on the whole, it is a critical and well-written review.

in his youth. [...] Adolf Hitler is the first Führer and at the same time the first artisan of our *Reich*.[4] After the war, however, the dominant opinion on Hitler's art took a 180-degree turn. Franz Jetzinger, one of the earliest biographers who, right after the war, concerned himself with Hitler's younger years, stated that his paint work in Vienna consisted mainly of copying, meant to make some money on the side.[5] Something similar had already been said before the war by Hugo Rabitsch, who wrote in a disparaging way in a book from 1938 about Hitler's youth that only ungifted drawers would make copies.[6] The pranks and jokes that circulated before and during the war about Hitler's attempts at becoming a painter were not always based on facts. Illustrative of the anti-Hitler feelings soon after the war, and of the misconception about Hitler's painting ability as well, is a picture that was taken at a liberation march in the Dutch province of Noord-Brabant in 1945. The picture shows a man dressed in a white coverall complete with a Hitler parting and moustache, walking around with a ladder and a tin of paint. The caption of the picture reads: 'If only I had remained a house painter.'[7] The joker didn't degrade Hitler to the usual failed artist but to a completely normal house painter.

The genius cult

It is impossible to discuss Hitler's artisanship in a sensible way without considering the genius cult in the Third Reich. Yet, after the war, this occurred frequently. Birgit Schwartz points to this in her book with the significant title *Geniewahn*, a detailed book about Hitler as an artist. Schwarz claims the notion of the genius was banned from Hitler research because the wounds of the war were still fresh.[8] Right after the war, nobody wanted to talk about Hitler as a genius, not even as a hypothesis. Meanwhile, decades have passed and while during the period of National Socialism in Germany, Hitler being a genius was taken for granted, it makes sense to consider the genius cult at that time along with the analysis of Hitler's artisanship.

In Germany, Hitler was being presented as a genius and he had initiated this himself when writing *Mein Kampf* in the 1920s. Among National Socialists the notion existed that such a genius was needed in the leadership

---

4. Giebels, p. 141
5. Jetzinger, p. 135
6. Maser, ALW, p. 98
7. Film- en Fotobank Noord-Brabant, www.thuisinbrabant.nl
8. Schwarz, p. 13

of the country as a polar opposite of the treacherous politicians who had created the chaos the country was in. It is all the stranger maybe that Hitler acknowledged in *Mein Kampf* that he hadn't been admitted to the Art Academy. With a little adaptation, he succeeded in bending the rejection in such a way that it seemed as if he was a natural and undervalued genius. There were, of course, many more of these misjudged geniuses. Some very successful ones, too.

Hitler was critical about his own painting but he never failed to point out that true genius was always inborn and never acquired.[9] The real soul of an artisan couldn't be cultivated in an academy of art; you either had such a soul or you hadn't. In his opinion, German artisans were better than their colleagues in other countries in every way possible and that was a question of genes: non-German elements in arts were rejected and eventually often labelled as Jewish. This kind of 'degenerating German art' could be seen – according to some – in impressionism but became fully visible in expressionism, a movement that was considered the direct result of genetic neglect.[10] Hitler himself was a genius, his talent was inborn. And that showed in his biography.

Much later, when Hitler was the leader of the German Empire, a true art mania emerged in the country. Göring, Goebbels and many other prominent Nazis started collecting works of art or visited expositions frequently. Furthermore, the state did all sorts of things to promote the experience of art: theatres and new museums were built, large art expositions were held and music festivals funded. Not only the upper classes should enjoy art, the man in the street should also be able to go and see an opera or visit an exhibition. The National Socialist art mania went completely out of hand. Robbing of art became daily practice in the Third Reich and the staff of Rudolf Hess, for instance, judged works of art stolen from Austrian-Jewish collectors to see whether there was anything Hitler would like to have.[11] In the end, works of art from all over Europe ended up in German hands, either through forced sale or some other illegal manner. In that respect, Hermann Göring's art collection in particular was notorious.

The German population was presented with another side of the Nazi conception of art at the travelling exhibition *Entartete Kunst*. It showed works of art considered un-German and mainly made by expressionists. Apart from an interesting, cynical show for the public, it was a smart form

---

9. Schwarz, p. 207
10. Schwarz, p. 211
11. Schwarz, p. 237

of censorship and propaganda at the same time. The population was allowed to look at it and at the same time they were made aware this was not art anymore but 'degeneration'.

The young artist

At primary school Hitler had good marks for drawing[12] and as a young adolescent he still drew and painted a lot. Apart from that, he is said to have written poetry, too.[13] When he was a little older, he often had talks with his friend, August Kubizek, about artistry, music, visual art and architecture. At the time, Hitler was already a great lover of music. In Linz in Austria he frequently visited a theatre along with his friend, operas by Wagner being the most favourite. He never managed to master an instrument, though. He probably lacked persistence because, apart from his famous overestimation, he must have been quite lazy. He never kept up his piano lessons longer than four months, even though his mother had rented a grand piano especially for him.[14] Yet he thought he could achieve something in music. When he lived in Vienna as a young adult, he learned from his friend August, who meanwhile had become a music student, that Wagner once intended to put the saga of *Wieland der Schmiede* to music. Hitler then decided to take it on himself. He looked for the saga and started to work on it immediately.[15]

Apparently, it never crossed his mind that without any knowledge of music and technique, composing an opera was an impossible task. Consequently, the project was a downright failure and later on he never talked about it anymore with his friend.

Art Academy in Vienna

In September 1907, Hitler moved from Linz to Vienna to take the entrance exam for the Art Academy. He passed the pre-selection with drawings he had made earlier but the second exam, consisting of a mandatory subject, ended in disappointment. He was rejected. Hitler said himself he was rather confused and therefore he asked the rector why he had been rejected. The

---

12. Giebels, p. 19, 21
13. Kershaw, Hoogmoed, pp. 47–48
14. Kershaw, Hoogmoed, p. 47. Kershaw mentions the 'buying' of a piano. Giebels, p. 37. Giebels states his mother rented a piano. In Giebels' opinion, it could be that Hitler stopped playing because his mother fell ill.
15. Kershaw, Hoogmoed, p. 76

rector said it was obvious Hitler had no talent as a painter but he was far more gifted in the field of architecture.[16]

The story of the rejection, as told by many biographers of Hitler, is mainly founded on *Mein Kampf*. It isn't usually pointed out that this anecdote of Hitler may well have served a purpose other than telling the truth. This story may well have been meant to portray him as an undervalued painter, Birgit Schwarz says.[17] After all, it is part and parcel of the artisan's cliché that born geniuses are frequently undervalued but come floating to the surface nonetheless. The response of the professor at the academy to Hitler's question, as included in *Mein Kampf*, as to why he had been rejected is suspect, according to art historian Schwarz. The professor assumed Hitler had already graduated from a study in architecture, at least according to *Mein Kampf*. That would explain his talent in that area. However, he hadn't been educated to become an architect at all so it is likely the professor had discovered a hidden talent in Hitler, which neatly matches the National Socialist notion of the born genius Hitler tried to bring out in his book.[18] From that moment on, Hitler thought he was going to be a builder. At least, that is what he wrote. But neither in the period afterwards in which he stayed in Vienna, nor during his pre-war period in Munich, did he do anything to make this come true. Hitler's wish to become an architect was pure fantasy. 'Architecture was a dream, painting for a living reality.'[19]

Actually, Hitler must have been quite frustrated about being rejected. It seems he suffered from severe bouts of anger in the period in which his dream to become an artisan had been blown to pieces. About the academy, he said for instance: 'It was a place where nobody had the slightest idea of artisanship.'[20] Actually, not being admitted to the academy wasn't such a dismal failure. Out of 113 applicants, only twenty-eight made the grade and so rejection didn't automatically mean he had no talent at all. The written argumentation, which has been preserved, was also very short: 'Few views, test drawings insufficient', so the assessment read. Historian Lambert Giebels assumes there had been a need to reduce the number of applicants to a predetermined total.[21]

---

16. There are various versions of this story. In the catalogue of Hitler's works by Price, it says that Hitler was told he was better at architecture after his second rejection. Ian Kershaw takes this more or less for granted.
17. Schwarz, pp. 11–12
18. Schwarz, p. 58
19. Schwarz, p. 61
20. Kershaw, Hoogmoed, p. 53, 75
21. Giebels, p. 39. After the first round, there were ninety-five applicants left.

Despite the rejection, Hitler didn't give up on drawing and painting. The reason to continue changed, however. Hitler switched from painting out of passion to painting for a living. In the years that followed, he usually copied Viennese city views to have them sold by a friend with whom he had set up shop. When he moved to Munich in 1913 he continued doing so but he sold his work himself or he had it sold by an art shop in town. The paintings provided him with a living in the first place and that was, also according to Hitler in later life, the main reason for his painting.[22]

When the First World War broke out, Hitler immediately reported to the army. This obviously influenced the number of drawings and watercolours he made as he had much less time to draw. The necessity of making some money on the side naturally didn't exist in the army either. Maybe this explains why some consider Hitler's work during the First World War much better than his previous work. In the introduction to the only catalogue of Hitler's work, published by Billy F. Price, it also says that this difference in quality was caused by Hitler no longer copying images but having to draw from reality. It is quite imaginable that his wartime work would have been far better than he had produced previously; on the other hand, the authenticity of his work during the war is in doubt.

The artist becomes a politician

After the First World War, Hitler occupied himself with politics more and more and he mainly made sketches in the field of architecture. In addition, in 1920 for instance he designed the emblem of the *Deutsche Arbeiterpartei* (DAP): a slanted swastika in black in a white background within a red ring, in fact an adapted version of an idea by another member of the DAP. It would become the best-known design of the twentieth century.[23] In the same way, he is supposed to have designed the first Volkswagen Beetle, one of the most iconic European cars ever, based on ideas by Jewish engineer Josef Ganz.[24]

When Hitler became known as a politician, he had, of course, much more money at his disposal than before. He could afford to buy a spacious apartment on *Prinzregentenplatz* in Munich and in addition to the financial means to buy works of art, he also had the space to hang paintings. Later on,

---

22. Maser, ALW, p. 96
23. Giebels, p. 126. The Aryan and occult Thule Society, the origin of the DAP, had a swastika as its emblem as well.
24. Schilperoord, p. 8

in his villa the *Berghof* in Berchtesgaden as well as in his official residence in Berlin, he collected various works of art. In the long run, he had many more buildings at his disposal that he could furnish after his own taste, such as his office in Munich and the *Reichskanzlei* in Berlin. Hitler had his own art hung there or paintings he had on loan from various museums. He painted less and less himself but he continued making architectural sketches almost throughout his entire life. Albert Speer possessed a number of them, which were also included in Price's catalogue. These were sketches of bridges, a mantelpiece, a stadium, theatres and, for instance, the large dome hall for the new capital city of Germania. Hitler is supposed to have made between 2,000 and 3,000 drawings, watercolours and oil paintings in his lifetime.[25] After the invasion of Poland, he drew gradually less; in any case, the Price catalogue contains much less of the years of war after 1939 than from the previous period. Sketches from these later years involve architecture. Hitler's last vague architectural sketch dated from 1943.[26] Although he hardly drew anything anymore himself, he retained his love for art, in particular visual art, all his life. When German cities were increasingly subjected to Allied bombardments, he ordered his *Gauleiter* to protect works of art as much as possible against these air raids and erupting fires.

Devotee

Hitler was an art lover but he hardly had eyes for anything beyond his own taste. Where music was concerned, he loved composers such as Bruckner, Beethoven, Liszt and Brahms, but Wagner in particular.[27] During his early years in Linz and Vienna he attended a large number of operas by this composer. His friend, August Kubizek, also loved the then popular music by Verdi but Hitler didn't share this preference at all. He talked condescendingly about Verdi and, as Kubizek said, there was little sense in entering into a discussion with him about it.[28]

Wagner offered everything Hitler looked for in music. 'What appealed to him so much was the mood of the Germanic myths with their exalted drama and spectacle, their gods and heroes and their titanic struggles ending in salvation, victory and death.'[29] Hitler's chief of press Ernst Hanfstaengl, an

---

25. Price, pp. 6–9
26. Price, pp. 246–251. Hitler's last sketches are mainly about the reconstruction of Linz.
27. Kershaw, Hoogmoed, p. 78
28. Kershaw, Hoogmoed, pp. 78–79
29. Kershaw, Hoogmoed, p. 79

amateur pianist with a wide range of light and classical music at his disposal, pleased Hitler most with his renditions of Wagnerian music. He played for him at almost every visit, sometimes for two hours on end.[30]

In 1923, Hitler visited the house where Richard Wagner once lived, *Villa Wahnfried* in Bayreuth. Siegfried and Winifred Wagner, the composer's son and daughter-in-law, personally welcomed Hitler and showed him things like the grave of the old master, who had been buried in the garden near the house.[31] Hitler was to become a personal friend of the family and for years on end he saw to the financial support of the performance of Wagner music at the *Festspielhaus* in Bayreuth, with the Führer in frequent attendance.

Hitler also loved the music of Anton Bruckner, who came from the region of Linz where he had lived during his youth as well. Along with his friend Kubizek, he once went on a walking trip from Linz to Sankt Florian, to the abbey where Bruckner lay buried. They visited the holy surroundings where Bruckner had played the organ, but of course they only found his tombstone. Hitler was very much impressed by this excursion, but it seems it was only because of the Baroque building.[32] In April 1943, he visited the abbey anew.

As Führer, Hitler frequently arranged musical evenings. During them he and his guests listened to the songs of Brahms, Hugo Wolf, or symphonies by Bruckner, List and Beethoven and also to excerpts from the operas by Wagner. But Hitler also liked the lighter work by Johann Strauss and Franz Léhar, so the operettas by these two were played frequently. After the fall of Stalingrad, these nights hardly took place anymore.

When Hitler was in his villa on the Obersalzberg, he and his guests frequently watched all sorts of movies as well. In particular those movies that had been banned by Goebbels' Ministry of Propaganda drew an eager crowd. The majority shown would have been light entertainment, including cowboy and adventure movies and musicals.

Joseph Goebbels is supposed to have presented Hitler with a number of Mickey Mouse movies, a present he appreciated very much. According to Albert Speer, experimental or artistic movies were not played at all. Later on, during the war, movies were not watched frequently anymore, a gesture of frugality in accordance with the situation at the front.

---

30. Conradi, p. 75
31. Hamann, WW, p. 84
32. Kubizek, p. 35

The art of painting

Hitler loved paintings from the nineteenth century. He preferred German Romanticists like Anselm Feuerbach and Eduard von Grützner. He also liked the work of Hans Makart very much. For instance, Hitler owned the painting *Pest in Florence* by this nineteenth-century painter.[33] Makart and Feuerbach are supposed to have been banned from the academy as well, just like Hitler. However, the idea of Makart and Feuerbach being undervalued geniuses who had been rejected by the academy is a myth, and it also fitted all too neatly into the genius cult surrounding Hitler.[34]

During his stay in Vienna, Hitler's great example was Rudolf van Alt, a watercolour painter who was known for his Viennese city views.[35] Heinrich Hoffmann, the photographer who saw Hitler in his home, said he regularly commented that he loved van Alt's work. Hoffmann further said Hitler had once looked in admiration at a painting of an old monk by Grützner in his home. Later on, Hitler possessed some thirty paintings by Grützner.[36]

The prudish Hitler

The notion that Hitler was an extremely prudish man is belied by sketches of nude women he sometimes made but also by his admiration for a particular erotic painting by Paul Mathias Padua entitled *Leda mit dem Schwan*. The painting is based on the myth of Zeus who, in the form of a swan, impregnates a girl named Leda. It is an image of the spiciest part of the myth. Hitler's photographer Heinrich Hoffmann found it a stark painting but because of the offensive image he didn't dare to include it in an exhibition in the *Haus der Deutschen Kunst* for which he was responsible. He first wanted Hitler's permission. Hitler found it a fabulous painting as well but he doubted whether a part of the public wouldn't find it too offensive. Gerdy Troost, widow of architect Paul Ludwig Troost, was asked for her opinion. After some thinking she said the painting could be exhibited as usual and Hitler decided to have it displayed. Although Troost changed her mind the same evening, that didn't change anything as Hitler didn't go back on his

---

33. Maser, ALW, p. 106
34. Schwarz, p. 5
35. Giebels, p. 66; Maser, pp. 106–107. In addition, he liked the works of Carl Spitzweg, Hans Thoma, Wilhelm Leibi and 'forgotten painters' such as Friedrich Stahl and Karl Leipold.
36. Hoffmann, HH, p. 28

decision.[37] But an image of a swan copulating with a, naturally naked, young woman obviously caused much discussion among the public. Gauleiter Adolf Wagner, for instance, was very troubled by the painting, notwithstanding Hitler's personal approval. Others liked it very much and wanted to buy it. Eventually, the work was bought by Martin Bormann. The reaction of the public is rather less interesting than Hitler's opinion of the work of art because he obviously had no aversion whatsoever to nude paintings, the only issue was how the body was being portrayed. The expressionist form of eroticism and the bodily decay that sometimes went with it, for instance, wasn't at all liked by the Nazis, however, images of nude women or men were not prohibited. Hitler had various nude paintings in his collection.[38]

Arnold Böcklin and the discussion about German art

Artisans who had suffered from the 'misunderstanding of the masses',[39] could, of course, count on Hitler's sympathy, in view of his rejection by the Art Academy. Anselm Feuerbach is one example but artisan Arnold Böcklin is also supposed to have suffered from this misunderstanding. Böcklin was a symbolist who produced most of his work in the second half of the nineteenth century. This famous artisan is mentioned only rarely in the major biographies[40] of Hitler and that is strange because he was being discussed in even the top echelons of the Nazi party. Alfred Rosenberg, the ideologist of the NSDAP, considered it impossible to have Böcklin's painting *Der Toteninsel* hanging on the wall.[41] The work, based on an Italian legend, didn't match the spirit of German art, according to Rosenberg. But Hitler couldn't be bothered that much. At the time of publication of the book in which Rosenberg had voiced his criticism of the artisan, Hitler was just furnishing his new apartment in Munich and the first work of art he bought was one by Böcklin. Later on, Hitler had paintings by Böcklin in all of his homes, and eventually *Der Toteninsel* hung on the wall of the old *Reichskanzlei* in Berlin.

---

37. Hoffmann, HH, p. 135
38. Hitler possessed for instance the 'Thief of Honey' by Lucas Cranach, 'Perseus and Andromeda' by Franz von Stuck and 'The Four Elements' by Adolf Ziegler, which hung over the fireplace in the Führerbau in Munich.
39. Schwarz, p. 23
40. He is not mentioned by either Joachim Fest or by Ian Kershaw.
41. Schwarz, p. 25

Albert Speer about Hitler's favourite painters

There are two lists of Hitler's much-loved painters. One of them was made by historian Joachim Fest based on the statements by Hitler's principal architect Albert Speer, the other by Henri Picker, the man responsible for taking notes of Hitler's so-called table conversations in the 1940s. The difference between the two lists is that Speer's mainly consisted of artisans from the first half of the nineteenth century while Picker's also contains names of artisans from the second half including Böcklin, who does not appear on the Fest list at all. According to Birgit Schwarz, the Speer list (and so the Fest list) is incomplete. In her opinion, Hitler saw the Romanticists from the second half of the nineteenth century as the pure interpreters of German art.[42]

Speer's reason to keep silent about some of the artisans admired by Hitler is, according to Schwarz, because he wished to distance himself from Hitler after the war as much as he could. So, Speer said Hitler loved neo-Baroque in particular and that he was no real classicist, and Speer was just that. According to Schwarz though, Hitler did not like neo-Baroque that much and considered the excessive decorations tasteless. Hitler admired the opera house in Paris very much, especially its exterior, but he didn't like the interior, which was overcrowded with decoration.[43] When Hitler as Führer moved into his official residence at the *Wilhelmstrasse* in Berlin, he refurbished the entire building, which was once occupied by Wilhelm II and Bismarck. He had carpets and gilded ornaments removed, along with the dark, neo-Renaissance and neo-Baroque furniture. The result of the work was sober and sleek, which matched the neo-Classic tradition far better than that of the Baroque.[44]

For the most part, Hitler was an admirer of classic, romantic and classicist art. He preferred art that showed the soul and heroism of the German population over that of the Renaissance and the Gothic that, according to Hitler, had too many ties with Christianity.[45] Modernistic and expressionistic art did not appeal to him at all.[46]

---

42. Schwarz, p. 34
43. Schwarz, pp. 33–34
44. Schwarz, p. 133, 135
45. Maser, ALW, p. 106
46. Only a few out of the enormous number pieces of work that Hitler possessed and the painters he liked are named in this chapter. There are just a few books that offer a complete overview of it. A positive and recent exception to this is *Geniewahn* by Birgit Schwarz, frequently referred to for this chapter.

Books

Hitler is supposed to have been an avid reader. In the past however, it has been said he was a bad reader, for instance because of the way he wrote about reading in *Mein Kampf.* He would read the table of contents, the introduction and the epilogue of a book but mainly in order to find ideas that fitted into his own way of thinking. Whether or not Hitler was a thoroughbred intellectual is an open question. He would have especially bragged about the books he read. He is supposed to have told Leni Riefenstahl once that Schopenhauer appealed more to him than Nietzsche, but even his secretary Christa Schröder indicated that he especially wanted to create the impression he was a profound thinker. In Lambert Giebels' words, books by Karl May appealed more to Hitler than those of well-known philosophers.[47]

Hitler read a lot in Linz, Vienna, Munich and during the First World War, as confirmed by numerous witnesses, but they couldn't always give details about what he read. A fairly recent book, *Hitler's Private Library* by Timothy Rybeck, offers a clarification about what was in Hitler's library. He possessed, for example, a book about sagas, he read *Don Quixote* and he owned a book about Frederick the Great by Thomas Carlyle. His library was very extensive and he received many books as presents, which he hardly ever read. The book about the Prussian king Frederick the Great was very important to Hitler. Until shortly before his death he hoped that in the future people would look back on him and those around him in the same way that people in his time would look back on a hero like Frederick.[48]

Hitler had his own vision on literature. He considered books like *Don Quixote, Robinson Crusoe, Uncle Tom's Cabin* and *Gulliver's Travels* important works in world literature.[49] In a certain sense, he was right but with this kind of book in mind, it isn't strange that he was seen as a lover of adventure books rather than as a connoisseur in the field of literature. His enormous admiration of the books by Karl May only confirm this image.[50] Yet he is supposed to have been crazy about the German translation of Shakespeare's *Hamlet* and he owned a copy of the stage editing of *Peer Gynt* by his good friend Dietrich Eckhart.[51] It doesn't look like Hitler was a true lover of literature but it is more than likely he read much about non-fiction subjects such as architecture, warships and German history.

---

47. Giebels, pp. 60–61
48. Ryback, p. 227
49. Ryback, p. 9
50. Ryback, p. 11
51. Ryback, p. 45

Architecture

Hitler loved beautiful architecture. Much of his drawings and paintings involved views of buildings, ruins and houses. In Vienna he admired the classicistic buildings and the neo-Baroque on *Ringstrasse* such as the *Hofburg*, the parliament building by architect Theophil Hansen, the Opera building by Eduard von der Nüll and the *Burgtheater* by Godfried Semper.[52] In Munich, he greatly admired the Glyptothek museum, which resembled a Hellenistic temple, and the classicistic Propylaën on *Königsplatz*. Those stood in the square where Hitler's office, the *Führerbau*, would later be built. He also liked the *Wittelsbacher Residenz*, which stood close to the spot where his attempt to overthrow the Bavarian government had failed.

The First World War did not mean the end of his interest either. In November 1915, for instance, he bought a book about the architectural history of Berlin[53] and during the Great War he visited Brussels twice. He returned in 1940 in order to drive past the *Palais de la Justice* he admired so much. He considered the *Opéra* in Paris, at least when he was there, to be the most beautiful building in the world.[54] That is to say, the exterior. He liked the *Sacré Coeur* a lot less.[55]

In his early years, Hitler designed theatres, museums and town halls.[56] In Berlin and on the *Obersalzberg*, Hitler could often be found in the workshop of architect Albert Speer, the successor of Paul Ludwig Troost, Hitler's favourite architect from the early years. Troost designed for Hitler both the *Führerbau* and the *Haus der Deutschen Kunst* in Munich and after the death of Troost in 1934, Speer took over. He built a new *Reichskanzlei* for Hitler and he designed the stadium for the party rallies in Nuremberg. Speer had a successor as well. After Speer was appointed *Reichsminister für Rüstung und Munitionen*, Hermann Giesler became Hitler's new court architect. Giesler was responsible for, among other things, the conversion of the town of Hitler's youth, Linz. The scale model that went with the blueprints was taken to the cellar of the *Reichskanzlei* in Berlin just before the end of the war. For Hitler, it was a welcome diversion from reality.

---

52. Giebels, p. 62; Speer, p. 54. According to Albert Speer, Hitler showed a special love for the theatres designed by Hermann Felmer and Ferdinand Feliner (late baroque) and the more rigid work of Gottfried Semper and classicist Theophil Hansen.
53. Ryback, p. 25
54. Kuypers, p. 29
55. Kuypers, p. 43
56. Jetzinger, p. 119

Germania

In planning the conversion of Berlin into the new capital, Germania, Albert Speer played the most important role. The construction of Germania was a mammoth project in which the centre of town would be rebuilt in the tradition of classicism,[57] complete with two huge boulevards: the east–west aisle and the north–south aisle. An enormous dome hall, in principle based on a sketch by Hitler, was to be erected close to the *Reichstag*, making that building shrink to matchbox size in comparison. On the other side of the north–south aisle, an immense station would be built with a triumphal arch so gigantic that the gates that were to be constructed beneath it would be just as tall as the *Brandenburger Tor*. The arch itself would be 394ft high and the names of the 1.8 million victims of the First World War would be engraved in its granite walls. The arch was also based on a sketch by Hitler. Anything in between had to make way for the new buildings of the capital city of Germania. 'It was an unbridled dream, constructed with elements alien to the city itself which took no account whatsoever of the historic structures of Berlin and only aimed at erecting monuments of architectural self-glorification.'[58]

Germania would only be comparable to ancient Egypt, Babylon or Rome[59] and the city should have been realised in a very short time. Speer managed to build a new *Reichskanzlei* very quickly but as to Germania, he did not get past a lot of preparatory work. When war broke out, construction ground to a halt. Along the east–west aisle only Speer's street lamps remain and a strange chunk of circular concrete, lying somewhere near a railway track close to Tempelhof airport. It was meant to determine whether the soggy ground in Berlin was strong enough to carry the weight of the immense buildings. The object, quite unfit for any purpose, is one of the few 'remains' of project Germania.

Megalomania

Many of Hitler's building projects were megalomaniac art expressions. Speer's buildings for the party rallies in Nuremberg were meant for mass meetings with much flag waving and lighting effects, making Hitler's speeches even more impressive for his followers. The new *Reichskanzlei* in

---

57. *Mythos Germania*, p. 14
58. Pest, SH, p. 105
59. Maser, ALW, p. 9

Berlin was to impress international guests even before they entered Hitler's office. Entering his office, they had to cover quite a distance before reaching him, so they must have been duly impressed. Architect Clemenz Klotz was in charge of the construction of a holiday resort, 2.8 miles long, on the Rügen peninsula for the Nazi organisation *Kraft durch Freude*, which provided holidays for workers. It was not meant as a quiet holiday resort.[60] The Nazi buildings on *Königsplatz* in Munich were subtle in comparison but, then again, they were not designed by Speer but by Paul Ludwig Troost. Incidentally, Troost also applied many classicist elements in his architecture: the existing buildings on *Königplatz* are identical and stand symmetrically on either side of a street that connects to the square.

Yet historian Joachim Fest dared to say Hitler was not a true follower of this art trend, but liked it because it was a very useful way to recall memories of the grandeur from the past.[61] Albert Speer, with whom Fest had many conversations, said the *Führerstihl* in architecture that the party press was continuously writing about didn't really exist. What was elevated to the style of the Third Reich was, according to Speer, the neo-classicism of Troost, but Hitler was too pragmatic a man to pin himself down on a style of building based on ideology.[62] It was mentioned earlier that Speer had reasons of his own to name Hitler's style different from what it actually was. The reason Fest accepted Speer's vision was probably due to his lengthy contact with him. When Speer stated that Hitler loved neo-Baroque the most and had remained in the world of his youth from 1880 to 1910,[63] this was an attempt to distance himself from Hitler.

Hitler had little stomach for modernistic paintings, architecture and new music. When, for instance, the first blueprints of the Berlin Olympic Stadium were completed, it appeared that Hitler couldn't appreciate the modern design. Initially a glass shell was foreseen and Hitler was so displeased with it he said the Games couldn't continue because he refused to enter such a 'glass cubicle'. Thereupon, Albert Speer quickly drafted a sketch in which the glass was omitted and replaced by granite. Only then was Hitler pleased.[64]

---

60. The building still exists and part of it was actually used after the war, but it has never been a holiday resort. When war broke out, the buildings were not yet finished and they were never finished. Since 1992 the building has been a protected monument.
61. Fest, SH, p. 113
62. Speer, p. 55
63. Speer, p. 55
64. Speer, p. 94

It is likely Hitler didn't like modernistic architecture but Speer calling him a lover of the neo-Baroque style was a smart way to distinguish between Hitler's taste and his own. After the war, Speer had distanced himself from Hitler in other fields and with that in a certain sense he managed to save his own skin.

Hitler was no genius

Hitler was no artisan but he wanted to become one. The first setback, however, made him a painter for a living. Of course, it is likely that with the appropriate guidance by the teachers of an art academy he would have evolved into an able artisan but his life took a different turn. For that reason alone, Hitler didn't belong to the real geniuses in arts at all. At best, he could look at their work in admiration.

Hitler's own paintwork has always met with much criticism. The people he drew or painted always came across as very clumsy and the watercolours he copied were rather dull. The fact he copied photographs and paintings didn't show any originality but he didn't care. He made money selling paintings and as long as they sold well, he was doing his job well. He himself said, by the way, that he wasn't that good as a painter; in any case, he didn't consider his work good enough to have it exhibited in the *Haus der Deutschen Kunst* as he indeed saw it as a means of sustenance.[65] He also said his meticulously copied images lacked special qualities.[66]

If it is true what papers all over the world wrote in 2008, Hitler would even have drawn beautifully colourised images of Walt Disney figures. The drawings of two out of the seven dwarfs from the movie *Snow White* and one of *Pinocchio* were reported to have been discovered on a painting signed by A. Hitler. William Hakvaag, manager of a war museum on the Lofoten in Norway, bought the painting in Germany in 2007. The drawings of these figures are supposed to have been made in 1940. The story is too beautiful to omit but the record of the purchase is so vague it can't be determined whether this painting, bought by the Norwegian, is a genuine Hitler. Because of this, the origin of the Disney figures is hard to ascertain. The drawings can therefore not be accepted for the time being as evidence of the superficial 'art' Hitler produced during his life.

Some of the sketches and designs Hitler made were successful. Two of his designs, the Nazi version of the swastika and the Volkswagen Beetle, have

---

65. Price, pp. 10–11
66. Kershaw, Hoogmoed, p. 131

been defining images over a long period and are still iconic. As mentioned earlier though, those were not original ideas; Hitler had copied them from others. He did have ideas of his own but he needed others to finalise them. Albert Speer, among others, helped him translate his artistic ambitions into real projects, although the best-known of them were never realised. Therefore, it can only be guessed at what the triumphal arch and the dome in Germania would have looked like. Hitler's idea to adapt the bridge on the Danube in the Austrian town of Linz has materialised though and this still exists. German architect Friedrich Tamms built the so-called *Nibelungenbrücke* for Hitler. Here again, Hitler played the role of the building master and not of the creative genius he might have wanted to be.

Werner Maser said that, even after the war, people said Hitler's work wasn't so bad after all. They pointed, for instance, to the watercolours Hitler made during the First World War, which were a remarkably artistic achievement.[67] In 1935, Hitler's court photographer, Heinrich Hoffmann, published seven of these watercolours from Hitler's wartime period with an introduction by Professor H. Nasse, who made the following remark about Hitler's painting entitled *Haubourdin* from 1916: 'Here, through the eyes of a German landscape painter, the strange evolves into an intimate, familiar, inspiring and poetical experience. The painting is especially breezy, mobile and flowing. The building master of the Third Reich puts blame on the former Viennese academy.'[68] The academy didn't have to feel ashamed for rejecting him though, and could hardly be blamed. The admission policy was strict and Hitler obviously was not among the most talented applicants.

The publication of Hitler's paintings from the war were nothing more than propaganda and even if Nasse had criticised Hitler's art, he would never have said so in the introduction to this publication. Anton Joachimsthaler said about the watercolours that in a strange way they were in marked contrast to other work by Hitler, before and after the First World War. While Hitler usually worked meticulously without any fantasy, his war paintings were much more skilful as to technique and colour, so it is said.[69] One of the works published by Hoffmann is a watercolour of the Holleweg near Wytschaete. It was more or less where Hitler, along with another soldier, saved the commander of their regiment from a certain death, so the story goes. Propaganda wise, it was an excellent choice, of course, requiring stark images that 'might need some help'. Lambert Giebels described the war

---

67. Maser, ALW, p. 99
68. Maser, ALW, p. 97; Giebels, pp. 140–141
69. Joachimsthaler, KB, p. 136, 139–140

paintings as the work of a painter looking for an 'impressionistic form of expression that almost led in the direction of expressionism'.[70] But was it Hitler who was looking for something here or was it somebody else's hand that can be seen in the painting? The conclusion seems premature that the vast difference between Hitler's works was mainly caused by himself as he no longer copied but worked with nature during the war. It is assumed that these watercolours were adaptations by another artisan, who colourised or adapted Hitler's drawings. The book *Korrektur einer Biographie* by Anton Joachimsthaler contains examples of sketches from the First World War by Hitler that must have been adapted at the time of publication.[71]

Hitler had a very limited view of art. In the Third Reich, many 'modern' issues were rejected, for instance. Abstract art and modern plays were considered Jewish, jazz was 'negro music' and Hitler hardly ever watched experimental movies. The logical result of this attitude was a cultural impoverishment in some aspects.[72] When there is little room for modernisation, free spirits that keep art alive get insufficient chances and opportunities. It could be said that the Nazis mainly retained art from the past. In spite of the supposed artistic genius of the Führer, only art that fitted within the Nazi ideology was granted space.

In his later years, Hitler seldom visited theatres, so Speer said, and he enjoyed the lighter forms of art more and more, like the operetta and variety shows. Speer even suggested Hitler would have attended variety shows more often but that he had to be very cautious as the questionable content didn't match the image of the artistic genius he liked to be seen as. He did, however, dispatch one of his subordinates to such a show sometimes to tell him about it afterwards. Speer also said that Hitler attended the *Bayreuther Festspiele* every year and that his power of judgment in the field of music still seemed authentic to him, but it struck him that Hitler often talked far more about the direction of the opera than about the music. Furthermore, Speer said, Hitler would have attended operas only very seldom during the war and he hardly listened to music by Bruckner any more either. 'In public however, he had the image spread around of his strong feeling for art.'[73] As unreliable as this later testimony by Speer may have been, in this case he could have been partly right.

---

70. Giebels, p. 112
71. Joachimsthaler, KB, p. 138, 147
72. Kershaw, Vergelding.
73. Speer, p. 145

Nonetheless, Hitler did possess knowledge of architecture and the art of painting. He just didn't like 'messy paintings of which you can't distinguish up from down'.[74] He had no stomach at all for modernistic art but he did like classicist art and Romanticism. The notion that Hitler was only interested in architecture after 1933 isn't true either. Although he may have become the self-proclaimed building master of the Third Reich and mainly made architectural sketches himself, his interest in visual art remained.[75]

Hitler's alleged aptitude in the field of art was the main result of the cults of Führer and genius surrounding him: his work of drawing didn't offer any reason at all to think he was a true genius. Hitler was a drawer who was denied admittance to the world of art as a young man and who in his productive years as an 'artisan' sold paintings only for additional funds. After his time as a painter, he became a courier in the army and subsequently turned to politics. He continued drawing but much less frequently. Whether real artisanship had ever been in him can't be said with any certainty.

Hitler's still lives were interchangeable, he had his architectural drawings finalised by real architects and his view on art was limited. Because he had never been a free artisan full time, he never created an oeuvre. Further investigation into Hitler's painting would only be sensible to determine how his work could be compared to that of other amateur painters and drawers. Additionally, more thorough research is required into the falsifications and later adaptations of Hitler's work.

Although today Hitler's work is usually rated negatively, he did pass the first selection of the Viennese Art Academy. If he had had no talent whatsoever, he would not have made it that far. After the second round he was rejected though, but then the selection was fairly tough. Hitler could certainly draw and paint and it has been said that he mainly copied, not from lack of talent but out of laziness. Ian Kershaw may have called Hitler's art uninspired and lifeless[76] and yet he said that the work Hitler sold in Munich was a match for the work of other sellers of works of art who were often students at the Art Academy.[77]

In his book about Hitler's artisanship, Lambert Giebels also stated that Hitler had a certain gift for drawing but that those he made during his puberty varied in quality. Giebels also pointed out, however, that Hitler sometimes made far better drawings and he describes him as someone who

---

74. Hoffmann, HH, p. 133
75. Schwarz, p. 203
76. Kershaw, Hoogmoed, p. 131
77. Kershaw, Hoogmoed, p. 131

might have become a 'locally and regionally recognised painter'. He would never have made it, though, as a visual artisan 'with the power to create a world instead of copying it'.[78] The notion that Hitler was a genius in the field of art was pure propaganda. In full agreement with the tradition of Joseph Goebbels, who made a sharp distinction between talent and genius,[79] we can state with certainty that as an artisan Hitler never made it beyond the status of an unsecure talent and that he was never a genius.

---

78. Giebels, p. 142. The book was published posthumously and was finished by his son Robert
79. Schwarz, p. 131

Chapter 12

Did Hitler Suffer from a Sexual Disorder?

The strange love life of the Führer

In 1944 American Secret Service agents came up with a plan for a weird attempt on Adolf Hitler. A massive amount of pornographic material would be dropped over his villa on the Obersalzberg in order to make the prudish Hitler so crazy he would no longer be able to function normally, bringing the war to an end much sooner. The material was ready and the agents were busy selecting a suitable type of aircraft when their colonel labelled their plan as insane and swept it from the table.[1]

The idea, bizarre as it may seem, didn't emerge out of the blue entirely but was based on stories about Hitler's struggle with his sexuality, stories that still circulate more than seventy-five years after his death. He is supposed to have been homosexual, impotent, frigid or a necrophile; he had incurred a venereal disease after a visit to a Jewish prostitute, he had a suspiciously strong aversion towards that kind of women, he forced his lover into sadomasochistic acts; he had a love for young girls, bordering on paedophilia; he was ashamed of his missing testicle or he was a faeces fetishist. Historian Robert Waite: 'Hitler would have had bizarre sexual preferences so repulsive to women they were driven to suicide.'[2]

Little is known about the sex life of most people, let alone that of Hitler, who was always very taciturn about his private life. The only people who were able to talk from personal experience have long since passed away and except for some loose remarks by his loved ones, Maria Reiter and Eva Braun, there are few sources. Yet, the myth of Hitler's all-explaining sexual disorder is so persistent that it is still hard to distinguish fact from fiction.

---

1. Moorhouse, p. 215
2. Rosenbaum, p. 164

'Budding' love

Some remarks about the first tentative steps on the path of love taken by the youngster Hitler have been recorded by his boyhood friend, August Kubizek, who wrote that Hitler fell in love on a certain moment with a girl the boys saw walking on the arm of her mother down the main shopping street in Linz. Hitler did fantasise about a future with the pretty Stefanie but he never mustered the courage to talk to her. When he had already left for Vienna, he still sent picture postcards mentioning her name. When his mother died in the same period, Stefanie would have been standing on her balcony watching the funeral cortège pass by. Kubizek saw her and he presumed Hitler saw her too but Kubizek didn't know whether she stood there especially because of Adolf or just because a cortège happened to pass by.[3] Hitler's first love remained platonic and, according to witnesses, at the age of twenty Hitler was still hardly active in the field of love and sexual activity.

From the time of Hitler's late adolescence, stories are known on which presumptions about his sex life have been based. When for instance, he and his friend August were looking for a room in Vienna during an inspection, the dressing gown of the landlady fell open and underneath she was wearing nothing but a pair of tiny knickers. Hitler jumped up, took his friend with him and left the house. Once outside he would have exclaimed: 'What a Potiphar!'[4]

During that period, Hitler rejected everything related to sexuality, although he was rather popular among the ladies, so Kubizek said. He assumed that between 1904 until the summer of 1908 Hitler had nothing to do with girls[5] and he named various situations in which girls tried to get in touch with Hitler but he always turned them down. He wouldn't have anything to do with masturbation and homosexuality either.[6]

A lot has been invented about Hitler's sex life in Vienna. Examples are Hitler attempting to rape the girlfriend of a half-Jew, and his alleged visit

---

3. Kubizek, p. 143
4. Kubizek, p. 159 The story of Potiphar is taken from the Bible. He is the man Joseph worked for when he had been sold as a slave. Potiphar's wife tried to seduce Joseph but when he did not give in, she accused him of abuse and Joseph was imprisoned. Hitler made a mistake here by calling the woman Potiphar while in the Bible, Potiphar was the woman's husband. A spicy detail: it has been suggested that Joseph and Potiphar had a homosexual relationship. It simply goes too far, however, to turn Hitler's remark into a far-fetched Freudian slip of the tongue.
5. Kubizek, p. 230
6. Kershaw, Hoogmoed, p. 82; Kubizek, pp. 228–239

to prostitutes in Vienna.⁷ One of these visits would have left him with syphilis. These concoctions should help explain Hitler's abnormal sex life or his later aggression on the world stage but evidence is still lacking and later during medical examinations traces of syphilis were never established.⁸

The only witness who once walked through the red light district of Vienna with Hitler after having attended an opera was his friend August again, who said, however, that he and Adolf had only been looking at the prostitutes and that Adolf, after they had left the place, had started a long discussion about this pool of vice.⁹

There is no evidence for a normally budding sex life of Hitler but this doesn't automatically mean that he was abnormal sexually because it isn't clear at all whether Kubizek knew everything about his friend's sex life. He was in Hitler's company frequently but not always and his avowed rejection of masturbation, for instance, doesn't mean he also stuck to it in practice. We know nothing about that. Ian Kershaw concludes, however: 'It does seem almost certain that Hitler had no sexual experience when he left Vienna at the age of twenty-four.' He also assumes, based on stories in *Mein Kampf* and by Kubizek, that at the time Hitler suffered from an 'extremely disrupted, suppressed sexual development'.¹⁰ Kershaw clearly indicates though that this is an assumption and not an established fact. Repression of sexuality can lead to all sorts of aberrant behaviour but whether this actually applied to Hitler can't be said with certainty. Nonetheless, it remains an interesting issue and with regard to the attention still being paid to the nature of Hitler's relationships, it is important to take a critical look at the evidence for any disorders.

Munich and the Great War

In 1913 Hitler left Vienna. Along with a friend named Rudolf Häusler, he left for Munich, where the two boys shared a room until mid-1914. Häusler left quite soon as Hitler sometimes lay reading throughout the night. Little is known about Hitler's possible sexual contacts in Munich. 'During the months leading up to the First World War he hardly met anyone in Munich, apart from people in beer halls and cafés.'¹¹

---

7. Kershaw, Hoogmoed, p. 81
8. Kershaw, Hoogmoed, p. 110, foot note 146
9. Kubizek, p. 236
10. Kershaw, Hoogmoed, p. 81
11. Kershaw, Hoogmoed, p. 132

The war offered him an escape from a life that lacked direction. He hadn't completed any education, he had no job and only temporary money from the inheritance of his parents. He was unable to enter into true, lasting friendships.[12] The regiment to which he was posted became his substitute family as he hardly had any contact with his real family. At the time, he mostly served behind the lines in Belgium and northern France. Many of his regimental friends visited the cafés and prostitutes in nearby villages when they were away from the trenches for a while. Despite his close ties to his regiment, he didn't take part in this, so many historians state. During the First World War, his life seems to have progressed devoid of sex. Contrary to some of his comrades, he did take the warnings against infected prostitutes and riotous women seriously.[13] Whether that was the only reason why he preferred to wander through town on his own, can't be determined.[14]

Return to Munich

When the war was over, Hitler went back to Munich after being treated in the military hospital in Pasewalk in northern Germany. He stayed in the army as long as he could and only left his regiment after it was disbanded. Meanwhile, he had turned to politics and as he gained success, the first gossip about him soon emerged. This was rather innocent at first, compared with today's standards. For instance, in 1920 it was said he amused himself with women and even with cigarette-smoking ladies![15] The allegations against him grew more severe as he became more famous and had more and more enemies.

In order to obtain money for his party, he kept in touch with higher circles in Munich, in particular with rich men's spouses such as Lotte Bechstein, Viktoria Dirksen, Elsa Bruckmann and Carola Hoffmann. Suggestions have been made about his relationships with these women but they mainly involved useful and aged mother figures rather than serious sexual partners for him. He is supposed to have had a long relationship with the pretty sister of Ernst Hanfstaengl,[16] but that is also an ancient gossip that pops up on the internet again and again and which was published initially by the anti-Hitler

---

12. Kershaw, Hoogmoed, p. 135
13. Weber, p. 140
14. One piece of gossip about Hitler from the same period is the intriguing story of a child he may have fathered on a girlfriend in northern France. This is dealt with in more detail in the chapter 'Did Hitler have a son?'
15. Kershaw, Hoogmoed, p. 221
16. Gun, p. 73

paper the *Münchener Post*. It is to the historic merit of the contributors to this paper that they attacked Hitler heavily but this was one of their stories not based on truth. Modern historians therefore haven't mentioned this possible relationship for a long time. By the way, Hitler is supposed to have had feelings for Ernst Hanfstaengl's wife but she seems not to have taken him seriously as a man.[17]

Even before Hitler attempted to forcibly dethrone the Bavarian government in 1923, he was known well enough to be able to contact the family of his favourite composer, Richard Wagner. This contact remained over the years and about Hitler's relationship with the widow of Wagner's son Richard, Winifred Wagner, whispers circulated there was more to it than just friendship. About a marriage to the Wagner widow, Hitler said it would be one with historic importance but the two never had something with each other. Winifred herself said that rumours about a marriage was just 'meaningless garbage' in the papers.[18] The numerous stories about this impending marriage between Hitler and Wagner, but also about many other women, are 'exaggerated or concocted stories' not based on Hitler's 'deeper' feelings.[19]

Hitler as homosexual

Hitler lived with a young man twice, with August Kubizek in Vienna and Rudolf Häusler in Munich, and this fuelled rumours about his homosexuality. Some anecdotes Kubizek wrote down could be the reason for thinking Hitler had feelings for men. When Kubizek, for instance, took a girl to the room the two boys shared in order to give her piano lessons, Hitler became very angry as he thought Kubizek could have a relationship with her. Later on, various conclusions were based on the weird reaction by the young Hitler. First, Hitler's irritation, as noted by Kubizek, could offer the possibility that Hitler was indeed the asexual figure August Kubizek presented in his diary. In addition, there is the possibility that Hitler was afraid that the girl would come and take away the only friend he had. In his book *Hitler's Intimate Circle*, Lothar Machtan emphasizes the possibility that Hitler was Kubizek's jealous lover[20] and the homoerotic tendency of a part of a description of a walk the two took in the mountains near Semmering is, so Machtan states,

---

17. Kershaw, Hoogmoed. p. 457
18. Sigmund, FN, p. 603
19. Kershaw, Hoogmoed, p. 45
20. Machtan, pp. 44–45

proof of the 'romantic love affair' between the two friends.[21] When the two sought shelter in a barn against the rain Hitler, who had become soaking wet, would have stripped completely, after which Kubizek wrapped him in a dry cloth. In particular, Kubizek's description of Hitler's body who, Kubizek said, resembled an Indian ascetic with the cloth wrapped around his groin and shoulders, would point to more than an ordinary friendship. If this rumour is based on truth, then Kubizek had been lying when he talked about Hitler's asexuality, probably in order to cover up his sexual relationship with him.

Another one of Kubizek's stories is about a man the two boys met one evening in Vienna and who took them to dinner. After the meal, Hitler found a card in his pocket containing an invitation. Only after Hitler's explanation, would Kubizek have understood it was an invitation by a homosexual. The card disappeared in the stove in their room[22] but the fact that Hitler had found out, even before dinner, why the man had invited them, can be explained in different ways. Kubizek did so by pointing out that he and Hitler had had a decent meal in any case: the two had just used the older man to have a nice dinner. The story was somewhat strange, however, and is rich pickings for those who thought Hitler was a homosexual.

Hitler's relations during the First World War would also be suspicious. The best friends of war courier Hitler, apart from the dog Foxl he had found, were couriers like Anton Bachmann and Ernst Schmidt. Hitler is supposed to have had a relation with the latter. At least, that is what Hans Mend said, one of Hitler's fellow couriers. After Hitler had become a well-known person in Germany, Mend said it soon stood out that Hitler never looked at women and many soldiers thought he was a homosexual. Sometime in 1915, they would even have caught him red-handed when he and Schmidt were rolling about in the hay.[23] Mend, however, as mentioned earlier,[24] was totally unreliable as a witness. Before 1933, he had been sentenced ten times, mainly for 'fraud, intimidation and forgery of documents'.[25] Historian Thomas Weber pointed to the fact that Mend had produced two documents contradicting each other: one in which he praised Hitler and the other criticising Hitler and declaring he was a homosexual. For Weber the question is obviously which document is to be taken seriously.[26]

---

21. Machtan, p. 44
22. Kubizek, pp. 236–237
23. Weber, p. 155
24. In the chapter 'Was Hitler a hero?'
25. Weber, p. 156
26. Weber, p. 156

Machtan's book about Hitler's homosexuality stirred up a lot of sensation. Machtan claimed Hitler had led the life of a homosexual in secret for years. Aside from the stories already mentioned, he also pointed to Hitler's adoration for Wagner and the regular visits by Adolf Hitler and August Kubizek to performances of operas by this composer, which would have been very popular among homosexuals. Bayreuth, where the Wagner family lived and where operas of Wagner were staged during the yearly *Bayreuther Festspiele*, was a meeting place for homosexuals. One of the regular visitors was Hitler, a fanatic admirer of Wagner and, after he had turned to politics, the most famous attendee.

Furthermore, Machtan views Hitler's love for his mother through a pink magnifying glass, and he points to the numerous contacts he had with homosexuals. The men's shelter in Vienna where Hitler stayed when he had too little money to rent a room for himself was a place visited by many homosexuals. Here Hitler is supposed to have had sexual contact with his companions Reinhold Hanisch and Joseph Neumann. The evidence seemed to be stacking up. Not only Hanisch and Neumann, who sold pictures and paintings for him, but also some of the men to whom Hitler sold his paintings himself were homosexual.

After the First World War Hitler had contacts with men of whom it could be assumed that they were homophiles. As to Ernst Röhm, this was a certainty. Machtan assumed, however, that Hitler and Röhm were not a couple. Hitler's relationship with his much older mentor, Dietrich Eckart, was suspect as well. Hitler worshipped the man and Eckart in turn saw Hitler as a young man with a lot of potential, but it isn't clear whether there was a question of a relationship. With men like piano player and chief of the press Ernst Hanfstaengl, party comrade Rudolf Hess and drivers Emil Maurice and Julius Schreck, the list of potential partners grows longer and longer. In the case of Maurice, Machtan describes an interesting triangular relationship between Geli Raubal, her lover Emil Maurice and the so-called lover of both, Hitler. His frequent visits to the Hotel Bube in Bad Berneck, at the time very popular among homophiles, seems to complete the evidence.

Making a list of men who probably or almost certainly were homosexual is just as easy as making a list of friends who were avowed heterophiles. Such a list would include, for instance, Goebbels and Bormann. The fact that young Hitler, when he lived in Passau, played cowboys and Indians rather than with the puppets of the girl next door could put another myth to rest but the major point remains that Machtan's work is also about an interpretation of evidence, not irrefutable facts. During the First World War, Hitler never rose above the rank of corporal – rather unusual for someone with such a long service record. This was the result, so Machtan claims, of Hitler's wish to stay with his homosexual cronies but it could just as well have been the result of something else: Hitler was a weird man and promotion, resulting in a transfer to another unit, probably was not so obvious. As mentioned before, at the time Hitler was still seen as a weak leader.

It is almost too good to be true: Hitler as a secretive homophile, frustrated to the core as he could not come out of the closet. It would not only explain his strenuous association with women but also his tendency toward secrecy and his talent as a liar, because in his time he probably had the idea he had to lie about his orientation. Hitler having feelings for men is an assumption though and is far from certain. Notwithstanding the views of other historians, Machtan did succeed in making Hitler suspect. At the end of his book he said himself that Hitler's orientation could not have been the key to his life but could have been the cause of other interpretations of issues in his life, for instance the Röhm crisis.[27] We don't know for sure, however, whether Hitler was homosexual or even bisexual.

Women yet again

After the failed putsch in Munich in 1923, Hitler became instantly famous outside Bavaria as well. From that moment on, the list of women who are supposed to have had a relationship with him grew longer and longer. Especially in the foreign press, much was speculated about Hitler's loves.[28] In the mid-1920s, the stories began to trip over each other. At that time, Hitler often attended operas and it seems that after the performance he sometimes took a female singer to his home. The speculation was that nothing other than cuddling would have taken place during the few hours he spent with them.[29] However, how people think they know such things in detail remains an open question.

Hitler also showed up frequently at dance shows and made acquaintances with several female dancers. He sometimes visited the Art Academy, where he wandered freely among the nude models completely at ease.[30] In his biography of Eva Braun, Turkish-American journalist Nerin E. Gun

---

27. The fragment about Hitler has been taken from Machtan's *Hitler's Intimate Circle*.
28. Once Hitler had risen to power and the press had been brought into line, this kind of story obviously did not get reported anymore.
29. Lambert, p. 121
30. Gun, pp. 73–74

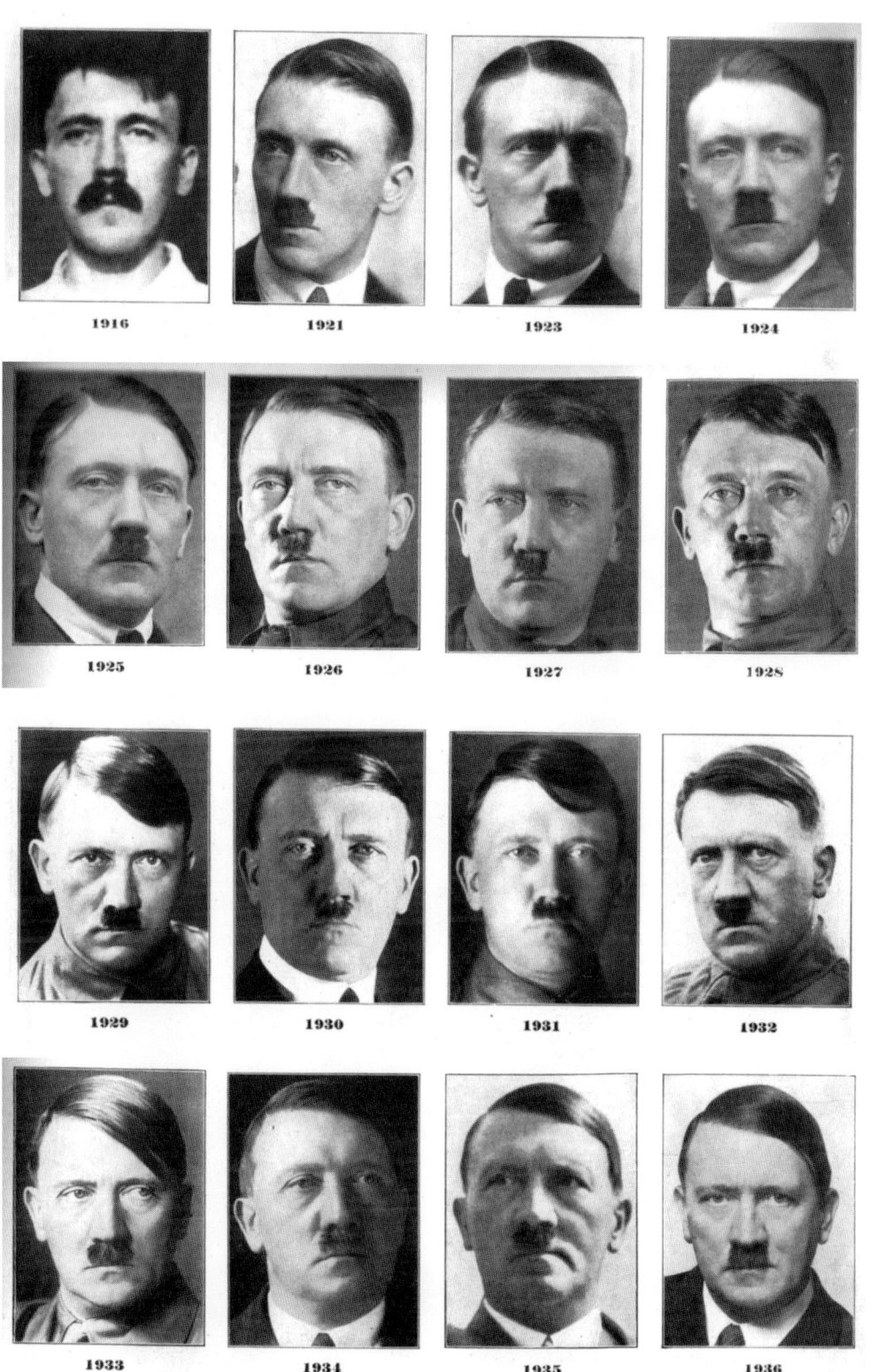

A series of photographs of Adolf Hitler from 1916 onwards. On the first photo Hitler is seen with the broad moustache he wore during the First World War. (*Pictures: Illustrierter BeoBachter*)

Hitler leaving the bunker of his headquarters Felsennest on 16 May 1940. From there he coordinated the attack on the Netherlands, Belgium, Luxembourg and France. (*Picture: Heinrich Hoffman*)

A propaganda photo of Hitler from 1927. taken in the Munich studio of his personal photographer Heinrich Hoffman. (*Picture: Heinrich Hoffman*)

Hitler's office on the Königslatz in Munich. Next to it are the two temples of honour for the victims who fell during the Hitlersputsch of 1923. (*Picture: Illustrierter Beobachter*)

Adolf Hitler arrives at an airport. Next to the girl who is handing him flowers is his minister of aviation Hermann Göring. (*Picture: Heinrich Hoffmann*)

During the 1920s and 1930s Hitler made many speeches around Germany. This decreased considerably during the war. (*Picture: Heinrich Hoffmann*)

On his way to a meeting somewhere in Germany, Hitler fell asleep. (*Picture: Heinrich Hoffmann*)

A parade at the Brandenburg Gate in Berlin, after France had been defeated in 1940. (*Picture: Heinrich Hoffmann*)

The people cheer for Hitler on 6 July 1940 after the defeat of France. Hitler is standing on the balcony of an extension to Berlin's Old Reich Chancellery. (*Picture: Heinrich Hoffmann*)

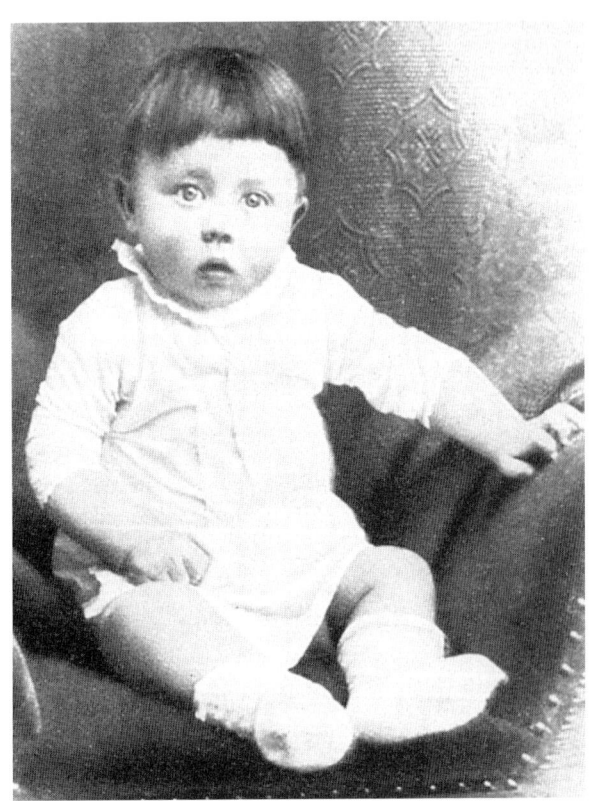

Adolf Hitler as a baby. The innocence he radiates in this photograph was not always appreciated immediately after the war. Some people were shocked by it. (*Source unknown*)

Visiting Braunau am Inn in 1938, Hitler is driven into the town of his birth from the bridge over the river Inn. (*Picture: Heinrich Hoffmann*)

Hitler during a speech to the Austrian people on the Heldenplatz in Vienna after the 'Anschluss' in 1938. (*Picture: Heinrich Hoffmann*)

Hitler visited the so-called Vimyhöhe in Northern France on 2 June 1940. His regiment had fought there during the First World War, but he had not been there himself because he was being treated in a German hospital at that time. (*Picture: Heinrich Hoffmann*)

At the beginning of the First World War, Munich residents gathered on Odeonsplatz in Munich. Adolf Hitler (apparently shown with a square around his head) is said to have been present ... (*Picture: Illustrierter BeoBachter, 1914*)

Private Hitler (seated, right) with his comrades and his dog Foxl in the garden of a German headquarters in Fournes-en-Weppes in 1916.

In 1940 Hitler revisited the places he had been during the First World War. Here he is at the German cemetery in Langemark. (*Picture: Heinrich Hoffman*)

Hitler and his regiment never fought at Langemark, but the commander of his regiment was buried there. (*Picture: Heinrich Hoffmann*)

Top left: Hitler (standing, second from left) as a station guard in Munich, just after the First World War.
Top right: The mythical 'Blutfahne (Bloodflag) at a parade taken by Hitler.
Centre: Hitler wrote most of the second part of Mein Kampf in this so-called 'Kampfhäusl', a small mountain house belonging to a hotel on the Obersalzberg.
Below: The NSDAP headquarters in the late 1920s. The Bloodflag hangs in the middle, against the wall. (*Picture: Heinrich Hoffmann*)

In 1923/24 Hitler was imprisoned in Landsberg am Lech for almost a year after a failed coup d'etat. In 1934, as Reich Chancellor, he visited the prison. (*Picture: Heinrich Hoffmann*)

The Führer of Germany and Austria at the start of the construction of the Salzburg-Vienna motorway. (*Picture: Heinrich Hoffmann*)

An enthusiastic crowd outside the Opel factory of Rüsselheim cheers Hitler as he passes. (*Picture: Heinrich Hoffmann*)

As a young man Hitler had lived in Vienna. In 1938 he returned there as a celebrated leader. Here he is being driven in front of the Vienna Burgtheater. (*Picture: Heinrich Hoffmann*)

The Alter Hof in Munich, which Hitler painted as a young man. He made money painting and selling postcards like this.

A perfect propaganda picture of admiring SA members looking mesmerised at their Fuhrer. (*Picture: Heinrich Hoffmann*)

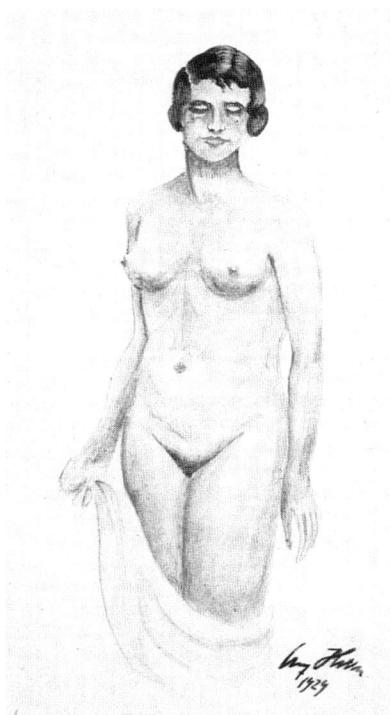

This is supposedly a drawing that Hitler made of his niece Geli Raubal, though it is not certain that he did it himself.

A picture with interesting symbolism. Hitler leaves a church in Wilhelmshaven with his head bowed. The cross is exactly above his head. (*Picture: Heinrich Hoffmann*)

In a hospital in Beelitz, south of Berlin. Hitler (top row, second from right) healed from an injury he sustained in the First World War.

Hitler's new Reich Chancellery in Berlin only functioned for about six years. By May 1945 it was so battered that it was demolished by the Soviets a few years later. (*Picture: Boston Public Library*)

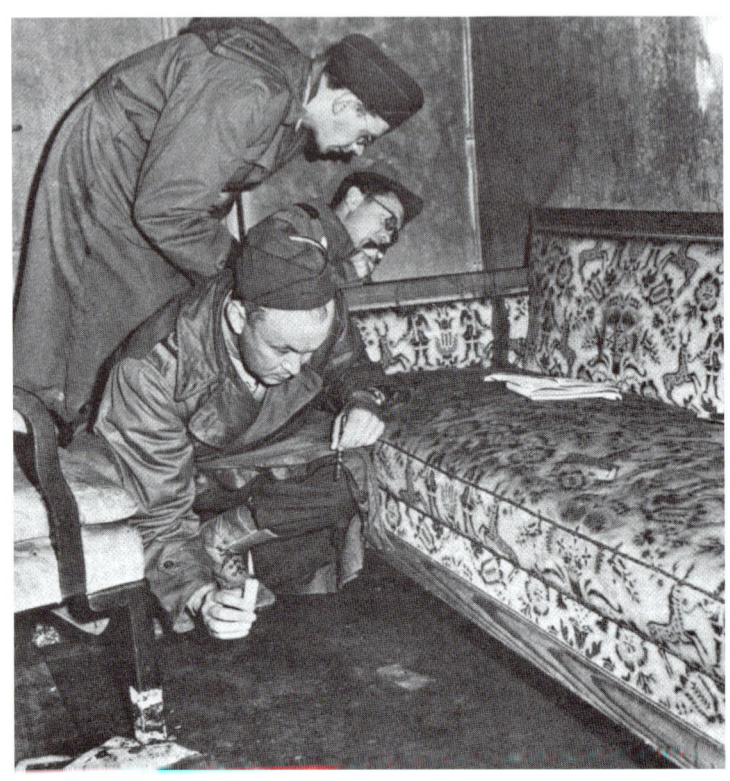

The sofa in the Führerbunker where Adolf Hitler and Eva Braun committed suicide. (*Picture: National Archives*)

The ruined Old and New Chancellery after the war. Behind the building the cylindrical guardhouse and the square emergency exit of the Führerbunker are visible. (*Picture: Library of Congress*)

names several women about whom gossip circulated to the effect they had a relationship with Hitler. A certain Suzi Liptauer, for instance, is supposed to have attempted suicide after Hitler cut off their relationship. Jenny Haug, sister of one of Hitler's drivers, is supposed to have been his girlfriend for a period around 1923. After 1934 Hitler is said to have had an affair with Gerdy, widow of Professor Paul Ludwig Troost. In addition, a Mrs Bouhler was mentioned, probably the wife of Hitler's fellow putschist and the later chief of the *Parteikanzlei* Philip Bouhler, and the actress Pola Negri, about whom it was published incorrectly in 1937 that she had a relationship with Hitler. Eleonora Bauer is supposed to have given birth to Hitler's child.[31] It isn't so hard to prove that Hitler had known and met these women but there is no proof whatsoever that he had a relationship with any of them.

The name of Inge Ley, the beautiful wife of Nazi big wig Robert Ley, the head of the *Reichsarbeitsdienst*, appears on the list of Adolf Hitler's lady friends as well but there is no certainty about her in that respect at all. The suggestion that her suicide in 1943 could have had something to do with Hitler can still be found here and there, but it looks like far-fetched gossip. It is very likely that her suicide had more to do with personal problems or with her husband, who drank too much.

About Unity Valkyrie Mitford, a member of the British nobility, it was said, especially in the English press, that she had had a relationship with Hitler. Unity got to know Hitler personally by literally thrusting herself upon him. When Hitler had lunch in one of his favourite cafés, she always sat down in full view of him. Soon Hitler invited her to his table. It didn't come to intimacies between the two but Hitler did use Unity for political and propaganda purposes. Eva Braun, with whom Hitler already had a relationship at that time, would have felt irritated by the obtrusive Unity. In a diary entry by Braun about a *Walküre* (Valkyrie), she writes that she had learned from Frau Hoffmann, spouse of photographer Heinrich Hoffmann, that Hitler had somebody else. *Walküre* would have applied to Unity Valkyrie Mitford but later on Eva's sister Ilse thought Winifred Wagner was meant.[32] Unity was more or less the symbol of the positive German–

---

31. Gun, p. 74
32. Gun, p. 87. In view of the date of the fragment, 10 May 1935, it probably concerns Unity Mitford. He had already had a long relationship with Winifred Wagner and only a short one with Unity. The remarks Eva Braun makes about the bars of *Walküre* would probably indicate Wagner. 'But he loves that kind of music. Well, if it is true she'll probably soon lose 33 pounds as he will put her to work naturally.' Possibly, Eva Braun herself did not know who Mrs Hoffmann was talking about and she thought it was Winifred Wagner, the daughter-in-law of the composer of *Die Walküre*.

British relationship so much desired by the Germans. Apparently, Unity felt so strongly about this that she made an attempt at suicide by shooting herself in the head when Great Britain and Germany went to war. Initially, the bid to take her own life failed but a few years after the war she died in England from meningitis caused by the bullet still lodged in her brain.

In her autobiography, Heinrich Hoffmann's daughter, Henriette, told an interesting story about Hitler. She also was in the queue of Hitler's possible lovers, but in her own words, it didn't go beyond a clumsy attempt to seduce her. She saw nothing in him. In 1929, when she still was a young girl, the much older Hitler once asked her if she would kiss him. She responded with something like, 'Better not, mister Hitler,' and Hitler left irritated.[33] According to her father, she had got something into her head but the scene that unfolded between the young girl and Hitler might be characteristic of the obtrusive and clumsy way in which Hitler sometimes tried to seduce young women.

The list of women of whom it is only suggested that they had a relationship with Hitler is a long one. Magda Goebbels is the best-known of them. She is supposed to have been in love with Hitler but it never evolved into a relationship, although later on it was claimed he had fathered one of her children.[34] At the end of the war, she first poisoned her children, then she and her husband committed suicide.

Mimi Reiter

One of the first of Hitler's alleged relationships, which is generally considered true, was that with Maria, or Mimi, Reiter from Berchtesgaden. Their relationship began in 1926 when Hitler was already 37 years old and the girl only 16. After they had met in the *Kurpark* in Berchtesgaden, they saw each other more frequently. The young girl must have got the idea that an important man was in love with her[35] as Hitler was a well-known figure in the village. He was the most important man at the party rallies of the NSDAP, one of which she attended right at the start of their relationship.

During the short relationship between the two, Hitler was often away, to the frustration of his lover. In the periods when they didn't see each other, Mini wrote long letters to him. He responded with picture postcards from the various places he visited during his political trips all over Germany.

---

33. Schirach, p. 8
34. Basti & Van Helsing, p. 394
35. Sigmund, FN, p. 694

Some uncertainty exists about the way the relationship came to an end. It is said, however, that in early March 1927, in the NSDAP paper the *Völkische Beobachter*, Hitler denied speculation in the press about his possible engagement and relationship with a minor.[36] Another source claims the two were in each other's company frequently until the summer of 1927.[37] Whatever it was, Hitler began to avoid the girl at a certain moment and when he turned up in Berchtesgaden once without telling Mimi, her world collapsed and she made an attempt at suicide. Her brother-in-law was just in time to save her from hanging herself. This would be the first in the series of suicide attempts by women surrounding Hitler.

The reason why Hitler distanced himself from the girl was probably a political assessment. In an anonymous letter, likely written by an acquaintance of both Hitler and Mimi, the NSDAP Führer was charged with fornication with minors and a threat was made to inform the police. The story made the press in February or March 1927. The *Leipziger Nachrichten*, for instance, reported the affair and a possible engagement of Adolf Hitler. Naturally, Hitler feared the end of his political career and he ended the relationship with a Dear John letter.[38] Mimi was told she would have to accept her fate as Hitler strove towards a higher goal: *Deutschland*. She complied and a year later she married a boy from Innsbrück.

Mimi thought this would not necessarily mean the end of her relationship with Hitler. Her marriage was not that good and as a married woman she would have visited him a few times in Munich and Berchtesgaden between 1931 and 1933. Precisely during the period in which two other young women, Geli Raubal and Eva Braun, already played a role in his life, she, in her own words, spent the night in his apartment.[39] The next morning, Hitler may have asked her to move in with him. As marriage was out of the question and, contrary to him, she did want children, she turned down Hitler's offer and returned to her husband. According to Ian Kershaw, this story is more than likely a fairy tale. In 1931, Geli Raubal, his other and much better-known possible lover, already lived with Hitler in his spacious apartment on *Prinzregentenstrasse*.[40] It is highly unlikely that Mimi had spent the night with the Führer unnoticed.

---

36. Bruppacher, p. 159
37. Sigmund, FN, p. 707
38. Sigmund, EN, p. 708
39. Sigmund, FN, p. 713
40. Kershaw, Hoogmoed, pp. 372–373

Whether the two had had sex or not, Maria Reiter's story doesn't offer any evidence to support the theory that Hitler led a bizarre sex life.[41] The reason for the termination of the relationship, and therefore for the attempt at suicide, was political and not sexual. A few similarities between other relationships Hitler had stand out though. First off, there was an unequal relationship between an older man and a young girl. Regarding the difference in age between his father and mother, Hitler would not have felt this as unnatural. The other two best-known women with whom Hitler would have had a sexual relationship, Geli Raubal and Eva Braun, were also much younger than Hitler. The advantage of such a relationship was, of course, that Hitler's earlier restraint in his dealings with women played a much smaller role. In contrast to his early love Stefanie, he could impress them with his experience and the status he enjoyed among his followers. The basis of their attraction couldn't be anything other than the young girls being impressed by the fact his political friends held him in such high esteem.

Hitler's neglect of the relationship with Mimi became a recurring pattern in his later love life. He considered his political career far more important than his relation with a woman. The attempts at suicide, successful or not that the three women, Mimi, Geli and Eva, made during their relationship with Hitler probably had more to do with him neglecting them and the personality of the girls themselves.

Geli Raubal

In 1927, when Hitler was still winding down his short relationship with Mimi Reiter, his niece, Geli Raubal came to Munich with her class to meet him. This would be the beginning of a strange relationship, about which speculation ran wild until long after the war. In September 1931, when the Nazi party was on the rise and was finally being taken seriously as a national party, the body of Hitler's niece was found in his apartment in Munich. She had committed suicide shortly after Hitler had left the property. The anti-Hitler paper the *Münchener Post* soon reported that Geli had left the apartment after a furious argument over an engagement for which she had to travel to Vienna. The next day, so the paper reported, the body of Hitler's niece was found. She had a broken nose and was holding Hitler's gun in her hand. Hitler stated that shortly before his departure nothing remarkable had occurred and his staff confirmed his story. Why the girl committed suicide, nobody knew.

---

41. Rosenbaum, pp. 171–172

Did Hitler Suffer from a Sexual Disorder? 121

After graduating from high school, Geli came to Munich in 1927 to study medicine. She soon entered into a relationship with a good friend of Hitler, his driver Emil Maurice, whom she took more seriously than her studies.[42] Eventually, Maurice asked Hitler for Geli's hand. Hitler, who had been imprisoned in Landsberg along with Maurice, flew into a rage. He obliged the couple to postpone their marriage for two years, probably hoping the relationship would evaporate in that time.[43] Hitler's anger was explained in various ways. One of the best-known was that Hitler was in love with the girl himself, or in any case felt sexually attracted to her.

Whatever the explanation, after the proposal the relationship did not last long, mainly because of Hitler's interference. He had fired Maurice in the summer of 1928 and banned him from his circle. After he also had put Geli under pressure by threatening to stop his financial support of her and her family if she didn't break the relationship,[44] the two didn't see each other anymore. Hitler's real motives for breaking off the relationship became clear in 1945, when it appeared that he might have come under political pressure. Emil Maurice was of Jewish descent and, being the leader of an anti-Semitic party, Hitler could obviously not allow a member of his own family, for whom he was responsible after all, to marry such a person.[45] This forced ending of their relationship might have been very unpleasant for the girl but it couldn't have been the reason for her suicide later on. After all, she did not end her life until a few years afterwards. The manner in which Hitler brutally interfered in the life of his niece as a jealous lover or a much too stern uncle is characteristic of his further dealings with Geli.

After her suicide, the *Münchener Neueste Nachrichten* wrote that Hitler had forbidden his niece to make a trip to Vienna in order to meet a man. The paper also suggested, however, that she had taken her life because she had to perform as a singer and couldn't stand the pressure.[46] Other sources suggested Hitler had murdered her or had her murdered. Another suggestion was that it had been an accident: Geli had been playing with Hitler's gun and had fired it unwittingly. After the war, it was often stressed that the girl might have committed suicide because Hitler had been an overprotective uncle, allowing his niece hardly any freedom, and that his consistent control, even when he wasn't around, had such a strangulating effect that it led Geli to kill herself. Kershaw, who isn't sure whether the two had a sexual

---

42. Sigmund, FN, p. 205
43. Sigmund, FN, pp. 208–20
44. Sigmund, FN, p. 213
45. Sigmund, EN, p. 213
46. Sigmund, FF, p. 177

relationship, does say it could have been possible that Hitler was emotionally dependent on the woman who lived with him and that she might well have been the victim of Hitler's possessive attitude and jealousy.

Geli was more or less imprisoned in Hitler's apartment and she had to consult him about each choice she made from possible partners to parties. Everywhere she went, she was watched over by her uncle or someone from his circle of friends. In September 1931, she may have tried desperately to free herself from the tight grip of her uncle.[47] The exaggerated way Hitler watched over her must have been so oppressing to the young woman; she called her uncle a monster and said nobody could imagine what he demanded of her.[48] Based on this statement, Ernst Hanfstaengl suggested Hitler had a sexual and perverse relationship with her. Hitler's former friend, however, drew this conclusion only after he had fled to America and had become his political opponent.

Another statement about Hitler's alleged perverse sexual behaviour was made by Otto Strasser and is demonstrably biased as well. Strasser,[49] a prominent Nazi, had emigrated after a violent argument with Hitler and tried to oppose the Führer from the outside. He stated Hitler was a sadomasochist who had forced his niece to perform certain perverse acts. But this, Strasser stated, wouldn't have led to Geli's suicide. He believed the SS had murdered her because she was pregnant by a Jewish student. Kershaw says this statement, separating Hitler's sexual disorder from Geli's death, is based on speculation and unreliable evidence as well.[50]

It still isn't entirely clear what role Hitler played in the events leading up to the death of his niece but it stands out that a second young woman in Hitler's entourage had made an attempt at suicide. Geli must have been extremely dependent on her uncle, financially as well as emotionally, but in her case, it was not neglect by absence but Hitler's strangulating presence that caused her to commit suicide.

Following her death, Hitler displayed erratic behaviour, to say the least. He may have felt extreme grief over Geli's suicide but he wasn't present at her funeral. It would have been too much for him. However, it was probably not his emotional involvement in the fate of his niece that caused his absence at the funeral. Actually, there was a political reason not to attend. That day, an important meeting was scheduled in Hamburg where he would

---

47. Kershaw, Hoogmoed, p. 458
48. Kershaw, Hoogmoed, p. 458
49. Kershaw, Hoogmoed, pp. 457–459, 490–491
50. Kershaw, Hoogmoed, p. 490

address thousands of people. Apparently, he wasn't grieving enough to call it off.[51] Furthermore, so the rumour goes, during the period of mourning Hitler stayed in the home of a friend for weeks, but this was a concoction as well. Hitler did retreat from Munich for a few days but this was to evade a confrontation with the press.[52] He also deemed it unnecessary to buy a grave or even a tombstone for Geli.[53] She was buried in a municipal grave in Vienna. Despite this display of disinterest, Hitler said Geli was the only woman he had ever loved. From the moment of her death, he felt himself married to Germany,[54] a fine but flimsy excuse for not answering questions about marriage from the press.

A third and final explanation for Geli's suicide, involving the third well-known woman in Hitler's life, came from his housekeeper, Anna Winter. Apart from a few contradicting statements about the suicide, she came up with the story that Geli had found a letter from Eva Braun in Hitler's room, which upset her very much. Eva is supposed to have shoved love letters into his pocket regularly, even though the possibility existed that Geli would find them.[55] Eva's mother, Fanny, also supposed Eva and Geli knew each other[56] and that would have led to a competition for Hitler's attention. Frau Winter supposed it had been one of these letters that Geli had read shortly before her suicide. However, Geli had known Eva since 1929 and it seems that on the day of her suicide Frau Winter had left in the afternoon, so she could not have known what had occurred in the apartment either.[57]

At the end of the day most of the speculation, except that of the uncle keeping his niece on an extremely short leash, remains unproved. There wouldn't have been any question of maltreatment either. The *Münchener Post* may well have stated that Geli's body had a broken nose but hard evidence is missing. Stories about Geli being impregnated by a Jewish student and wanting to go to Vienna for an abortion weren't correct either. Hitler's sexual relationship with Geli has not been proved either, let alone any question of sadomasochism or other forms of aberrant behaviour. Ian Kershaw concludes: 'It is hard to find out what kind of relationship this has been, in view of all stories being based on hearsay or just guesswork.'[58]

---

51. Sigmund, FN, pp. 226–228
52. Sigmund, FN, p. 226
53. Sigmund, FN, p. 230
54. Sigmund, EN, p. 232
55. Lambert, p. 128
56. Lambert, p. 123
57. Sigmund, FF, p. 169
58. Kershaw, Hoogmoed, p. 457

Eva Braun

In September 1929, 17-year-old Eva Braun got a job in the store of photographer Heinrich Hoffmann on *Amalienstrasse* in Munich, where after a month she met Adolf Hitler for the first time. It would have been obvious that she would have been impressed by Hitler. Hoffmann's entire business centred on Hitler and his NSDAP[59] and she must have been impressed by the pictures on display of the then 40-year-old Hitler. A letter by Eva about the Friday night she first met him reveals, however, that she didn't recognise him at first. Her boss came in 'with a somewhat older man with a weird small moustache wearing a light raincoat, such an English one, you know and a large felt hat in his hand'.[60] Her boss invited her to join them but she still didn't recognise Hitler. When she wanted to go home, she rejected his offer to escort her there and only when she put on her coat, Hoffmann told her the man was Adolf Hitler. 'Who is that?' she is supposed to have asked.[61]

And yet, her interest in the man awoke. He was obviously a well-known politician and that must have made him very intriguing to the young woman. Hitler was attracted by her joyful carelessness and naivety. Initially, this didn't immediately lead to a relationship. It was probably because at the time Geli was still living with Hitler. Eva was, however, able to go to the opera with him and as early as 1930 she went to dinner with him in his favourite café, Osteria Bavaria. For her, however, this wasn't good enough and she soon attempted to get closer yet to the NSDAP leader.

Prior to Hitler becoming *Reichskanzler* of Germany, Hitler couldn't afford new personal dramas in those years that were so politically crucial. Therefore in 1930, he had research conducted into Eva Braun to determine whether or not she was of Jewish ancestry.[62] She wasn't but that was, of course, no guarantee for an absence of great dramas in the relationship between him and Eva. Probably in reaction to the attention of the press to his relationship with Mimi Reiter and the suicide of Geli Raubal, Hitler decided to keep this affair secret. That was the fate awaiting the best-known lover of Hitler: being the secret love of the Führer. As long as she didn't stand in the way of his political ambitions, she could stay.

In December 1931, Eva was allowed to come to *Haus Wachenfeld*, the summer residence on the Obersalzberg, which was converted later into the

---

59. Sigmund, EN, p. 241
60. Gun, p. 56
61. Gun, pp. 56–57
62. Sigmund, EN, p. 243

Berghof villa. A few weeks earlier the house had been Geli's domain, where Eva was not welcome. At that time and place, the first intimacies between Adolf and Eva must have taken place, but they remained secret from the general public.[63] Most Germans found out about her existence only when the war was over and the couple were dead. Publications mentioning Braun and Hitler were withdrawn from the market and it was expected of Hitler's intimi that they would handle the situation with discretion. The former chambermaid at the *Berghof*, Anna Plaim, said that she was told at the beginning of her employment she had to keep silent about anything going on there, especially the relationship between Adolf and Eva. Furthermore, she couldn't recall whether the two had kissed or held hands in the presence of others.[64] There was speculation about the lover Hitler had in his villa on the mountain but Eva herself remained unknown. Albert Speer said about it: 'He kept her hidden from everyone, except for his closest intimi.'[65]

This situation posed a problem for Eva. Initially, Hitler did not accept any responsibility for her and therefore her father did not agree with his daughter's relationship, also because Hitler had no marriage to offer. She had to keep working for Heinrich Hoffmann and lived with her parents for a long time. The pressure by her father and the absence of Hitler, who addressed crowds all over Germany during political campaigning, became too much for her in 1932. On the night of 31 October, the lonely young woman made an attempt at suicide by shooting herself in the neck. Her sister, Ilse, found her in time though. Hitler came to her speedily and decided to see her more often, out of a feeling of guilt or out of fear of a new scandal.[66]

Despite her attempt at suicide, the situation didn't get much better for her, all the more after Hitler had become *Reichskanzler* in 1933. Eva still didn't live on her own and therefore was dependent on her parents, while she was old enough to marry. What's more, she also had to keep her relationship secret because Hitler wanted it that way. All this led in May 1935 to a second attempt at suicide, this time by pills. Again, Ilse found her in the nick of time.

---

63. Lambert talks about this in his book about Eva Braun. Sigmund, EN, p. 245. Testimony of Mrs Winter, Hitler's housekeeper in Munich, in which she more or less confirms this. She says Eva Braun became Hitler's lover in early 1932 in Hitler's home in Munich. When the sexual relationship began is not entirely clear but it is estimated to have been in 1931 or early 1932.
64. Kuch, p. 56, 92
65. Lambert, p. 139
66. Lambert, p. 145

Following this second attempt, Hitler finally took over responsibility for her from her father and rented an apartment where she could live with her sister, Gretl. Later on, she was given a small villa in a well-to-do neighbourhood in Munich. Her bills were paid by Martin Bormann, who managed Hitler's assets, and she was given a monthly allowance so she didn't have to work for Heinrich Hoffmann any longer. Hitler sent her messages much more frequently, even later on during the Soviet campaign, or called her on the phone.[67]

They only married in 1945, shortly before their mutual suicide, when there were no more political successes for Hitler to achieve. Their marriage proved there was more between the two than just a good relationship and it seems as if Hitler eventually rewarded Eva for the special bond he had had with her.

During his lifetime, Hitler mentioned various reasons why he didn't want to marry. A marriage didn't match the exalted view he had of his leadership of Germany but the obligations inherent to a marriage didn't appeal to him either. In his opinion, it was far better to have a mistress. 'The burden is lighter and everything unfolds at the level of a present,' he is supposed to have said.[68] Journalist Nerin E Gun made a comparison between Hitler's vision on his function as leader of the German population and that of a pope. 'He had to guarantee the German people, he was ready for them day and night, not letting himself be distracted in any way. So, no parties, no vacations, adventures or a family with kids.'[69] It is hard to say whether his notion about marriage resulted from the behaviour of his father, who hadn't exactly been a worthy housefather either.

Very few pictures showing Adolf and Eva together appeared in public, and at official occasions when Eva was present, she never sat next to Hitler but often among the secretaries where she didn't stand out. During state visits to the *Berghof* on the *Obersalzberg* the lady of the house, Eva, was always the unknown absentee. She then spent most of the time in her room. Yet, the role of the secretive lover apparently suited Eva well. Hitler might well not be married to her but in the end, he had chosen her. Hitler providing her living and including her in his most intimate circle came closer to a marriage than she might have hoped for. In the long run, she was even allowed to accompany him on his travels, for instance on a trip to Italy. She always remained in the shadows though, even at the *Anschluss* of Austria to the

---

67. Gun, p. 90
68. Lambert, p. 130
69. Gun, p. 94

German Empire, when the two stayed in the luxurious Hotel Imperial in Vienna.[70] In 1939, she was given a room of her own in the *Reichskanzlei* in Berlin, a clear sign of recognition.

Little is known about the sex life of the couple. Entries in Eva's diary like: 'Yesterday he turned up unexpectedly and we had a wonderful evening'[71] are easily interpreted as hints for an amorous evening but the quote doesn't offer anything conclusive. This kind of remark is no proof of Hitler's so-called strange sexual preferences either.

On 11 March 1935 Eva wrote about him: 'He only needs me for a special reason. It can't be anything else.' Later on, she added the comment 'nonsense'. What that special reason might have been isn't hard to guess but what happened sexually between the two remains a mystery.

Angela Lambert, who wrote a book about Braun, also assumes they went to bed with each other.[72] She states Hitler deflowered Eva sometime at the end of 1931 or beginning of 1932, but evidence for this does not exist.[73] The fact that she became the most important inhabitant of the house proves that he increasingly appreciated her presence. Especially with a person like Eva, of whom many said she was no intellectual genius, Hitler could relax.

At the *Berghof*, she had a room next to Hitler's and there was a connecting door between the two. According to the housekeeper and her husband, the two frequently shared a bed in Eva's room and on occasion she had to get pills or a potion for Eva to suppress or postpone her menstruation when Hitler suddenly arrived at the *Berghof*.[74]

In a book compiled by historian Werner Maser, Hitler's personal adjutant Heinz Linge said about Hitler's alleged impotence: 'As far as I could see, the sexual relationship between Hitler and Eva was sometimes a very active one.'[75] Linge once caught the two red-handed when he entered the study at the *Berghof*. He saw Eva and Adolf tenderly hugging each other and left in a hurry.[76]

---

70. Gun, p. 134
71. An entry in Eva Braun's diary of 18 February 1935, referred to by Lambert, p. 163, and quoted in its entirety by Gun, p. 84.
72. For instance: Lambert, p. 189
73. Lambert, p. 136; Kuch, p. 126. The former chambermaid Anna Plaim says no one knew exactly where Hitler spent the night. This does not mean though that there was nobody who knew. After all, someone had to make the beds. People with the most intimate knowledge obviously kept it to themselves.
74. Lambert, pp. 215–216; Kuch, p. 94
75. Linge, p. 56
76. Linge, p. 40

Eva was also very young when she met the somewhat older Hitler. His power of attraction obviously was so strong, the difference in ages posed no problem for her. The lack of attention by Hitler was. She was last on the list of women neglected by Hitler who made attempts at suicide out of frustration. Due to Hitler's continuous absence, she even made two such attempts. Only then did Hitler accept his responsibility for her. Yet she never held a public function and the German population never got to know her in her lifetime. The secrecy might have been the cause of the abundant post-war speculation about the sex life of the two but there is no evidence whatsoever for alleged excesses in this respect.

Perversion

The wild stories about the sexually frustrated Hitler emerged early in his career. In 1931, the *Münchener Post* published an article about sex in the Third Reich. It was about the homophile leader of the SA, Ernst Röhm, and the ambiguous attitude of the Nazi party regarding homosexuality. The paper wondered why on the one hand the party was vigorously against it while on the other hand Röhm could continue his homosexual activities undisturbed.[77] The speculations about Hitler's own sex life really exploded on the occasion of Geli Raubal's suicide. Although it wasn't even certain whether there had been a question of an intimate relationship, rumours sprang up that Hitler had unleashed his sexual lust on her. Otto Strasser, along with his brother Gregor, a former important Nazi from northern Germany, claimed that Geli had told him privately in the *Englisher Garten* in Munich that Hitler regularly ordered her to undress and to squat over him, and subsequently urinate on him.[78] When Strasser told this story he had already left Germany and his brother had been murdered in the Night of the Long Knives in 1934 because both men had had ideological conflicts with Hitler. This probably explains why Strasser made statements to blemish Hitler.

Konrad Heiden, a Jewish journalist and historian, also had to leave Germany when Hitler became the boss. He suggested Hitler had had a fixation for excrement but his statements were not based on fact but on the desire to blemish Hitler just like Otto Strasser.[79] Ron Rosenbaum swept the

---

77. Rosenbaum, pp. 86–110
78. Rosenbaum, p. 189
79. Rosenbaum, p. 188

claims of Heiden and Strasser aside as simply being sexual fantasy[80] because evidence for these charges did not exist either.

Ernst Hanfstaengl, the former chief of the Nazi press, also escaped from Germany in 1937. After the previously excellent relationship between Hitler and him had cooled down for political and other reasons, Hitler ordered him to carry out a final and strange task in Spain, where a civil war was raging in which German forces participated. It dawned on Hanfstaengl that he would be dropped behind enemy lines by parachute, although he didn't speak a single word of Spanish and he wasn't trained for this kind of operation. Therefore, he presumed it had been intended that he was to be killed during this operation and so he fled to Switzerland. When he finally arrived in America, he wrote, under permanent observation by the army, an analysis of Hitler that also mentioned his sexuality. First off, he claimed Hitler's sexual life was a complete mystery to him. Nevertheless, he managed to report, without source or proof, that Hitler had contracted venereal disease in Vienna. Furthermore, he denied Hitler's homosexuality but he presumed psychic or physical obstacles stood in the way of his sexuality. With the little whip he often carried around with him, he dealt with his inferiority complex and erection problems, so Hanfstaengl wrote.[81] In an article in *Cosmopolitan* from 1943, he further claimed Geli Raubal hadn't committed suicide but had been murdered and that Goebbels, after her death, had arranged a number of blondes to help Hitler get rid of his 'mother complex'.[82] What exactly Hanfstaengl knew about Hitler's sexuality can probably best be summarised by his opening remark, when he said it was a mystery to him. As for the rest, Hanfstaengl uses vague interpretations with unclear origin. It is hard to imagine that Hitler let his chief of press in on his erection problems in a man-to-man talk. Moreover, Hitler's physicians never established anything similar.

The most conspicuous sexual speculation about Hitler stems from the period following Geli Raubal's suicide. Sometimes, a connection was even made between the alleged incestual relation of Geli and Hitler and his hatred of Jews because he would have been afraid to contaminate pure blood[83] as he thought he was a Jew himself. A beautiful thought, of course, but there is no one to confirm it and there wasn't a single psychiatrist who discussed this with him. Other rumours, such as the explanation that Hitler's aggression

---

80. Rosenbaum, p. 188
81. Conradi, pp. 375–376
82. Conradi, pp. 370–371
83. Rosenbaum, pp. 193–194

would have stemmed from sexual abstention or that his hatred of Jews was the result of syphilis he contracted when visiting a Jewish prostitute, have never risen beyond the level of speculation. Those who wanted to see in Hitler a homophile who had never come out openly could use the statement by Hermann Rauschning, who 'told the American Secret Service that a trial was pending against Corporal Hitler and an officer for sexual acts'.[84] Rauschning, however, like Hanfstaengl and Strasser, had fled Germany. The NSDAP politician left the country in 1934 and became a critic of the Nazi regime. He wrote a book, entitled *Gespräche mit Hitler*, which is supposed to have been based on hundreds of conversations he conducted with Hitler between 1932 and 1934. Years later, however, it turned out he had only talked with Hitler about four times and so this much-quoted book is less useful for historians.[85] And this, of course, sheds a very different light on the remarks he made to the American Secret Service.

The myth put to rest

According to journalist Ron Rosenbaum, people who have said something about Hitler's sexuality have placed this in three categories: perversion, asexuality and normalcy.[86] The category perversion often listed people who had been rejected by Hitler or were his enemies or critics; sometimes conmen who could make money with their concoctions. Whatever the case, members of this group didn't serve their interest by putting Hitler in a favourable light.

That was often the case in the second category: they worked or lived close to Hitler, had a relationship with him or earned a living as a member of staff or servant. Especially in that category, there was a high level of loyalty that often remained until long after the war. Historians who joined this category didn't have that loyalty, with the exception of a few. The underlying motives of the explanations of those who say Hitler was asexual must be judged critically. August Kubizek said, for instance, that Hitler didn't occupy himself with sex but if it were true he had a relationship with Hitler then he created an alibi for him as well as for himself with his statements. It could also be that Kubizek, with his remarks about Hitler's 'sexlessness', embraced the idea behind the Führer cult in which he was portrayed as a demigod who had more important things on his mind than women.

---

84. Machtan, p. 95
85. Kershaw, Hoogmoed, p. 10
86. Rosenbaum, p. 172

The statements made by those in the category of perversion about Hitler's sexuality were never based on know-how. A former press photographer who often took pictures of Hitler in Munich said, for instance, that everybody in town knew Hitler was a pervert and in 1934 the London paper the *Spectator* reported that he was a 'sexually abnormal man', that he probably wasn't heterosexual, that the only woman in his life had been his mother and that his possibilities with regard to love and marriage were few.[87] In an important report, published in America in 1944, psychologist Walter C Langer concluded that Hitler was a homosexual and lover of pornography and sadomasochistic sex, and that he had a fixation for excrement. Langer stated Hitler was a neurotic psychopath with a leaning towards schizophrenia. In addition, he would have unleashed his extreme perversities on his niece, Geli Raubal.

Although the report, in addition to these conspicuous issues, included some, to the point, traits about Hitler, such as the prediction he would commit suicide, it seems strange to draft a psychological report about someone to whom you have never spoken. Langer did talk to various people who knew or had known Hitler, but nearly all of them were either National Socialists who had arguments with Hitler or who didn't agree with the policy of the Third Reich and who often couldn't have known at all what sexual preferences Hitler eventually had. The report was actually based on conversations with, for instance, Eduard Bloch, William Patrick Hitler, Ernst Hanfstaengl, Kurt Lüdecke, Hermann Rauschning, Otto Strasser and Friedelinde Wagner – we met a few of them earlier on. Nearly all of them had fled Germany and nearly all of them had severed their ties with Hitler's Nazism or never had had anything to do with it, for instance the Jewish physician Eduard Bloch.[88]

The *Münchener Post* usually and rightly accused Hitler of everything under the sun and the personal feud between him and the journalists that made them even more eager to damage him was also true. Con man Hans Mend, who claimed Hitler maintained homosexual relations during the First World War, was utterly unreliable and his motives were far less noble than those of the journalists of the *Münchener Post*. His suggestion of Hitler's homosexuality has never been proved and the argumentation in this field by Lothar Machtan isn't convincing either. It is therefore senseless to fantasise about the idea that suppressing his homosexual leanings led Hitler to such

---

87. Rosenbaum, p. 159-160
88. Rosenbaum, pp. 159–160

frustrations that he just had to channel them by initiating all sorts of crimes against humanity.

According to the 'members' in the category asexuality, Hitler wasn't perverted but he wasn't entirely normal either. They assumed he hardly had sex or not at all. People who had seen Adolf and Eva together based this notion on the fact that, even in intimate settings, the two kept their distance. There were hardly any signs of intimacy in public either. Based on that, it could easily be concluded Hitler had few sexual feelings but it couldn't be known what happened in Eva's bedroom. Ernst Hanfstaengl's wife, Helene, thought that Hitler wasn't a man but more or less without gender, and impotent.[89] That means she was convinced of his asexuality.

Hitler's lack of sexual experience as a 24-year-old in Vienna would also indicate he had trouble with sex. The stories by his companion Reinhold Hanisch as well as those by his friend August Kubizek show a man who was deeply troubled by his sexuality,[90] although Kubizek claimed at the same time there was nothing wrong with Hitler. Frequently mentioned physical causes of Hitler's possible asexual life, such as missing a testicle or some other defect to his genitals, are not in keeping with medical files and statements by physicians. The most stubborn myth of the two, that of the missing testicle, comes from a questionable report of a Soviet autopsy on a corpse that wasn't Hitler's at all.[91] In a fairly recent publication of Hitler's personal physician during his imprisonment in Landsberg am Lech in 1923–24, however, an interesting note from a doctor can be found, namely the observation of a left-sided Kryptorchism, meaning Hitler had an unsettled testicle. It is not said that this made him completely infertile or that he couldn't have sex, but it may have made him reluctant in this area. Hitler's fear of dramas in his love life and the notion of the infallible Führer who is married only to Germany and who would be weakened by a human trait like sexuality could well be one of the few plausible explanations of his strange dealings with women.

The stories about Hitler's sexuality during the First World War are possibly even more confusing. On the one hand, Hitler is being portrayed as a young man who, in contrast to his comrades, never visited a brothel and who had no further sexual contact; on the other hand though, he supposedly impregnated a girlfriend[92] and was discovered making hay with a comrade from his regiment. The stories about the pregnancy and the comradely male

---

89. Kershaw, Hoogmoed, p. 255
90. Kershaw, Hoogmoed, p. 81; Fleischmann, p. 417
91. Kershaw, Hoogmoed, p. 81
92. See 'Did Hitler have a son?'

love in wartime were utterly unreliable, as became evident later. The only remaining notion is that Hitler had very little sex between 1914 and 1918 and that he might have been completely asexual.

However, Hitler was certainly not asexual. From the few diary entries by Eva Braun about sex with Hitler, historians could not conclude much else than that the frequency of their love making wasn't that high, but it did occur. In her biography of Eva Braun, Angela Lambert states in a down-to-earth manner: 'If a young woman starts getting regular visits and presents from an older man, the general assumption is that she has become his mistress. If he has no other "constant companion" and she, despite her charm and ebullience, no other recognised suitor or boyfriend, the general assumption is that she is his mistress. If in due course she is allotted a bedroom next to his, starts turning up in elegant and expensive outfits, is accepted by his friends (whether or not they approve of her) and treated by the domestic staff as head of his household, the general assumption would be that she is indeed his mistress. Theories can be constructed and anecdotes or opinions cited that seek to demonstrate that Hitler was impotent, masochistic or homosexual, and that Eva died a virgin, but if the contrary looks overwhelmingly more probable, then it is probably true.'[93]

Gretl Braun, Eva's sister, also says that Hitler wasn't shy at all about sexuality because 'still waters run deep'.[94] Eva herself didn't make any remarks in her diary beyond this kind of vague description either. Except for the cynical remark: 'He only needs me for special purposes, it can't be anything else,' nothing very substantial regarding sex can be found in it. The remarks of the Braun sisters, however, do show a man with a fairly normal sex life, even though Eva would have to miss her lover regularly for long periods on end. Historian John Lukacs agrees. He says the evidence for Hitler's unnatural sexuality is 'rare, not authentic and hard to assess'. 'In my opinion', Lukacs writes, 'Hitler's relations with women were entirely normal.'[95] After Hitler's death, Mimi Reiter tried to make this clear as well.

Hitler's lovers, chambermaids, housekeepers and, of course, Heinz Linge, Hitler's adjutant, who was in Hitler's quarters more than once every day, all had their say about the sexual relationship between Adolf and Eva. Naturally, it also struck them that whenever the two were in the company of others, they kept their distance. Linge said, however, he had seen the Führer

---

93. Lambert, Angela, *The Lost Life of Eva Braun*, p. 155. St Martin's Publishing Group. Kindle Edition, 2006.
94. Gun, p. 71
95. Rosenbaum, p. 208

and his lady friend hugging passionately and, as mentioned before, we know from maids that Eva postponed her menstruation with pills and such when she knew Hitler was coming. This may seem trivial but in the discussion about Hitler's sexuality, these are the only substantive indications that Hitler had sex every so often.

Other evidence for Hitler's sexual normalcy are of a medical nature. During examinations by physicians, nothing at all became evident in regard to the wild stories about syphilis he had supposedly contracted from a Jewish prostitute. He didn't suffer from venereal disease and there was no question of aberration of his genitals. Hitler's doctors, at the end of the day the only specialists in this field, belong to Rosenbaum's category of normalcy, even if one of them found he had an unsettled testicle.[96]

Many of those exonerating Hitler assumed he had a sex secret.[97] Actually, apart from a number of known relationships, many possible relationships and even more speculation, we know hardly anything substantial about Hitler's sex life. When an unsettled testicle is the only thing critical investigation turns up, then the only conclusion is that in the field of Hitler's sex life, demonstrable perversities are out of the question. The real perversities for which Hitler was responsible occurred in the concentration camps. The fact that we want to see a connection between what happened there and what happened in Hitler's bedroom is probably the result of the threatening thought that Hitler was more or less a normal man.

---

96. Hamann, HE, p. 464; Neuman & Eberle, p. 52
97. Rosenbaum, p. 208

Chapter 13

Did Hitler Always Get his Way?

His role as absolute leader

The most famous scene in Downfall, *the movie about Hitler's last days, is undoubtedly the one in which Hitler is sitting in a small room at his chart table surrounded by big wigs from the army and the party. As his last hope of rescue goes up in smoke and someone still dares to contradict him, he flies into an uncontrollable rage. This part of the movie is often ridiculed on the internet, especially the version of Hitler, the spoiled egocentric who doesn't want to be contradicted when planning a company trip. Although it is a joke, it matches seamlessly with the image we have of him: a dictator who always got his way. Hitler is after all the ultimate example of a lone ruler. The assumption that his power was exclusively based on violence and suppression of the German population is a misconception. The notion that anyone crossing his path did so at the cost of his life, wasn't always in keeping with reality either.*

The unnuanced image of the dictator Hitler was the direct consequence of the Führer cult of the Nazis themselves. Within that cult, Hitler was portrayed as the infallible leader who would finally steer Germany's fate in the right direction. In the eyes of the National Socialists, Hitler was coherent and consistent in his conceptions and he was a genius who was in fact incapable of making mistakes. It goes without saying that someone who was portrayed as he was would always get his way. But looking closer into how he gathered and maintained his power and to what extent he, being the leader, could ignore the wishes of the population or of his party comrades, this image of the absolute ruler Adolf Hitler turns out to be far from complete.

Pride

Long before Hitler took power, exalted ideas existed among German Nationalists about the characteristics the great, future absolute ruler and leader of Germany should have. They didn't appear out of the blue. There was already a Führercult surrounding one of Hitler's important political forebears, Georg Schönerer in Vienna. Not only did his followers literally call him Führer, they swore complete loyalty to him, sang songs about him, wrote poems in honour of him and every year, congratulations for the leader were published in the political paper under the heading *Heil dem Führer!*[1]

Years later, Hitler was honoured in the same way and in order to merit that honour over and over again, he should 'have a coherent view on the future – a view of how the world should be, based on a special insight into reality'.[2] Therefore, the Nazi propaganda machine did its utmost to present Hitler in such a way that he met the image of the ideal leader with this 'special insight'. The perennial emphasis on Hitler being a genius almost had to lead to an enormous level of haughtiness in him. Or was it the other way round and did Hitler in fact possess characteristics much earlier that matched the charismatic way in which the Nazi party and the country were governed?

Young Hitler

In order to find out whether Hitler became haughty or was born that way, we have to return to his youth. Part of the information about that period that exists is from *Mein Kampf,* though, and in order to paint the picture of the infallible Führer, Hitler looked at his youth in a certain way, as already mentioned in other chapters. Yet there are other sources that can help to determine if Hitler was haughty at the time.

In a book about Hitler published in 1958, Austrian author Franz Jetzinger dwelled on his youth. Ten-year-old Adolf is portrayed as the leader of a bunch of boys that could always be found playing outside. Hitler loved war games and if older boys didn't like it, he would search for a few younger boys who did want to join in.[3] There is no question yet of pride but rather of leadership. The qualification of 'leader' that Jetzinger used in his book was taken from *Mein Kampf,* however, and based on Hitler's politically coloured biographical elements in that book, it is hard to say whether he was a real leader as a boy. Hitler's former teacher of French, Dr Hümer, wrote of him in December 1923 that the adolescent boy he had had in his class was arrogant, lacking self-discipline and capable of being cranky, stubborn and irritable. Also, according to his teacher, he would have loved to see himself in the

---

1. Hamann, HW, p. 337
2. Rees, p. 53
3. Jetzinger, pp. 59–60

role of leader.[4] It must be said, however, that Dr Hümer's commentary was given right after Hitler's failed attempt at seizing power in Munich, which may have influenced his judgment, but it is an early description of a haughty, arrogant adolescent.

One of the richest early sources about Hitler's youth is the work of August Kubizek. Describing himself as a quiet young man, Kubizek describes his friend in contrast to himself as a restless, temperamental boy who had little respect for Kubizek's profession; he often helped his father who was a cabinet maker which Hitler considered a Brotberuf (a profession for money). He preferred to talk about Wagner. During one of their first encounters he wondered whether Hitler might be the child of rich parents, which he wasn't.[5]

Not only was a craft not good enough for Hitler, but neither was public officialdom. There is a famous story in *Mein Kampf* about the discussion between Adolf and his father, whereby father Alois thought the profession of official would suit his son. Adolf, however, got sick at the thought of having to sit at a desk as an unfree man; no longer master over his own time and being forced to make a living filling out forms.[6] Hitler considered himself too good for normal work, didn't want to exchange his freedom for the profession of an official and at school, if we take Dr Hümer's testimony seriously, he also stood out as a haughty boy. After his sixteenth birthday, however, he quit school because he managed to convince his mother he was too ill to attend.[7]

Apart from these examples, indicating some kind of haughtiness or arrogance, young Adolf Hitler could also be insecure, for instance when the beautiful young girl Stefanie from Urfahr was involved, who was seen regularly by August and Adolf when she walked down the shopping streets in Linz. Although Adolf said he had feelings for her, he never spoke to her. Why he never did is unknown. Did he fear being rejected, did he not want to make a fool of himself? Or did he dare not address her as he was still inexperienced in the field of love?

An entirely different side of Hitler unfolded in 1907 when he cared in a very loving manner for his mother, who was on her deathbed. He was with her almost all day long, slept in a room next to hers so she could always call him and he was visibly affected by the unbearable pain she suffered. When she passed away, he would have been so upset that the Jewish family

---

4. Jetzinger, p. 69
5. Kubizek, pp. 18–19
6. *Mein Kampf*, p. 6
7. Kershaw, Hoogmoed, p. 4

doctor Dr Bloch declared years later he had never seen anyone so shaken by grief as Adolf Hitler.[8] Apparently, Hitler could also be extremely emotional and caring.

Paradox

In Kubizek's descriptions of the young Hitler, there are many anecdotes, not exclusively indicating haughtiness. Kubizek also points to the paradox in Hitler's nature when he compares his grim humour or mockery to his capability to familiarise himself with the feelings of his friend. Hitler's secretary, Traudl Junge, confirms Hitler also had a friendly side. When she was tense while taking dictation for the first time, Hitler did his best to put her at ease, even admitting his own shortcomings: 'You don't have to be nervous at all, in my dictation I make so many mistakes you couldn't even begin to make more.'[9]

He was no stranger to self-mockery either. This is obvious, for instance, in a story Hitler told himself about his stay in Hotel Elephant in Weimar. There was no shower or toilet in his room so he had to walk down the corridor to make use of it. 'When I left my room, word spread through the hotel like wildfire and after I left that delicate room, people gave me an ovation and I had to run the gauntlet to my room, arm raised and a somewhat painful grin on my face. Later on, I had the hotel rebuilt.'[10] This last remark is testimony of Hitler's well-known haughtiness and it should also be said that his mockery was more often at the cost of someone else, yet this self-mockery sheds a somewhat different light on the cliché image of the infallible Führer who couldn't bear any form of criticism.

Hitler did sometimes accept he had little talent for certain matters. He admired the way Mussolini wrote in Italian but about his own book he said it was more like 'an exercise in fantasy, written behind bars' and that it was little more than a series of articles for the *Völkische Beobachter*. 'Because,' Hitler said, 'I am no writer. I can hardly keep my thoughts focused when I'm writing.'[11]

At the end of his life, not much was left of his mockery and the other side of him manifested itself when he dictated his testament to his secretary, Traudl Junge. It shocked her he had nothing to report other than the old

---

8. Hamann, HE, pp. 86–89
9. Junge, p. 43
10. Junge, p. 181
11. Ryback, p. 112

and worn out charges. To her great disappointment he didn't make a single confession and didn't justify any of his deeds.[12] Instead, he said that during his political career, 'he had to take the most difficult decisions ever presented to man' and that the struggle 'will live on in history as the most glorious and courageous expression of the will to live of a nation'. Shortly after these self-righteous statements, he committed suicide. The entire country lay in ruins from a war he had started himself but which in his opinion was caused by international Jewry. At that moment he formed a new government. This seems strange, especially in hindsight, as he apparently did not understand that the Allies would never co-operate with him while the Soviets were a few hundred yards away from his bunker in Berlin. Hitler must have known that negotiations about surrender were out of the question but he seemed to be totally blind about his own responsibility for those he had appointed in the 'new government' and for the hell he had created. The statement in his testament: 'I hope my spirit will always be with them and lead them',[13] in which it sounds like he is the Messiah addressing his disciples, no longer displaying any of his earlier self deprecation.

Vienna

From the period of Hitler's stay in Vienna, events are mentioned in which his haughty attitude would appear. First off, he neither worked nor studied in Vienna. Later, when writing *Mein Kampf* he was apparently ashamed of this and wrote that he had been employed in building work. Historian Brigitte Hamann is seriously doubtful about this employment and calls it propaganda.[14] In the period he still shared a room with August Kubizek, he did little other than sleep or wander across town by day and when he ran out of money, he lived on the streets or in shelters for the poor. Maybe his wish to become an artisan and his admiration for great architecture, painting and music gave him the idea that a normal life was not for him, but outwardly the shabby young man who had been rejected by the Academy of Arts had no reason at all for that kind of pride.

Of course, he did understand full well that he wasn't very successful when he, hungry as he was, knocked on the door of a shelter for the homeless.[15] Evidently pride did not prevent him from sending a letter to his family,

---

12. Junge, p. 212
13. Hitler, My political testament
14. Hamann, HW, p. 210
15. Hamann, HW, p. 225

though, asking for money to buy painting materials, when he wanted to set up shop with his friend Reinhold Hanisch selling picture postcards. It was also striking that the exalted art lover now employed his capabilities as a drawer and painter in order to earn money. Hitler fulfilled orders by shopkeepers and tourists and had taken on a *Brotberuf* after all instead of an education to become a painter of art.

Attempts by his friend Hanisch to have Hitler make more than the required number of paintings became bogged down in his unwillingness to work hard, however. Instead, he preferred to read the paper and to discuss politics.[16] An awkward moment for Hitler occurred when during such a discussion he talked about the favourite philosopher of the Austrian nationalists, Arthur Schopenhauer. Another wanderer, nicknamed 'the professor', asked him whether he had ever read anything by Schopenhauer. Hitler is supposed to have blushed and said he had read something once, to which the man responded he shouldn't be talking about things he knew nothing about.[17]

An occurrence showing another side of Hitler took place before he ended up in a male shelter and still lived together with his friend Kubizek. He once took him to a night of music in the home of well-to-do Jewish industrialist Dr Jahoda. Hitler is supposed to have presented himself so timidly and so ashamed of his clothing, it struck Kubizek. Because he was no musician, Hitler said, he couldn't join in discussions about music.[18] This timid attitude of Hitler in circles of the rich, the intellectual or nobility was also recognisable in his later life.[19]

More than pride

So, Hitler was not only haughty but also sensitive, inhibited, timid, caring, cynical and lazy, and all that made him look more like a human being than the myth of the haughty lone leader allows. Defining Hitler as someone looking down on others all day results in a one-dimensional and hardly realistic image of the man who later on would set the whole world on fire. Of course, Hitler's haughty attitude would be enhanced by the massive glorification lying in store for him later on, but there is more to say about the character of the young Hitler. The descriptions also show very different traits, of which

---

16. Hamann, HW, pp. 236–237
17. Hamann, HW, p. 238
18. Hamann, HW, p. 506
19. Kershaw, Hoogmoed, p. 255

some, like his empathy and the love for his mother, can rightfully be called positive. At the same time, the friend of his youth, Kubizek, wrote that among these other traits, there were also very dark ones: 'Almost suffocating from anger about everything he hated, he spewed his wrath over anything, over humanity in general that didn't understand him, didn't appreciate him and which pursued him.'[20]

Resistance

The young man with his haughty attitude who had lost both parents and who lived in Vienna in poverty with neither a job nor an education could, after a few years, finally exchange the Vienna he hated for the German city of Munich with the money of his inheritance. Initially, he also didn't do much more than wander around until the First World War broke out and he entered military service voluntarily. After the war, he remained in active service until his regiment was disbanded. One evening, he ended up in the pub *Altes Rosenbad*, which no longer exists, where a small Nationalist party named *Deutsche Arbeiterpartei* was having a meeting. This party was to be the foundation of all political successes he would achieve later on.

At the beginning of his political career, there was naturally no question yet of the glorification he would receive later on. He had to earn that himself and the only weapon at his disposal was the spoken word. With his orator's gift, he had to rally his followers and in order to do so, he had to say things that appealed to the masses. Whether consciously or unconsciously, he would have taken the wishes and desires of those he addressed into account. He could not flatly ignore the ideas of his party comrades, whether he approved of them or not. Precisely that hardly matches the notion of the egocentric, power-hungry Hitler who mainly did what he wanted.

Although soon after the First World War many people in Munich gathered to listen to Hitler's speeches, it took the National Socialists almost fifteen years to seize power. During the years in between, Hitler had to cope with various crises; the failed putsch of 1923 being the best-known political one and the death of his niece Geli Raubal in 1929 the best-known personal one. It is interesting to see how he dealt with that kind of setback. After the putsch he is said to have been so disappointed he threatened to commit suicide but this extreme reaction to the failure has never been

---

20. Rees, p. 17

proved.[21] Hitler's emotional reaction to the death of his niece is also open to discussion, as mentioned earlier.[22]

The way Hitler dealt with setbacks at the end of 1924, when he had completed his prison term after the failed attempts in the putsch, is also interesting. Ian Kershaw says that in this period Hitler's view of himself changed. Just like his followers, he started believing he was the one destined to save Germany.[23] In order to become the leader of Germany, however, he first had to get the rightist people's movement behind him. It may say something about his haughtiness that he wanted to impose his will on all these parties but it is also striking that he didn't just shove anyone aside who didn't agree with him.

In 1926, it was mainly the struggle for direction that raged between the so-called *Arbeitsgemeinschaft* (AG) of the NSDAP in the northern and western part of the country and the NSDAP in the south that became a problem for Hitler. The two prominent figures, Georg Strasser and Joseph Goebbels, wanted to adapt the party programme in a way Hitler didn't like. In general, Strasser wanted to create a kind of 'United States of Europe' with Germany as the central power, and that was against Hitler's ideas. A few people from the north hardly knew Hitler and thought he had to adhere to party principles as well. And those principles, co-drafted in 1920 by Hitler, had to be adapted. When Hitler heard about it, he realised his position was in danger and in such moments he always took action. In an especially convened meeting, he spoke out against the plans of the AG. 'Gregor Strasser was to promise Hitler to ask for all copies of the draft, circulating within the AG, be returned.'[24] Hitler's reaction was remarkable: instead of expelling the most important members of the AG from the party, for instance, three of them, including Goebbels, were put in charge of a joint *Gau* in the *Ruhr* area. In the period following the crisis, Hitler tightened the bond between him and Strasser. Naturally, Hitler made it abundantly clear to them that the policy suggested by him should be followed but there was no question of a hot-headed Hitler weeding out resistance by the roots. Strasser remained in regular conflict with Hitler and was dealt with later, during the Night of the Long Knives in June and July 1934.

---

21. Kershaw, Hoogmoed, p. 278
22. Sigmund, FN, pp. 226–228
23. Kershaw, Hoogmoed, p. 321
24. Kershaw, Hoogmoed, p. 363

Hitler and religion

The fact that Adolf Hitler was raised in a Catholic environment is the foundation of a discussion about his religion that is still raging extensively on the internet. It is not entirely clear why some want to prove Hitler was a devoted Catholic but it seems there is some sort of similarity between this discussion and the one about his sexual preferences, alleged psychic disorders or his supposed Jewish ancestry as possible explanations of his actions. Stories about the Jew who exterminated Jews, the homosexual who killed Ernst Röhm, the psychopath who murdered the mentally ill and the Catholic who committed the most serious sins imaginable, are apparently much more interesting than a sober analysis of the facts. Hitler's personal secretary, Traudl Junge, is very clear about Hitler's religious life: 'He had no ties whatsoever to any church and he considered Christian religion an overtaken, hypocritical and deceptive institution. His religion was the laws of nature. In those, he could far better incorporate his violent dogma than in the Christian teachings of charity and love for the enemy.'[25]

For someone with such an obvious aversion towards Christianity and so much dictatorial power it should have been easy to shove the church aside. Yet Hitler never succeeded in disabling the clerical power entirely and from his statements it appeared he didn't want to either. In 1933, in the *Reichstag*, Hitler even declared that the churches would retain all of their rights and that the relationship between church and state would remain unchanged as the churches were important pillars of the nation.[26] Hitler may well have suffered from overestimation but it wasn't so big yet that he thought he could defeat the church hands down. The majority of churchgoers, whether they were evangelic or Catholic, were also followers of Hitler. Many Nazi leaders did have plans to do away with the church in the long run and although Hitler had put the Catholic Church under a lot of pressure a few months later, nothing came of these plans for the time being. It was arranged through the Vatican that Catholic clergy were not allowed to get involved in politics, whereby the Catholic Church could only survive when the Catholic parties would disappear.[27] The power of the Catholic Church, however, remained a problem for the National Socialists, in particular for local party leaders.

When in 1934, an attempt was made to incorporate the independent churches into a newly established *Reichskirche* and consequently two bishops, admired by the people, were relieved of their functions, even National Socialist churchgoers protested against it. Eventually, Hitler stepped in

---

25. Junge, p. 126
26. Kershaw, Vergelding, p. 605
27. Kershaw, Hoogmoed, p. 616

himself by reappointing the two. He considered the situation politically risky and accepted the will of the people. Hitler hesitated to enter the power struggle with the Catholic Church because of his experiences with Austrian politics and his opinion of the 'Free from Rome' notion. This was the idea of his political example Georg Schönerer, who had actually tried to replace the Catholic Church with an Austrian pro-German movement. Hitler called these attempts at eliminating the church a grave political mistake by Schönerer as he had made the expansion of his party impossible among the common people. According to Hitler, Schönerer and his followers lacked understanding of the psyche of the masses.[28] So it is not surprising that Hitler told Goebbels in 1935 he wanted peace with the churches, at least for a certain period.[29]

Kristallnacht

There were more issues Hitler distanced himself from outwardly, although he approved them. Even for his closest associates, he was an excellent actor who sometimes pretended not to have been informed in advance when a certain issue didn't feel right among the population. He also did so during *Kristallnacht*. He had approved the pogroms on 9 November 1938, a symbolic date for the Nazis, namely the date of the failed Hitlerputsch in 1923, and organised by Goebbels but 'he preferred not to be openly associated with this anti-Jewish campaign'.[30] Local leaders instructed members of the party in advance to destroy Jewish possessions and set fire to synagogues. The police agreed to stand back. When the actions were in full swing Hitler, in Munich, pretended he was surprised by these 'spontaneous' actions by the population. Ian Kershaw rightly wondered whether Hitler's shocked reaction to the pogrom had been genuine and considered it to be fully in keeping with his intentions. But the negative reaction to the violence that unfolded during *Kristallnacht* probably shook him so much that he pretended he knew nothing about it. 'In so far as Hitler's rage was genuine, it was because the "action" of which he hadn't expected to be received so badly, threatened to devour him.'[31]

Hitler didn't want to be associated in advance with any anti-Jewish actions not desired by him and so tried to play dumb. Party members fell

---

28. Hamann, HW, p. 35
29. Kershaw, Hoogmoed, p. 742
30. Kershaw, Vergelding, p. 214
31. Kershaw, Vergelding, p. 232 MIR

for it and blamed Goebbels for the actions that had got out of hand. In this way, the unrealistically positive image the Germans had of their Führer remained intact. The fact that Jewish people were obliged to pay for the damage caused by the Nazis and the statement of a few months later in which self-proclaimed prophet Hitler warned that a new global war would result in the extermination of the Jewish race in Europe, made clear what he really thought.

Aktion T4

It also occurred that Hitler's policy was entirely carried out in secret or even partly revoked. In 1939 for instance, a programme, ordered by Hitler and code-named *Aktion T4*, was initiated in which, under the veil of mercy, some 200,000 psychiatric patients were euthanised. The medical staff and the psychiatrists responsible for this did so with extreme caution but an action of this magnitude could not be kept secret forever. Under pressure from the churches and relatives of the patients, Hitler had to suspend the programme temporarily. When relatives of patients found out what had happened to their next of kin and published obituaries in the papers or as a precaution took patients out of hospitals and institutions, Hitler's hands were tied.[32] Bystanders watched patients being unloaded from grey vans and taken into institutions where chimneys of the crematoriums kept smoking.[33]

This outside pressure on the government unfortunately wasn't strong enough to stop the assassination of psychiatric patients entirely. The murdering was transferred from the institutions to the concentration camp, farther away from public view. It appeared that 'common' citizens and even Protestant and Catholic religious leaders did not reject these 'murders out of mercy'.[34]

Whether the population would have been able to stop these killings, provided it had wanted to do so, is hard to find out as a general revolt against Hitler never occurred, but it may be obvious that Hitler did understand that he just couldn't openly do everything he wanted. He took the reactions of the German population into account and adapted himself whenever he thought it was necessary, especially when something was detrimental to the positive image the German population had of him.

---

32. Gellately, p. 120
33. Kershaw, Vergelding, p. 585
34. Gellately, p. 122

Extermination of the Jews[35]

The most important and most confusing example of Hitler's secretive behaviour is the lack of a substantial *Führerbefehl* for the extermination of the Jews. In public Hitler made extremely derogatory remarks about the Jewish race but it seems that in the period in which plans were drafted for the *Endlösung* – final solution – he didn't interfere with the *Judenfrage* (Jewish problem) any longer. He intentionally indicated, in no other way than orally and only to a few high-ranking Nazis, what the exact fate of the Jews was going to be. The lack of a written order may have perfectly been in keeping with the way he ruled his empire,[36] but it also indicates he knew very well this was an issue that would evoke massive indignation at home and abroad. The tactic he had applied before, giving his permission in secret and subsequently keeping his distance as much as possible, was applied again: 'It involved a *Geheime Reichssache* – state secret – of the highest order and even the people most closely involved were expected not to talk about it. In discussions on the highest level, veiled language was maintained. Hitler himself never spoke about the killing of Jews, not even in his most intimate circle.'[37]

Naturally, there was no misunderstanding whatsoever about Hitler's attitude towards the Jews: in the early 1920s, he had already spoken of their removal from Germany. When he took power in 1933, his speeches might have sounded a little less anti-Semitic but that was more of a tactic by Hitler adapting himself to the prevailing situation. Whenever local Nazi leaders interpreted his remarks about Jews as anti-Jewish measures, he agreed, for instance in the form of anti-Jewish legislation. But it was striking that Hitler didn't sign the documents of 28 March 1933 that called for a boycott of Jewish enterprises and service providers. The signature only read: *Leitung der Natioalsozialistischte Arbeiterpartei* – Leadership of the National Socialist workers party.[38] Ian Kershaw typifies this order of business as a 'continuous interaction between "wild" actions from below and orchestrated discrimination from above'.[39] Hitler said or had written something in *Mein Kampf*, local leaders concocted substantial plans and Hitler or other prominent Nazis saw to the 'legal implementation'. By signing nothing

---
35. This fragment is mainly based on the article by Ian Kershaw 'Hitler's role in the Endlösung', in his book *Hitler, the Germans and the Holocaust*.
36. This will be dealt with in the next paragraph.
37. Kershaw, KP, p. 469
38. Rees, p. 97
39. Kershaw, HDH, p. 111

himself, Adolf Hitler consciously kept his distance from policy that could be detrimental to the Führer's image.

The discrimination as actually ordered from above became effective as from 1 April 1933, and meant that Jewish artisans, journalists and public officials, to name a few, were banned from working.[40] Subsequently, the *Nürnberger Rassengesetze* – Nuremberger racial laws – of 1935 stipulated who was Jewish and who wasn't and prohibited sexual relationships between Germans and non-Germans. Germany radicalised very quickly but there was no question of systematic extermination of Jews for years yet.

In January 1939, right after the November 1938 pogrom, cynically called *Kristallnacht* by the population as so many windows of Jewish shopkeepers had been smashed, Hitler made a somber prediction in a speech before the *Reichstag* as to the fate of the Jews: 'Today I want to be a prophet again: if the international financial Jewry in and outside Europe should once again succeed in plunging the nations into a global war once again, then the result will not be the Bolshevisation of the earth and simultaneously the victory of Jewry but the extermination of the Jewish race in Europe.'[41] He said this in a time there were not yet any extermination camps. Written orders for that kind of extermination would never be issued but such a prediction would make any order superfluous. All high-ranking Nazis knew the statement and it was repeated regularly by Hitler as well as by his followers. It was striking that Hitler again kept silent about his own contribution to the issue. The Jews would plunge the world into war again, so Hitler said, but he said nothing about who was to see to the extermination of the Jewish race. He was sure it was going to happen anyway ...

After the invasion of the Soviet Union in 1941, Hitler's prophecy started to come true. Even before extermination camps were established, Jews in the occupied areas were slaughtered in brutal fashion. For this a written order wasn't necessary either although, according to Heinrich Himmler, Hitler had made the decision himself to deport the Jews from German territory to the east.[42] The assembly-line murder of Jews in the extermination camps came later. The actual occasion was the slow progress of the war against the Soviet Union. As the Germans could not achieve results fast enough, desired deportations of Jews to the Soviet Union couldn't continue and this led to an accumulation of problems in Poland as the need to provide for food, housing

---

40. Rees, p. 97
41. Kershaw, HDH, p. 113
42. Kershaw, HDH, p. 115

and diseases called for a solution. The cynical note, of course, was that the Germans had created these problems themselves.

When in December 1941, Hitler declared war on America as well, global war was a fact. Precisely in that month, Governor-general Hans Frank of Poland said he had trouble shooting 3.5 million Jews so other solutions had to be found to solve the problem. To this end, the Wannsee conference was called in January 1942, chaired by Reinhard Heydrich, at which decisions were taken as to the final solution of the Jewish problem. A few months later, the existing murder programme of the Nazi was expanded by the use of extermination camps.

It was Hitler's idea to exterminate the Jews but the initiative from below was taken by men such as Hans Frank and the confirmation in the form of agreements came from Reinhard Heydrich. Documents about the *Endlösung* of Himmler and Heydrich were burned by the Germans towards the end of the war,[43] but in those documents probably nothing of Hitler himself was ever recorded. The *Führerbefehl*, which must have been the base of the *Endlösung*, was untraceable. Hitler did have his way but he took great care not to get involved in any way in this unprecedented crime against humanity.

When Hermann Göring stood trial in Nuremberg after the war, he said during a discussion in his cell with American psychiatrist Leon Goldensohn about the missing *Führerbefehl*: 'The order to exterminate certain groups of people was never discussed as otherwise, a lot of resistance against this idea would certainly have been evoked.' Here, Göring admitted Hitler didn't always get his way but he also stated he couldn't believe he knew about it. 'Of course, what has happened is bad enough but the numbers are so large I can't imagine anything.' It goes without saying, he knew nothing about it himself. Göring blamed Heinrich Himmler for the crimes and men like Auschwitz camp commander Rudolf Höss. Göring suggested Himmler had a free hand as he exerted a wrong influence on Hitler or that Hitler didn't know anything about it.[44]

It is quite incredible though that only Himmler, Höss and the actual perpetrators of the *Endlösung* knew about such an immense operation. Göring seemed to have manoeuvred himself into a tricky position. On the one hand he didn't want to turn against Hitler as, in his opinion Speer did, on the other hand he had to defend himself against the most serious charge against the Nazis: Auschwitz. Hans Frank, the former governor-general in the occupied areas in Poland, while in his cell told the American prison

---
43. Kershaw, KP, p. 487
44. Goldensohn, p. 146

psychologist Gustave Gilbert: 'Don't be bothered by those telling fairy tales, *Her Doktor*! It wouldn't even have crossed Himmler's mind to carry out his programme of mass murder without Hitler having ordered him accordingly.'[45] Chief of the *Sicherheitsdienst* Otto Ohlendorf said something similar in the dock: 'It was all carried out by Himmler on orders from the Führer.'[46]

If Hitler really didn't know anything, he was a weak leader from whom such an enormous operation could be kept secret. And that was something Göring surely did not want to say. If Hitler had known what was going on in the east, he would be responsible for something that, in Göring's words, was 'too bad to imagine'. That responsibility was denied by Göring as well. Apparently, Göring wanted to sweep his own doorstep without being called a coward, thereby assuming all indicted Nazis would form a closed front. The result, however, was that his statements and similar ones by other Nazis became the base of the myth of Hitler's ignorance about the extermination of the Jewish race.

Hitler's leadership

Hitler was a dictator and his Third Reich was a police state. What did this mean though? That he always got his way because he was the boss? That he therefore put his opponents under such pressure that they had to make way? It is hard to understand the lack of a *Führerbefehl* for the extermination of the Jews when we have the image in our minds' eye of a Hitler who didn't have to be bothered by anyone and who, roaring like a lion and stomping his feet like a toddler, put so much fear into his subordinates they just had to give in. Why should someone in charge of a state apparatus with which he could exert maximum pressure, be bothered in the least by what the population thought of him and eventually keep secret his responsibility for what he had always said?

In order to be able to answer that question we must look at how Hitler worked normally and what was the base of his authority. Hitler, for instance, was a different kind of dictator than his Soviet colleague Joseph Stalin. The latter took over power in an existing Communist regime and he was a bureaucrat meddling in everything. He sent many letters and directives, creating some sort of monopoly within the *Politburo* (executive committee of the Communist Party) that, in Kershaw's view was more comparable to the way Martin Bormann operated than to Hitler's own way of work.

---

45. Gilbert, p. 23
46. Gilbert, p. 91

Within the Nazi state, Bormann controlled the secretariat of the NSDAP. Hitler himself wasn't all bureaucratic, he read only half his files and he often assumed things would turn out right as long as he didn't interfere with them. He preferred to direct policy orally rather than in writing and he didn't chair official organs.[47] Whereas in 1937, Stalin had a high-ranking army officer shot who didn't suffice any longer, in 1938, commander-in-chief Werner von Blomberg was given a golden handshake after a crisis involving his marriage to a former prostitute and his criticism of Hitler's plans for attack. Hitler left them alone after Blomberg and his wife returned to their villa in Bavaria after a trip to Italy.[48]

According to Ian Kershaw and Laurence Rees, Hitler was a typical example of a charismatic leader. Charismatic authority is based on the leader's personality and the admiration of his followers.[49] In particular, a charismatic leader can rise to power in a confusing situation of rapid changes and power relationships under great pressure. It is also said of charismatic leaders, including various gurus and religious leaders, they can be unpredictable. They often don't follow rules or bend them according to their personal views. Hitler's NSDAP was a 'classic movement surrounding a charismatic leadership' with a saviour in distress on a mission and followers falling in behind the great leader: the direct opposite of 'the bureaucratic, legal-rational authority' of modern regimes.[50]

When a charismatic leader takes over a state as its lone ruler, it goes almost without saying that something emerges that can be called a lack of system. The only system that is ultimately left over is, of course, the personal conviction of the leader himself. So, in Germany, Führer Adolf Hitler became the system to which judges, public officials and local politicians had to conform. This system only works when key positions are occupied by as many party members or other believers as possible, as was the case in Germany. Hitler's authority was based on the belief of his followers in their leader, on the so-called infallibility of his words and on the presumed truthfulness of those words.

Hitler needed people who were willing to believe in his charisma and the mass of believers increased in time. Historian Rees pointed out it often happened that in the 1920s people who were not impressed by Hitler at all, thought very differently later on. Fridolin von Spaun, an early Nazi follower,

---
47. Kershaw, HDH, pp. 41–46
48. Rees, p. 133
49. The German sociologist Max Weber coined this phrase long before Hitler came to power.
50. Kershaw, HDH, p. 48

had once seen Hitler as early as 1923 and considered him a little, non-descript figure. When he saw Hitler ten years later, however, he felt Hitler's eyes boring into him and he felt a vibration running from Hitler's fingers into him as the Führer laid his hand on the armrest of his chair although the Führer was talking to someone else. It must have been von Spaun himself whose vision of Hitler had changed but apart from the fact he had risen to chancellor, Hitler hadn't changed significantly. Apparently, von Spaun himself was now willing to believe in Hitler and that was the main difference.[51]

Minister of Propaganda Joseph Goebbels considered the conscious sculpting of Hitler's image one of his greatest achievements:[52] 'Despite the fact that in peace time more money was spent on armament than in any other state, despite a series of economic and political problems, despite the fact that the NSDAP regularly turned to unproductive arguments about who was responsible for what, despite the emergence of concentration camps and the persecution of minorities, despite this and much, much more, Hitler's authority and prestige increased between 1934 and 1938 until he was being glorified to a level unheard of in the modern history of Europe.'[53]

Working towards the Führer[54]

The consequence of this almost god-like status of the Führer was that he wasn't allowed to make any mistakes. That is why he often hesitated so long before intervening and rather waited until an issue had solved itself or conflicts of power between subordinates had been settled. In this way, the image of him indeed being unable to make mistakes remained. This, in combination with his aversion towards bureaucracy, led to a relative administrative chaos in contrast to the idea we generally have of the Third Reich,[55] which could only be compensated by initiatives from below. Thereby it had to be taken into account that the Führer's authority was autonomous and the order of business in the Reich was not always determined by the remnants of the old regime, nor by righteousness or another traditional political principle. The argument 'Hitler wanted it that way' became the most important argument with which Nazi leaders got things done with other leaders or subordinates. In this context, the Nazi habit of working towards the Führer came about.

---

51. Rees, p. 99
52. Rees, p. 107
53. Rees, p. 107
54. The Nazi habit to work towards the Führer is explained extensively in various works by Ian Kershaw. For this part, I made use of the books enumerated in the bibliography.
55. Kershaw, HDH, p. 50

This consisted, so to speak, of the practical realisation of Hitler's visions from below. The things Hitler had proclaimed in general terms, had written in *Mein Kampf* or had mentioned during meetings with party leaders, were translated into substantial policy. Local problems could also be tackled in this way in the spirit of the Führer. In this manner a lot of things were done in Hitler's name, sometimes with and sometimes without his permission. If that was the case, measures were supported or approved afterwards but it also happened that 'subordinates were apt to promise much more than they could accomplish'.[56]

In 1934, a Nazi official said: 'Whoever makes mistakes will soon notice it but who really works towards to the Führer, in his spirit and aimed at his goal will one day receive the best reward for it in the form of a sudden legal ratification of his work.'[57] A favourable side effect for Hitler was that among Nazi leaders a competition often arose for Hitler's favours. This applied to the *Gauleiter* in Poland as well. One attempted to realise Germanisation much sooner than the other and, it goes without saying, this provoked further radicalisation.

Working towards to the Führer didn't only apply to administrative issues but to private matters as well. Two well-known examples of this unfolded on the *Obersalzberg* where Hitler's summer residence, the *Berghof*, was located and where the most famous lip servant among the Nazis, Martin Bormann, was often present. He was there when Hitler, greeting a group of admirers passing by, which happened often in the 1930s, said that he was bothered by the sun. Bormann immediately had a tree planted on the driveway of the *Berghof*. On another occasion, when Hitler was admiring the view of the mountain from his terrace, he would have complained about a farm building obstructing the beautiful view. A few days later, when Hitler returned from Munich, the farmhouse had disappeared. Hitler didn't have to issue a substantial order. A hint or a loose remark was enough.

In this way, Hitler could always hide behind something. He kept all possibilities open and could always withdraw from something at the last moment.[58] On the occasion of the *Kristallnacht*, which as described earlier had, according to prominent party leaders and other Germans, run out of control, it was Goebbels who was blamed. After all, Hitler hadn't given permission for the 'spontaneous' uprising by the people and thus, the damage that had been done wasn't his fault.

---

56. Rees, p. 234
57. Kershaw, HDH, p. 55
58. Rees, p. 233

The smaller actions aimed against Jews in Poland were also approved time and again while already going on until trainloads of people were transported from Europe to the extermination camps. Of course, such a mammoth operation couldn't elude Hitler.

An order to exterminate the Jews wasn't necessary. Instead, Hitler had prophesied about the Jews that something terrible would happen to them when a global war would erupt. After he had unleashed this war himself, he only had to repeat his prophesy to make his subordinates think about a solution of the problem of the Jews in Poland, created by the Nazis themselves.

The Nazi state

It is misleading to view 'the Third Reich as a dictatorship with a coherent, centralised command structure that provided a tightly orchestrated fulfilling of Hitler's wishes'.[59] The image of the Reich, as we see in a number of more recent works by historians, is much more than that of a state depending on the personal whims of the dictator. And because he let so many things just pass or left them to his subordinates, the state functioned mainly because of initiatives from below. This way, Hitler had his way, of course, but in a different manner than is still thought. Within these relations, Hitler's 'friend' and *Minister für Rüstung und Munitionen*, Albert Speer, could see to a massive increase in the production of arms. At the same time, Martin Bormann, chief of the *Parteikanzlei*, was one of the mightiest men in Germany and not only to Speer's displeasure. In 1943, following the lost battle of Stalingrad, a power struggle erupted with Bormann wanting that he, *Feldmarschall* Wilhelm Keitel and Hans Lammers, chief of the *Reichskanzlei*, would seize almost all power in Germany. He found Speer, Hermann Göring, Joseph Goebbels and Heinrich Himmler in his way, however. Hitler did nothing and although Goebbels spoke about a leadership crisis in this period, everyone remained where he was and Hitler in the saddle. It looks like Hitler's style of leadership had both a challenging and crippling influence on his subordinates. The imminent war against France, for instance, was a major challenge for the army leadership but the way in which Hitler, despite the many existing objections and without consultation, decided to continue the attack anyway, 'was deadly for the self-confidence of all who disagreed with him'.[60]

The Nazi state is often referred to as the ultimate example of a police state in which everything and everybody was kept under control. Yet, there

---
59. Kershaw, HDH, p. 289
60. Rees, p. 203

are examples of states where far fewer people were employed to keep the population in hand. Melching writes about this: 'Of course, the Third Reich was a dictatorship and a police state but at the same time it is remarkable that the regime could stay in the saddle with relatively little suppression.'[61] He proves this by pointing out that the Gestapo, with just 10,000 men, kept watch over more than 80 million Germans, whereas the DDR needed no fewer than 100,000 Stasi agents to keep just 16 million people in check.[62] Melching's comparison, by the way, applies to the Germany of the 1930s when the Germans were relatively satisfied and there was no question of neighbouring countries where everything was 'better' and 'more liberal', as was the case with the GDR. Yet, these figures are remarkable and they show a Germany other than the cliché of a state entirely controlled by the Nazis.

Party religion

The Nazi party had an almost religious aura with Hitler as the prophet, *Mein Kampf* as the Bible, the party top as disciples and, way down below, the common followers and maybe a few irresolute persons. There was also some sort of religious calendar with yearly recurring festivities such as the *Reichsparteitag* and a harvest day. There were memorials like the yearly commemoration of the dead on 9 November – the day of the 1923 putsch – with party members walking through Munich in procession.

Hitler was a pseudo Messiah though, responsible for the emergence of competing power cells in a state that had hardly any system left. There was no functioning parliament, the press was controlled by Joseph Goebbels and the judiciary was anything but independent. It was precisely in this context that the will of the Führer could become law[63] and evolve into a 'system'. Within this system, actually anything could happen – with war and genocide as the most important consequences.

Was he the ultimate dictator?

Hitler's leadership and the structure of the Third Reich were far more complex than some abridged stories suggest. Whoever wants to describe the Third Reich or any other state in short terms will soon revert to generalities and superlatives. Even the term 'dictatorship' is relatively useless without

---

61. Melching, p. 17
62. Melching, pp. 17–18
63. Kershaw, HDH, pp. 56–57

further definition. Within his version of dictatorship, Hitler couldn't just get everything done, contrary to what the term suggests. If whatever he wanted did happen, he sometimes had to do his best to keep matters secret from the population, in particular when he thought it would endanger his impeccable status. The fact that he did manage to realise many of his plans was the result of more than just dictatorial power and putting pressure on the population, in particular in the first half of the 1930s, although that pressure increased steadily as the war became a steadily growing disaster for the Germans.

Hitler sculpted the existing political and state judiciary by appointing party comrades in important posts. Within his one-party regime, this was the base of working towards the Führer. His charisma and method of ruling earned him his great successes but he certainly had to do his utmost to overcome various problems and sceptical opponents. It turned out he wasn't entirely blind to his surroundings: he understood full well he had to take the opinion or belief of the population into account.

'Hitler's totally unbureaucratic style of leading, his tendency towards secrecy, his usually veiled language and the hidden hints with which he, instead of substantial orders incited others to act, hide his interference.'[64] The lack of a *Führerbefehl* for the mass extermination of the Jews is used by some as proof of the lack of responsibility for the Holocaust. This is a misunderstanding. Here, Hitler also did his best not to be openly associated with the dark sides of his leadership. The lack of this *Führerbefehl* was entirely in keeping with his habitual method of working.

At the end of the day, the principle of working towards the Führer seems to contradict what Hitler had written in *Mein Kampf* about the responsibility in the state, which in his opinion shouldn't lie with a parliament but with only one man. He criticised parliamentary democracy because such a parliament never bore responsibility as there always was a changing majority that made the decisions.[65] Once Hitler came to power himself, he circumvented his responsibilities by often keeping himself aloof from issues, by covertly facilitating initiatives from below and interfering only when absolutely necessary. And with that, he was actually never accountable for anything as he could always blame his subordinates for failures. As this actually was his way of ruling, there is only one possible conclusion and that is that Hitler had been fully responsible for the Holocaust. The lack of a *Führerbefehl* makes no difference whatsoever. Hitler didn't need this order to get his way.

---

64. Kershaw, KP, p. 487
65. *Mein Kampf*, p. 8

Chapter 14

Was Hitler Ill?

The psychic and physical disorders of the Führer

Early 1945, little was left of the man who roamed all over Germany by plane prior to the seizure of power in 1933 to deliver no fewer than five speeches a day sometimes. Adolf Hitler couldn't control the shaking of his arm any longer and his bouts of anger were said to grow steadily worse. His subordinates searched for explanations for this massive change, as how could it be that the Führer, who had inspired them so much in the past, had turned into a sick, old man who was no longer the alleged genius he had been a long time ago. Was Hitler so much affected by the imminent end that he fell ill or did he display, at the end of his life, the symptoms of the mental patient he had been for a long time? It was even claimed that Hitler had been poisoned by his personal physician, Dr Morell, and that he made important military decisions while under the influence of obscure substances. People who looked to exonerate Hitler after the war looked for the key to his depraved soul, at a possible mental disease within the family or at some sort of a personality disorder. To the irritation of others, a discussion arose about Hitler's responsibility for his own acts. If he had been mentally ill, was he fully accountable for his own actions?

In October 2014, the Dutch paper *Trouw* published an article entitled 'Hitler on crystal meth, for tirades and against pain'. Hitler was called a fervent user of this drug and the article referred to a report of the American Secret Service that was shown in a documentary on the British TV station Channel 4. Hitler, who used seventy-four different drugs, could have become addicted after having visited the physician Dr Theodor Morell. But was the documentary not just the umpteenth television programme with sensationally presented 'news' about Hitler?[1] Or did the documentary actually present something new about Hitler's health and drug addiction?

---

1. According to Neumann & Eberle, every week some 350 TV programmes about Hitler are aired via the Astra satellites, some being presented as sensational and new.

In the past, various books have been published listing the drugs Hitler used and overviews of his ailments, but this kind of complete information was hard to obtain by doctors in Hitler's time. His various physicians, of course, knew what they prescribed themselves but sometimes weren't informed at all about the treatment by his other doctors. His silence about personal issues and his tendency to provide his subordinates with only the most needed information in order to play them off against each other when necessary manifested itself as well in his relationship with the physicians who treated him. Partly as a result of this, all sorts of speculation emerged about Hitler's possible ailments.

Young Hitler

From Hitler's early youth on, there are descriptions of the ailments he had. When they are taken from *Mein Kampf* they must be assessed with some caution, as was apparent in remarks about other subjects in Hitler's book, but it is clear that in the Hitler family great medical dramas unfolded. Adolf was raised in a family in which four children had died at an early age.[2] Just he and his sister Paula, the fourth and sixth child respectively, survived. Hitler's mother didn't live long either, she died at the age of forty-seven. Adolf wasn't a child any more at that time.

Apart from the scarlet fever he must have contracted in 1897, Hitler didn't suffer from serious diseases in his early youth.[3] This is apparent from the work of medic Hans-Joachim Neumann and historian Henrik Eberle, who wrote a book on the subject. In *Mein Kampf*, Hitler wrote, however, that after the death of his father, he had contracted a severe lung disease that saved him from a future he didn't like at all.[4] Young Adolf didn't want to become a public official as had been the wish of his father, so it suited him rather well not being able to go to school for a year owing to a disease.[5] Instead, he went to visit his family in the rural Waldviertel in Lower Austria to recuperate. At least, that's what he wrote in *Mein Kampf*.

It is highly questionable, however, whether he had spoken the truth about his severe lung disease. It is said that sometimes Adolf only fell ill when he was with his family and so he hadn't gone away to recuperate.[6] Much

---

2. Kershaw, Hoogmoed, p. 40
3. Neumann & Eberle, pp. 166–167
4. *Mein Kampf*, p. 16
5. *Mein Kampf*, p. 16
6. Neumann & Eberle, pp. 166–167

more important, however, were the findings of the family doctor, the Jewish physician Eduard Bloch, who never found any indication of a severe lung disease in young Adolf.[7] Based on this, it was concluded long ago that Hitler had used a mild disease to persuade his worried mother to allow him to drop out of school. There's a more than even chance that it had been a common flu or an infection, although the possibility exists he had contracted bronchitis.[8]

Thus, Hitler probably never suffered from a serious lung disease but proof of this, the notes of Dr Bloch, had been handed to an associate of Rudolph Hess by Bloch himself in 1938.[9] Like so many other medical records, this record also disappeared on account of the Nazis. Dr Bloch's findings were preserved, however, as, thanks to protection by Hitler himself, he was allowed to leave Europe at the start of the war. Living in America as he did, he had been interviewed by a journalist of *Colliers* magazine. During this interview, which was about the ailments of Hitler as well, Bloch did say something about Hitler's tonsils, his coughing bouts and flu but nothing about the serious lung disease he is supposed to have contracted. That was really conspicuous.[10] Ian Kershaw concluded: 'By pretending a disease or, more probable, to exaggerate a real disease, he succeeded in convincing his mother he didn't have to go to school anymore.'[11] Years later he managed, using the same white lie, to dodge conscription in Austria.

Meanwhile, Hitler had grown into a young man and he lived in Munich. He had left Austria, though, without fulfilling his conscription and it is assumed he did so on purpose. The Austrian authorities managed to track him down and on Sunday, 18 January 1914, a criminal investigator of the Munich police suddenly appeared on his doorstep and told him he was to report within two days to Linz in Austria in connection with his conscription. The following day, Hitler went to visit the Austrian consulate to apply for a postponement until the next recruiting day, 5 February.[12] His request was denied but he received the written reaction as late as Wednesday, so he was unable to report. In a long letter he admitted he should have reported as early as 1909 but he also indicated he had serious financial troubles at the time and he tried to get understanding for his situation. He requested an examination in nearby Salzburg instead of Linz. It is striking he also pointed to the old

---

7. Neumann & Eberle, p. 169, Hamann, HE, p. 465; Katz, p. 50
8. Neumann & Eberle, pp. 166–167
9. Katz, p. 49
10. Katz, p. 50
11. Kershaw, Hoogmoed, p. 4
12. Kershaw, Hoogmoed, p. 134

lung disease that would still bother him. The sad story was accepted and Hitler was declared unfit for military service.[13] In the same year it turned out he wasn't in such bad physical shape when he reported for duty in the Bavarian army at the beginning of the First World War.

Inbreeding

His severe lung disease had either been made up or exaggerated, but it would probably be correct to say his mother would have been duly impressed.[14] After all, she had already lost four children and she tried to care for the surviving ones as well as possible. There was something to remark though about the relationship into which they had been born. After all, Hitler's parents were related, something that occurred often in the region they came from, resulting in a higher risk of genetic aberrations.[15] This gave birth to the notion that, if among Hitler's forebears there had been any question of a mental disease, it could have been stronger in Hitler's generation. And again, that would have been a possible explanation for the crimes of which Hitler was capable, apparently.

Hitler's parents were healthy though, and there were only two family members who were mentally deranged: the sister of Hitler's mother, Johanna Plölzl, and a distant relative named Aloisia Veit. Based on these two separate cases, it is impossible to establish a hereditary disease, according to Neumann, and in Hitler's direct line of descent as well, nothing is known about the existence of such a disease.[16] The chance of Hitler being out of his mind was no greater than in any other family. As the presence of a mental aberration was never been established in Hitler himself, we have to assume he was fully accountable.[17]

The buck

No significant diseases or accidents are known from the period of Hitler's early puberty. One strange and painful story, both literally and figuratively, became known in 1981[18] though. Dietrich Güstrow, the lawyer who had

---

13. Neumann & Eberle, p. 170; Katz, p. 56; Kershaw, Hoogmoed, p. 134
14. *Mein Kampf*, p. 16
15. Bullock, p. 9; Rosenbaum, p. 60
16. Neumann & Eberle, pp. 40–41
17. Farther on the possible paranoid personality disorders Hitler would have suffered from, pass review.
18. Rosenbaum, p. 28; *Der Spiegel* is, 1981

defended the perpetrators of the attempt on his life by Claus von Stauffenberg in 1943, told in his memoirs about Private Eugen Wasner, whom he had defended in Germany after he had defamed the Führer by the words: 'Adolf is no good since a buck has taken a bite out of his cock.'[19] Wasner told his army comrades Hitler and he had attended school in Leonding together and one time Adolf had wanted to proof he could pee in the mouth of a buck. The goat had bit him so hard on his penis that he yelled out loudly and subsequently went home crying. The lawyer saw in this incident an explanation for the abnormalities Hitler displayed later on and he believed the soldier's tall story.[20] Private physician Bloch, mentioned earlier, was positive to recall in 1943 in America, without having known the story of the goat, that he hadn't established any physical deformations and that there was nothing wrong with Hitler. Therefore, there can be no question of Hitler's frustration over a bite by a goat that could have bothered him all his life. Historian Brigitte Hamann concludes, just like many other researchers,[21] there is no evidence whatsoever of Hitler's physical abnormalities, neither is there any substantial evidence for the story about the goat.[22]

The First World War

Up to the First World War, Hitler's health seems to have progressed rather well. Just like the previous period, little or nothing is known about visits to doctors and nothing is being said about it in *Mein Kampf* either. From the moment Hitler went into active service in 1914, it is known that he had been treated regularly for injuries he had sustained. There is, however, no question of him suffering any injury that affected his life until shortly before the end of the war. Neither is there a connection between shell shock, a neurological condition many veterans of the First World War suffered from, and Hitler's later Parkinson's-like condition at the end of the Second World War.[23] There is, however, an interesting story about Hitler's experience in the first war and the consequences thereof.

Pasewalk

At the end of the First World War, on the night of 13–14 October 1918, Hitler and his regiment were stationed in Wervicq-Sud in *Parc Dalle*

---

19. Rosenbaum, p. 29
20. Rosenbaum, p. 29
21. Neumano & Eberle, pp. 58–60
22. Hamann, HE, p. 464
23. Neumann & Eberle, pp. 210–215

Dumond, where he fell victim to a gas attack by the British. Because of this gassing, Hitler could hardly see and he had to leave the battlefield.[24] He was transferred to Pasewalk, north of Berlin, where he was treated in the psychiatric ward of the military hospital. He wrote in *Mein Kampf* how his vision returned. At the moment the news came in that Germany had lost the war, his vision went black again: 'I groped and stumbled my way back to the dormitory, throwing myself on my bed and pushing my face in my blanket and cushion. I have never cried more than the day I stood at my mother's grave. (...) Everything had been in vain.'[25]

In his book, Hitler presented his stay in Pasewalk as a turning point. He is supposed to have decided there and then to become a politician. This concoction has been mentioned before,[26] but the First World War must have had an enormous influence on his personal development.[27] The nature of his blindness, in particular the one that occurred in Pasewalk for the second time, became the subject of widespread discussion. Historians including Kershaw, Maser and Fest assume it was a sort of delayed gas glare,[28] but according to others this would have been a case of hysterical or simulated blindness.[29] If this were true, it could mean Hitler had inherited a certain predisposition for mental illness after all.

Indications for hysterical blindness certainly exist. In a book by author and lawyer Bernhard Horstmann it becomes clear, for instance, that Hitler was admitted to a psychiatric ward,[30] where he was supposed to have been treated as a psychopath and hysteric.[31] His physician, Dr Edmund Forster, could even have hypnotised him, from which he never woke up. Horstmann claims that could have been of essential importance for the rest of Hitler's life and it could also have been the explanation for the imposing and spellbinding look in his eyes.

The simple fact that Hitler had been in a psychiatric ward was reason enough for the Nazis to see to it that his medical records from that period disappeared. But that wasn't all. The building that once housed the institution was razed to the ground in 1934. It had to make room for a memorial hall in which Hitler's statement from *Mein Kampf*: '*Ich aber beschloss Politiker zu werden*' ('I decided however to become a politician'), was given a prominent place. The building, in memory of an unpleasant period in Hitler's life, was

---

24. Kershaw, Hoogmoed, p. 144
25. *Mein Kampf*, pp. 230–233
26. In the chapter 'Was Hitler a socialist?'
27. Kershaw, Hoogmoed, p. 149
28. Kershaw, Hoogmoed, p. 151; Neumann & Eberle, pp. 42–43
29. Neumann & Eberle, p. 43
30. Horstmann, p. 201
31. Horstmann, p. 202

replaced by one that should support the myth of Hitler's great transformation to politician.

Still more traces had to be erased though. When Hitler was searching for his medical record of the time, his former psychiatrist, Forster, was put under so much pressure that he committed suicide.[32] The death of general and former *Kanzler* Kurt von Schleicher, who had been ousted under mysterious circumstances during the Röhm crisis in 1934, could have been involved as well as he knew Hitler's medical record.[33] It is only because the shorthand notes of the record ended up in the hands of Jewish physician and author Ernst Weiss[34] that more is known about Hitler's treatment in Pasewalk; that is to say, if we can believe the novel Weiss wrote about it. One of the figures, named patient A.H., was treated in the city of P. but he remained in the last hypnosis that was part of his treatment.[35] The novel doesn't deal with the consequences and after the war nobody could question Weiss about the issue any more as he had committed suicide when the Germans entered his home city of Paris.[36]

Of course, the First World War and its aftermath were important to Hitler, and obviously he didn't want to be confronted with any emerging health records after his seizure of power. It is very likely that Forster would have been put under pressure, but the idea that his suicide had anything to do with the hypnosis he hadn't ended may well have been described in a novel but it hasn't been proved anywhere. The treatment in a psychiatric clinic may of itself have been ample reason for Hitler and other high-ranking Nazis to put the doctor under pressure.

Neumann and Eberle conclude in their book about Hitler's ailments that the discussion about his hysterical blindness is certainly justified but the story about the hypnosis of psychiatrist Forster isn't convincing enough. In addition, they state it can no longer be proved whether Hitler's clinical picture in Pasewalk looks more like a bout of hysterics or the delayed consequences of a gas glare.[37] The theory about Hitler's hysteric blindness that would have occurred when Hitler heard the war was over is swept under the rug by historian Ian Kershaw. As mustard gas doesn't cause permanent blindness but a short, recurring loss of vision when one wipes ones eyes or cries, it is

---

32. Horstmann, p. 169
33. Horstmann, p. 187
34. Neumann & Eberle, pp. 44–45
35. Weiss, pp. 141–146
36. Horstmann, p. 206
37. Neumann & Eberle, pp. 43–44

more likely that the second blindness was a delayed result of mustard gas as well.[38]

As open as one can be as to the possibilities of hypnosis, the likelihood of it playing a key role, as suggested in the novel, is highly questionable.[39] To put it even stronger, based on a fictitious report it is impossible to determine whether Hitler was actually hypnotised. Neumann and Eberle point out that, within that story, Hitler had fallen victim to a hypnosis that wasn't ended[40] and as a result he would have simply lost control over his own functioning. Hitler would have been unaccountable then. And that, as Neumann and Eberle say as well, is a far-fetched and, in the eyes of many, an undesired effect of this story. It actually exonerates Hitler in part from his responsibility for everything he did later on under the influence of this supposed hypnosis.

The key role that Pasewalk played in *Mein Kampf* and for Hitler himself is exaggerated. It is almost certain that he didn't decide in Pasewalk to become a politician at all. Once back in Munich, initially, he didn't undertake anything at all.[41] He remained in active service and he only became active politically during the period when his army career was almost over. The importance of Pasewalk in his political awakening is therefore an antedated finding of his own.

The Hitlerputsch

Hitler was subjected to more medical treatment following the failed putsch of 9 November 1923 to dethrone the Bavarian government. In an exchange of fire between the putschists and the police near the Feldherrnhalle in Munich, his left arm was pulled down by a man walking beside him who had been shot in the heart. Whether he broke anything in this incident is unknown but he probably sustained a dislocated shoulder.[42] He didn't sustain permanent damage from it and the prison doctor in Landsberg am Lech didn't notice anything conspicuously of a permanent nature either.[43]

In 1924, Hitler was imprisoned for most of the year and wrote part of *Mein Kampf.* Based on certain passages in the book, certain disorders or

---

38. Kershaw, Hoogmoed, p. 151
39. Neumann & Eberle, p. 46
40. Neumann & Eberle, p. 46
41. Kershaw, Hoogmoed, p. 152; Joachimsthaler, p. 184 e.v.
42. Neumann & Eberle, p. 83
43. Neumann & Eberle, p. 84

diseases were assumed and from pages where he wrote about syphilis[44] it was concluded he had contracted venereal disease in Vienna after visiting a Jewish prostitute. There is no evidence for this either. Hitler was never diagnosed with venereal disease and it is far more likely that in his book in the passages about Vienna he joined the social groups from that period that wanted to prevent young men contracting the disease.[45] During the First World War the problem of venereal disease increased owing to the high number of soldiers visiting prostitutes. Of course, Hitler was aware of this but it is generally accepted he didn't make use of such services himself.

The 1930s

Little is known about Hitler's possible visits to doctors during the remainder of the 1920s. When he made a stop in Berlin in 1932 during his election campaign, he saw a physician for the first time because he suffered from hoarseness.[46] Later on this would occur more often and it is known he had polyps removed from his vocal chords at some moment. What is conspicuous in the 1930s is his treatment in a hospital in Berlin for a headache, double vision and ringing in his ears. This treatment would have been initiated by symptoms of poisoning and therefore Hitler stopped using the drug Neo-Ballistol he used against the intestinal cramps that had bothered him during a big part of his life. The examination in the hospital yielded little result. Therefore, Hitler's court photographer recommended Dr Theodor Morell might well be able to help him.[47]

Dr Morell

Personal physician Theodor Morell was the most controversial doctor in Hitler's entourage. Various historians were convinced that, in time, Hitler became increasingly dependent on Morell's medicine and that he sometimes made decisions under the influence of those drugs.[48] Many people in his circle questioned Morell's role or simply disliked him. Those included tank general Heinz Guderian and Hitler's physicians, Hans Karl von Hasselbach and Karl Brandt.[49] If Morell did indeed administer more than injections with

---

44. *Mein Kampf*, p. 285 e.v.
45. Neumann & Eberle, p. 52
46. Neumann & Eberle, p. 84
47. Neumann & Eberle, pp. 86–87
48. Neumann & Eberle, blz, p. 88
49. Neumann & Eberle, pp. 88–93

dextrose and vitamins he was known for, as was suggested, he could well have been the cause of Hitler's bad decisions during the second part of the war. It has even been suggested that Hitler had been given hard drugs and some presented Morell as some kind of Rasputin in Hitler's court.[50] In the documentary *Hitler's Hidden Drug Habit*, which was broadcast on the British TV station Channel 4 in 2014, the authors did their utmost to confirm the images of Morell as a dealer and Hitler as a junkie. They claimed they even possessed fresh evidence. The charges against Morell, usually voiced behind Hitler's back, became publicly known after the war. At that time, Morell could hardly defend himself as his health had deteriorated quickly and he died shortly after it. Hitler's former and possibly jealous physician Karl Brandt felt free after Hitler's death to shine his light on the Morell case. Brandt said Morell injected Hitler daily with a substance that supposedly contained morphine or Pervitin (a substance with amphetamine that was used at the front to suppress fear)[51] but an addiction to it has never been established. Historian Ian Kershaw states it is out of the question that Hitler had been addicted to opiates or cocaine. About amphetamine, he said it has never been proven that he used it or that his behaviour was affected by it.[52] Hitler did use Vitamultin, which may have contained Pervitin, but it isn't even certain whether it contained this substance.[53]

In the British documentary, Hitler's addiction to hard drugs is heavily emphasized nonetheless. A somber voice-over makes all kinds of statements about the drug crystal meth (or Pervitin), Brom-Nervasit, Vitamultin and Eukodal. Hitler is supposed to have taken them all along with some seventy other 'drugs'. In the documentary, various specialists are paraded, including Timothy Ryback and Henrik Eberle. The latter is particularly interesting on Hitler's use of drugs. He was co-author of a book about Hitler's ailments and, together with Christian Neumann, he had confirmed Kershaw's statement by saying that Hitler had indeed not been addicted to opiates or cocaine.[54] There is more discussion about Hitler's use of amphetamine, though, but Neumann and Eberle conclude that Hitler can't have been addicted to Pervitin[55] and that he didn't need Vitamultin to sit out his meetings.[56] Obviously, he wasn't that dependent. In the documentary, Eberle gets his say

---

50. Katz, p. 360
51. Katz, p. 360
52. Kershaw, Vergelding, p. 947
53. Neumann & Eberle, p. 156
54. Neumann & Eberle, pp. 155–156
55. Neumann & Eberle, p. 159
56. Neumann & Eberle, p. 160

a few times but he doesn't speak a word about Hitler's use of amphetamine. And that is conspicuous as he has a clear opinion on this.

The news value of said documentary is low though. All uppers and downers mentioned in it already appear in the book by Neumann and Eberle of 2009 and in an overview of medicines in a book about Morell by Ottmar Katz from 1982 as well.[57] What did look new, however, was a report from the American military intelligence service that was presented, but its content is based on statements by Hitler's other doctors and they too were eager to paint Morell as black as possible after the war. Even if Morell had been a quack, without convincing evidence to the contrary it is too far-fetched to present him as Hitler's drug dealer. In the documentary, everyone does his best to enlarge Morell's influence on Hitler with funny rhymes such as *Under the spell of Dr Morell*. It is also striking that the voice-over makes statements about Hitler's drug addiction and that, apart from some interesting remarks by Eberle, it doesn't contain a single statement by him about hard drugs. Could Eberle's commentary have been too detailed?

In the documentary, Hitler's shaking hands are shown last as if it were the greatest discovery since the death of the Führer. And that, of course, isn't the case. Hitler's physical deterioration at the end of his life has been well-known for a long time and his shaking hands are always mentioned. These hands, by the way, can't have been a symptom of a Pervitin addiction but are symptomatic of the Parkinson's-like disease Hitler suffered from at the end of his life.[58] This is admitted in the documentary in so many words as well. The possibility of Hitler's Parkinson's being the major cause of his physical deterioration and this having had less to do with Morrell's injections is left open.

The negative manner in which doctors and other witnesses around Hitler talked about Morell later on is very likely unfair. Almost no one among them knew exactly what was administered to the Führer. Morell did have close ties with Hitler and Hitler in turn had great confidence in the doctor who had regularly helped him back on his feet with injections, but other doctors didn't know exactly what was in Morell's syringes. The assumption made that Hitler depended on hard drugs was unfounded and unscientific. The extensive discussion about it has partly been caused by Hitler himself though, who was known as a patient that was difficult to treat.[59] He selected

---

57. Katz, p. 389. He mentions Vitamultin, Brom-Nervacit and Eukodal but omits Pervitine, which is mentioned in the documentary.
58. Neumann & Eberle, p. 160
59. Katz, p. 48

his own doctors and he didn't want professors around. He preferred a trusted physician who could keep silent.[60] The treatments by Hitler's various doctors were not tuned to each other as Hitler wouldn't allow it. It looks like no one had a complete picture of the drugs Hitler took and that was, of course, the source for all sorts of suggestive comments, as well as for the mutual distrust among the various doctors around Hitler. There was hardly a specific reason, though, for the charges against Morell.

Führerschwäche

In the past, the disappointing results of the invasion of the Soviet Union were sometimes attributed to a disease suffered by Hitler. The decisive mistake to postpone the attack on Moscow until after the winter[61] was supposedly taken by Hitler because he was ill when he took it. Ian Kershaw confirms this: 'Hitler taking a decision as to Moscow, albeit with many ifs and buts and in fact immediately revoking it, could have been influenced by the serious dysentery he suffered from in the first half of 1941.'[62]

When in 1941, Joseph Goebbels paid a visit to Hitler in his field headquarters, the *Wolfsschanze* in Poland, he discovered that Hitler had been ill indeed; this is evident from his diary entry of 19 August, in which he writes Hitler had suffered from a *Ruhranfall* (abdominal loop).[63] He suffered from intestinal cramps, diarrhoea and nausea.[64] It was assumed incorrectly that with Goebbels' later statement about a *Führerschwäche* – leadership weakness – this period was meant, but at that moment Goebbels also wrote in his diary: 'The past four weeks have been an outspoken bad time. But pursuant to the ancient law of low and high tide, flood is sure to follow such a period.'[65] About Hitler he said that, despite his illness, he was as vital and worked as hard as ever. During this period, Goebbels never questioned Hitler's leadership.

The theory that Hitler's dysentery in 1941 was the cause of the first losses on the Eastern Front is also supported by David Irving, a British historian generally maligned as he is well-known for his denial of the Holocaust and has been attacked for his glorification of the Third Reich. It may be obvious for him not to blame Hitler for the German losses but a disease, the army

---

60. Katz, pp. 101–102
61. Kershaw, Vergelding, p. 569
62. Kershaw, Vergelding, p. 571
63. Goebbels, p. 1653
64. Neumann & Eberle, p. 174
65. Goebbels, vol. 4, p. 1652

leadership or, if necessary, any other external factor.[66] Irving might not have been entirely wrong here. Ian Kershaw, whose opinion unlike Irving's, does carry weight, points out for instance that Hitler, probably influenced by his illness, even considered accepting a peace proposal from Stalin.[67] In his analysis of all that went wrong during the invasion of the Soviet Union, Kershaw mentions far more than Hitler's dysentery. The extreme optimism with which the principle of *Blitzkrieg*, so successful in the Low Countries and France, was repeated was a catastrophic miscalculation and, moreover, the German equipment was too limited to make the speedy attack a success. That was, according to Kershaw the gravest mistake of Hitler and his 'military planners'.[68]

The *Führerschwäche* or Führer crisis as mentioned by Goebbels stems from 1943, by the way. In his own diary of that period,[69] as well as during a conversation at which Albert Speer was present, Goebbels criticises Hitler's modus operandi.[70] Apart from the understanding he had of Hitler's remark that death didn't frighten him anymore in regard to the dire situation at the front, he doesn't say anything about an illness of Hitler that could have been the cause of the German losses.[71]

Hitler's illness in August 1941 can't have been the major cause of the ultimate defeat the Germans suffered against the Soviets. If he had been fit, Hitler might have taken other decisions but even a direct attack on Moscow wouldn't have solved the lack of German equipment and incorrect military planning. 'And even if Moscow had been captured, then the war wouldn't have ended just yet. It is unlikely the opponent would have collapsed in a psychological, political, economic and military sense.'[72]

Cocaine intoxication and competition among doctors

A subsequent important stage in the Führer's medical history is the attempt on Hitler's life by Claus von Stauffenberg on 20 July 1944 in the *Wolfsschanze* in Poland. The attempt failed but Hitler didn't escape unscathed. His eardrums were damaged, blood ran out of his ears, he suffered from a balance

---

66. Neumann & Eberle, pp. 175–176
67. Kershaw, Vergelding, p. 571
68. Kershaw, Vergelding, p. 579
69. Goebbels, vol. 5, p. 1905
70. Kershaw, Vergelding, p. 767
71. Goebbels, vol. 5, p. 1905
72. Kershaw, Vergelding, p. 579

disorder and he had a bloody taste in his mouth.[73] As his hearing problems increased, Dr Brandt saw to it that Dr Erwin Giesing commenced treating Hitler. From 21 August 1944 onwards, Hitler was administered a 10 per cent solution of cocaine against his headache, applied directly to his nasal mucosa. As this had a favourable effect, Hitler immediately wanted two to three applications per day. By early September, his eardrums had healed but his cold remained. And even though his vision went black following a treatment on 12 September, and during the following days he reacted badly to the cocaine solution, the treatment was continued up to 1 October. That day, things went really wrong: Hitler collapsed. His personal adjutant, Heinz Linge, assessing the situation incorrectly, told Giesing Hitler just needed rest. He had the doctor leave for Berlin, where the next day he was informed that Hitler still wasn't doing well. The big question, still posed after the war, was whether Hitler had been given too much cocaine and whether his life had been endangered by it.[74]

Giesing himself must have thought earlier that he should suspend Hitler's cocaine treatment but as the headaches returned when the effect of the treatment had worn off, Hitler insisted it should continue. Giesing's conviction, voiced later by the way, that he should suspend the treatment apparently wasn't strong enough for himself to actually do so. During that period, both Giesing and Morell were struck by the unnaturally reddish colour of Hitler's face. Giesing supposed Hitler had contracted jaundice, Morell thought he hadn't. When one morning Giesing saw the pills Hitler took at breakfast, he was struck by the anti-gas tablets, supposedly containing two dangerous substances: atropine and strychnine. According to adjutant Linge, Hitler took a lot of them daily. Giesing, who hadn't been informed of what Hitler was taking, subsequently became angry at Morell, accusing him of letting Hitler decide for himself how much of the drug containing strychnine he took. In Giesing's view, Hitler could well have suffered from the symptoms of intoxication.[75]

As Giesing didn't dare to discuss his misgivings towards the Führer's favourite doctor with Hitler himself, Giesing, Brandt and another physician, Hans Karl von Hasselbach, mutually agreed Brandt would take the reins. He travelled from Berlin to the headquarters in Poland and on 3 October he had Hitler's urine tested for traces of strychnine without him knowing it. Like the other two physicians, Brandt assumed Hitler had suffered from jaundice,

---

73. Neumann & Eberle, p. 177; Katz, p. 289
74. Katz, pp. 290–291
75. Neumann & Eberle, p. 181

caused by intoxication. Morell himself, meanwhile, was in the process of solving Hitler's problems with his liver and gall bladder with chamomile tea and oatmeal.

Brandt's urine test didn't yield anything spectacular. Yet, on 30 September, a conversation took place between Brandt and Morell in which Morell was blamed for the large quantity of anti-gas tablets and also for Hitler's supposed strychnine intoxication. Morell denied the latter. He still thought it was a normal obstipation (severe constipation) that could be solved by simple means.[76]

The incident led to a small dispute in which eventually Morell got his way. Hitler did suffer from obstipation and he hadn't been intoxicated, at least not by anti-gas tablets. The amount of strychnine in the pills was so low, intoxication was out of the question, even if Hitler took sixteen pills per day.[77] Hitler had always suffered with his intestines and obstipation, as had been the case again this time.

When Hitler had recuperated, he unequivocally sided with Morell and the so-called overseeing physicians were sent back to Berlin. A young physician by the name of Ludwig Stumpfegger was named Hitler's new overseeing physician.[78] That was probably more than enough reason for Dr Brandt to blame Dr Morell once again after the war for having intoxicated the Führer.

Paranoid personality disorder

Hitler's diseases and supposed psychic disorders would explain all sorts of things: his perverted sexuality, the loss of the war against of the Soviet Union, his bouts of anger, but also the origin of his hatred of Jews. A very interesting book that deals with Hitler's hatred of the Jewish race was written by Dutch historian Peter den Hertog.

Den Hertog suggests Hitler suffered from a paranoid personality disorder that could be the foundation of his hatred of Jews. One of the characteristics of a paranoid person is the unfounded aversion he has towards a certain group of people. Thereby den Hertog indicates that workers in psychiatry warn that behaviour belonging to the disorder doesn't stand out when that behaviour is being justified by the prevailing culture; in other words: the best place to hide a pine tree is a pine forest. And that the first, aversion, as well as the second, justification within the existing culture, did apply to

---

76. Neumann & Eberle, pp. 182–183
77. Neumann & Eberle, p. 161, 183
78. Neumann & Eberle, pp. 184–185

Hitler may be obvious. Aversion to Jews was almost common practice in Vienna and in Munich, the base of Hitler's rise to power. Den Hertog states, therefore, that Hitler, as a paranoid in his time, was invisible behind the protective colouring of the culture at that time. In order to find out whether Hitler really suffered from such a personality disorder, den Hertog looks first at the possibility whether in Hitler's case it wasn't just a question of a paranoid style of leadership, common in important leaders, that he adopted in order to have success with the voters.

In order to investigate this, den Hertog voices this interesting thought: if Hitler didn't only display paranoid traits where Jews were concerned but also in other fields, he may well have suffered from a paranoid personality disorder rather than an adopted specific style of leadership. In regard to this, den Hertog investigated situations that had nothing to do with a hatred of Jews but with other forms of paranoid behaviour such as extreme distrust, doubting the loyalty of people or feeling injured quickly. And it is apparent now from primary sources, according to den Hertog, there is hardly any witness from Hitler's entourage who didn't mention his extreme distrust. Ernst Hanfstaengl, for instance, spoke about paranoid traits in Hitler's character; in his youth he accused the state lottery of deceit when he didn't win the jackpot with his ticket; in the kitchen a guard was posted to ensure no one else but the cook came to within 10m of the stove, and near the end of his life, he even accused Dr Morell of attempting to drug him.

If it is true that Hitler displayed paranoid traits in various situations, then, according to den Hertog, the conclusion can be drawn that behind his hatred of Jewry, rationalised by himself, there was an unconscious tendency to 'interpret the world according to a paranoid model'. Paranoid Hitler wouldn't have been able to see it. There is, according to den Hertog, a connection between Hitler's non-anti-Semitic paranoia and his anti-Semitic paranoia. In other words, it matches a paranoid personality like Hitler's to distrust and hate a group of people like the Jews.[79]

It could be true. What can otherwise explain the obstinate statements in Hitler's testament that, to the amazement of his secretary Traudl Junge, consisted of nothing other than repetition of old charges against anything and everybody except against himself. Also, at the end of his life, Hitler's reaction to his generals, Hermann Göring, his doctors and anyone else he didn't trust could be proof of a paranoid personality disorder. What then to think of the way Hitler dealt with women, resulting in their various attempts

---

79. The content of this paragraph is taken from *Hitler's Protective Colouring* by Peter den Hertog

at suicide? He didn't have true friends either and that matches the image of a paranoid as well.

Without a thorough psychiatric examination, though, we don't know anything in fact.[80] The lack of such an examination in which Hitler was involved himself means that all kinds of assumptions can be voiced but we will never manage to prove that Hitler did suffer from such a paranoid personality disorder.

Chronic problems

Just like any other human being, Hitler suffered from diseases in his lifetime. Although he was ill at a decisive moment once or twice, none of these diseases was so severe they had a lasting influence on the decisions Hitler took. He did suffer from a few chronic problems, however. First, he had an intestinal disorder and consequently he was plagued by stomach cramps. Maybe tension and stress caused this disorder to develop into a chronic disease. Hitler never let himself be examined accordingly.[81] The suggestion that Hitler's cramps may well have had something to do with his vegetarianism could be true, according to Neumann and Eberle.[82] They further presume that as early as August 1941, Hitler started being plagued by symptoms indicating Parkinson's disease as his left arm began shaking, in addition to a possible heart problem, high blood pressure, problems with his vision and his teeth. Later on, his left leg started to shake as well. This wouldn't have had anything to do with his injuries from the First World War. A connection with Hitler's fall at the *Feldhernhalle* in 1923 seems out of the question as well. The assumption that Hitler suffered from Parkinson's disease is generally accepted today.[83]

There is no evidence as to Hitler's alleged addictions. The disastrous role his personal physician Dr Morell is supposed to have played in this seems to have had more to do with jealousy, distrust and Hitler's way of dealing with his doctors than with Morell's depraved nature. There was no question of a co-ordinating physician at Hitler's court, tuning the treatments of the various doctors in to each other. That role was played by Hitler himself. The discussions about all uppers and downers Hitler took is not new. Whereas in the recently discovered American report, a number of seventy-four different

---

80. See also chapter: 'Was Hitler a demon?'
81. Neumann & Eberle, p. 191
82. Neumann & Eberle, p. 195
83. Neumann & Eberle, pp. 210–215

agents are mentioned that Hitler took, earlier on Kershaw listed ninety and Neumann and Eberle eighty-two. They don't conclude, however, that Hitler had been addicted to hard drugs and they refuted claims that disease or an addiction influenced the course of the war.

It is never been proved Hitler had a psychic disorder, although Henriëtte von Schirach, who had known Hitler since her youth, thought differently. Her husband, Baldur, once leader of the *Hitler Jugend* and *Gauleiter* of Vienna, imprisoned in Nuremberg, stated his wife had said as early as 1943 that Hitler was insane. Thereby he described the 'straitjacket' of Hitler's weird day-and-night schedule he imposed on his guests on the *Obersalzberg*. At meals he seemed to shut himself off from his surroundings: he either kept quiet or started an endless monologue that should not be interrupted.[84] There are undoubtedly more witnesses of Hitler's monologues at the dinner table who questioned his communicative abilities and maybe even his mental capability, and they may even have been right, but substantial evidence is lacking.

So, Hitler can't be diagnosed with diseases, physical disorders or addictions that made it impossible for him to take decisions. Nothing of that has been established. And although den Hertog's assumption that Hitler was paranoid is likely,[85] that idea can't be confirmed by psychiatric examination of the subject himself. As ultimate evidence for whatever (mental) disease simply doesn't exist, there is also no reason to think Hitler wasn't fully responsible for the decisions he made.

---

84. Goldensohn, p. 281
85. Den Hertog, p. 219. Referring to the psychiatric publication *Diagnostical and Statistical Manual of Mental Disorders*, den Hertog writes: 'If paranoia is considered on such a gliding scale, Hitler may well be considered paranoid.'

Chapter 15

Did Hitler Really Commit Suicide?

The mystery of a missing corpse

'The headquarters of the Führer reports that our Führer Adolf Hitler, who has fought Bolshevism until his last breath in the Reichskanzlei, has fallen for Germany,' an announcer of Radio Hamburg said on 1 May 1945, introducing a speech by the new German leader Karl Dönitz. This statement was the first mistake that was made public about Hitler's death. It wasn't on 1 May he had fallen but on 30 April that he had committed suicide and he had never been on the barricades, certainly not in Berlin. Many more mistakes, deceptions and myths about Hitler's death were to follow.

The contradictions about Hitler's death that were put forward after the war in the press, by politicians, in eyewitness accounts and in books by historians, soon led to the myth that he had survived the war. The wildest stories erupted, often based on nothing more than uncertainty about his death. He could have been killed in action, murdered, escaped by aeroplane or in a submarine; he could still be alive in Spain, on an uninhabited island, in South America or in Albania. The Soviet soldiers who reached Hitler's bunker first said they had found his mortal remains, but in their later messages from the scene it became apparent he had had a double who had stayed behind in the bunker. It seemed Hitler himself had escaped. Still later, the Soviets appeared to have performed an autopsy on the almost complete body of Hitler but it became known in 2009 that the skull hadn't been his but of an unknown female.

One of the tallest stories was coined by Johannes von Müller-Schönhausen. He said Hitler survived the first months after the war and subsequently fled to Arabia, where he led the battle against the Zionists. Other wild speculations were about a Führer who had been taken to greener pastures by a V-2 or had been picked up by a UFO.

Despite shaky evidence, many assumptions about the death of Adolf Hitler and his wife Eva Braun became the subject of discussions between historians, partly caused by the growing distrust between East and West. The Soviets, who entered Berlin first and had investigated the government buildings and the bunker, had taken the most important witnesses of Hitler's final days into custody after the war but the Western Allies were hardly informed about the results of the interrogations of the survivors. Instead, during the Potsdam conference, Stalin spoke about the possibility that Hitler was still alive and that he had escaped to Spain or Argentina. Since then, serious historians and journalists have done their best to find the truth but even they couldn't stop the publication of questionable facts and conspiracy theories. There were too many uncertainties and the Soviets went out of their way to keep the West in the dark.

Hitler is alive

The German radio bulletin of 1 May 1945 in which Hitler was declared dead was taken by the Soviets as a cover up for Hitler's escape, just like the statements of the witnesses interrogated by them, who nearly all said he was dead. But the Soviets weren't consistent in their publications. On 2 May, *Pravda* published an article voicing doubts about Hitler's death, but shortly after a communiqué from Moscow revealed that Hitler and Goebbels had committed suicide. Meanwhile, the Soviets refused to allow the imprisoned witnesses to be interrogated by the Western Allies and in this period they continued to publish all sorts of contradictions in *Pravda* and in reports of the secret services.

Although the Soviets presented various corpses that were supposed to be Hitler's or showed a physical resemblance to him, Stalin said he thought the Führer wasn't dead and was in hiding, and that applied to Bormann, Goebbels and Krebs as well. These were probably intentional lies. On 2 May, General Katukov had seen the corpse of General Krebs and there was no doubt either about the death of Goebbels. Marshal Zhukov said at a press conference on 6 June that Hitler had died by poison and a corpse had been found in a corridor in the bunker, burnt by a flamethrower.[1] Because Stalin didn't agree and wanted to prevent Zhukov from making more of these unauthorised statements, he dispatched an associate who didn't leave the marshal's side. The result was that a few days later Zhukov said Hitler could still be alive. At a press conference on 9 June, Zhukov was ordered by Stalin to let it be known that the Soviets hadn't managed to identify Hitler's corpse and the possibility he had fled in an aeroplane was still open.

---

1. Joachimsthaler, HE, p. 23

When the disappearance of a large submarine was also connected to Hitler, a myth was born: with the help of Spanish General Franco, Hitler could have escaped to either Spain or Argentina.[2]

The explanation for the weird behaviour of the Soviets was Stalin himself. It was said that by suggesting that Hitler was in Spain he wanted to put pressure on the West to attack his enemy, Franco. At Zhukov's press conference on 9 June, nothing therefore was said about the statements of the witnesses who were held in custody in the Soviet Union. He also kept silent about the Soviets having found parts of Hitler's teeth. Instead, he reported that Hitler had married shortly before his death and that his corpse hadn't been identified. 'The door was wide open for speculation and the legends, lies and stories surrounding Hitler's demise were legion in the years after,' so Anton Joachimsthaler states.[3] The Soviets stuck to the idea of Hitler's possible escape until mid-1946.[4]

Heinz Linge, Hitler's personal servant who was arrested by the Soviets, had first-hand experience that they didn't believe in Hitler's death: 'A Russian lieutenant colonel, speaking German, meticulously interrogated me with endless patience, almost driving me to desperation. Time and again he asked me the same questions, time and again he thought he could convince me that Hitler was still alive. He denied my persistent testimony that I had carried the dead Hitler out of his room, doused him with gasoline in front of the bunker and set him on fire, saying I had been ordered by Hitler accordingly to save his own skin.' It got even more brutal later on. 'As someone was yelling monotonously "Hitler is alive, Hitler is alive. Tell the truth," I was lashed with a whip until blood dripped onto the floor.'[5]

Hitler's former driver, Erich Kempka, noticed that the Americans were doubtful as well when he was arrested by them after the war and dragged from one prison camp to the other. 'Each time, there was some fanatic officer who wanted to know during a lengthy interrogation what had happened to Hitler and his associates. At the time it was believed that Hitler was still alive.' The story that at least ten U-boats were standing by to take Hitler to a foreign country was also presented to him. 'Actually, fantasizers and dumb heads came running, making themselves look interesting and indicating during interrogations they had taken Adolf Hitler and his wife to some foreign country.'[6]

---

2. Joachimsthaler, HE, pp. 21–25
3. Joachimsthaler, HE, pp. 279–301
4. Joachimsthaler, HE, pp. 279–301
5. Linge, pp. 172–173
6. Kempka, p. 115

Anton Joachimsthaler, who probably wrote the best and most exhaustive book about Hitler's demise, said about this period: 'What goals Stalin might have had, the actions of the Russians clearly show that there was no confirmation in the form of Hitler's corpse. If that had been the case, the Russians wouldn't have had to exert pressure for a year to force a confession as to when, where and how Hitler would have disappeared from Berlin.'[7]

Hitler survived in Argentina[8]

One of the survival stories about Hitler is that of his escape to Argentina. Hitler, so the story goes, escaped through a tunnel connecting the *Reichskanzlei* to a subway tunnel, after which he and Eva Braun were put ashore in Argentina by a German U-boat, probably on 30 June 1945. There he found shelter in German colonies, of which many members were Nazis or Nazi sympathisers. Thanks to the support of the Argentinian government, American and English supporters, the CIA looking the other way, German money and the many Germans living in Argentina, Hitler managed to get away with this tour de force.

The argumentation as to this story also starts with Stalin's doubts about Hitler's death and the uncertainties about his corpse, but even in the West, the possibility of escape was kept open. In a speculative book by Basti and van Helsing about Hitler's flight, it transpires from FBI documents that Hitler's possible escape to Argentina was even taken seriously by the Bureau itself. That, however, and the presence of German U-boats in Argentinian waters is still no proof that Adolf and Eva were actually put ashore there. In order to prove this and the stories about the children he is supposed to have fathered there, direct witnesses, pictures and other hard evidence is needed. And that evidence doesn't exist. Meticulous assessment of the many witnesses named in said book[9] indicates that not only were most of them 'of old age or had passed away since' but that most of the stories about the surviving Hitler had been told by people who hadn't met him themselves but who knew someone who is supposed to have met him. One of the most convincing stories in the book is that by nurse Mafalda Falcon, who was present in a field nursing station in France in 1940 where Hitler showed up to visit injured soldiers. And it was exactly she who encountered

---

7. Joachimsthaler, HE, p. 301
8. This paragraph is based on Basti & Van Helsing, 2011. References to FBI reports and newspaper articles that seem to be correct were taken from their book.
9. In the book by Basti & Van Helsen, an extensive search for direct witnesses is started.

Hitler again in a clinic in Comodo in Argentina years later. But after an interesting introduction, the phantom emerges once again: the authors of the book had never spoken to the woman themselves. She had already passed away.

To take that kind of witness, of whom only a few would have met Hitler in person prior to 1945, more seriously than the direct witnesses who had worked with him, sometimes for years, and who were present in the bunker at the time of his death, is almost ridiculous. And yet, this kind of story keeps popping up today.

Hitler's last days[10]

Fortunately, there were people in the West who conducted serious investigations into Hitler's death right after the war and who didn't let themselves be misled too much by the Soviets. One of those was Hugh Trevor-Roper. Based on indications and witnesses in Western Europe, his famous report *The Last Days of Hitler* was published in 1947. In it, the English historian revealed what he had dug up about Hitler's death, based on conversations with witnesses who hadn't been arrested by the Soviets. In the West, this report became more or less the foundation of all research into Hitler's death.

Trevor-Roper says that on the morning of 30 April 1945, Hitler took part in the usual military briefing for the last time. Without any emotion, he listened to the messages about the Soviets, who were closing in fast on the *Reichskanzlei* from all directions.

At that moment, Hitler's adjutant, Otto Günsche, in response to Hitler's request to cremate his body after his suicide, dispatched Erich Kempka, Hitler's personal driver, to get 200 litres of petrol. Kempka found some 180 litres and placed the cans in the garden of the *Reichskanzlei*. In order to avoid unwanted witnesses, all those guards not on duty were sent away.

At 1400 hours, Hitler had lunch for the last time, without Eva Braun but with his two secretaries and his cook.[11] After lunch, Adolf and Eva took leave

---

10. Information in this section was taken from *Hitler's Last Days* by Trevor-Roper (7th printing, 2002). Matters which later proved to be not quite correct, are also included.
11. Hitler and Braun were married at the last moment, from then on her name was Eva Hitler. For reasons of identification and to avoid confusion about the surname of Hitler, I continue to call her Eva Braun from here on otherwise it may not be clear which Hitler is meant.

of the others in the bunker.¹² After shaking hands with all of them, they retreated into their room. Anyone who wasn't needed anymore was free to go.

After a shot was heard in the corridor, a few men entered Hitler's room.¹³ According to the witnesses¹⁴ Trevor-Roper had available, Hitler lay on a couch covered in blood. He had shot himself through his mouth. Eva Braun also lay dead on the couch. A pistol lay near her but it hadn't been used: she had died by taking poison. The time was 1430 hours.

Who exactly entered the room first isn't clear in the book. In any case, people did enter. Artur Axmann, who had arrived too late to say goodbye, entered the room later. After everyone had left the room, Axmann remained with the corpses for a while. Driver Erich Kempka, who had obtained the petrol, was informed by Günsche that Hitler was dead. According to Trevor-Roper, he also witnessed the funeral.¹⁵ Linge entered the room, where

---

12. Hitler and Braun bade farewell to Martin Bormann, Joseph Goebbels, Wilhelm Burgdorf, Hans Krebs, Walther Hewel, Werner Naumann, Hans-Erich Voss, Johann Rattenhuber, Peter Hoegi, Otto Günsche, Heinz Linge and the four women, Traudi Junge, Gerda Christian, Else Krüger and Constanze Manziarly. Magda Goebbels was not present. She remained in her room the whole day; according to Trevor-Roper she was desperate about the impending death of her children.
13. Trevor-Roper described very vaguely who was waiting in the corridor until the suicide. 'The high priests and those who were still required were waiting in the corridor.' Who heard the shot remains unclear though. 'A single shot was heard.' But who did hear the shot? It does not appear from this that Trevor-Roper was grossly speculating but that he could not make use of direct witnesses. This vagueness concerning witnesses remains throughout the whole fragment, even when Hitler's corpse was carried into the corridor. The main line of Trevor-Roper's story, however, matches with much later testimonies of Linge and Günsche, who remained in Soviet custody until the mid-1950s.
14. While direct witnesses of the suicide were either dead or in Soviet captivity, Trevor-Roper had to make do with the testimonies of Else Krüger, Traudl Junge and Gerda Christian. The first two had learned from bodyguard Otto Günsche what had happened, Gerda Christian learned it from Hitler's orderly, Heinz Linge. Furthermore, Trevor-Roper used the testimony of Erich Kempka, Hitler's personal driver, who told him, as a few other witnesses had done as early as 1946, that Hitler had shot himself.
15. Trevor-Roper, p. 179. Trevor-Roper is also vague here as it is not clear whether Kempka looked into the room or not. Probably not. He writes: 'At that moment the door of Hitler's suite was opened, and Kempka too became a participant in the funeral scene.' With this he leaves the possibility open over whether Kempka had entered the room. This, however, matches Kempka's vague statement when he told about a conversation he had with Otto Günsche when he was briefed about Hitler's death. Kempka wrote: *'Nur mühsam erfuhr ich den Ablauf der letzten Stunden. Der Chef hatte sich in seinem Arbeitsraum mit seine Pistole erschossen (...).'* 'I slowly learned about the end of the past hour. The chief had shot himself in his office with his gun.' (Kempka, p. 9) Next he describes what he saw in the room but whether he *erfuhr* – learned – it from Günsche, from someone else or saw it with his own eyes remains unclear. Later on, after the corpses had been taken away, he does say: *'Günsche und ich gingen noch einmal zusammen in das Sterbezimmer unseres Chefs.'* 'Later on, Günsche and I entered the room of our chief together once more.' (Kempka, p. 99) This 'once more' can have different meanings.

Axmann still was. They wrapped Hitler's corpse in a blanket to hide his injuries and carried him out of the room. Those present recognised him by his trousers. Two SS men carried the corpse upstairs. Next, Bormann entered the room to fetch Eva's corpse. She wasn't wrapped in a blanket as no injuries were visible. Kempka took over her corpse and took it to the stairs, where Günsche passed it to another SS man.

One of the guards, Erich Mansfeld, watched the corpses being carried out into the garden. He recognised Eva's corpse and he saw Bormann, Burgdorff, Goebbels, Günsche, Linge and Kempka standing near the bodies. The corpses were laid down side by side in the garden, which was under heavy Soviet fire at that moment.[16] They were doused with petrol. Günsche set fire to a rag and threw it onto the corpses, which caught fire immediately. All present saluted Hitler one last time and re-entered the bunker.

Another guard, Hermann Karnau, who wasn't allowed near the bunker, just like his colleagues, went there nonetheless. He saw two corpses that caught fire at that moment lying in front of the entrance. As he saw no one standing outside, he assumed somebody must have thrown a match from the entrance. Karnau walked to the spot where the corpses were burning and recognised them. He subsequently entered the bunker.

Once in a while, someone came out to throw more fuel on the fire. Late in the evening, *SS-Gruppenführer* Rattenhuber ordered an SS sergeant and three men to bury the corpses. None of them was allowed to talk about what they had seen. With a slight doubt, Trevor-Roper records the exact times in a footnote: the corpses were set on fire at 1600 hours, they still burned at 1830 and they were buried at 2300. Trevor-Roper doubts whether the corpses had burned to such an extent there was nothing left of them. The bones, which couldn't have been consumed by the fire, were never found, he writes. He assumed they had been smashed up and had ended among the bones of other corpses, such as that of Hermann Fegelein, husband of Eva's younger sister Gretl, who had been executed for treason by order of Hitler. Maybe, Trevor-Roper concludes at that moment, the remains had been put in a box that had been taken out of the *Reichskanzlei* but probably nothing was found by the Soviets.[17]

---

16. Trevor-Roper, pp. 181–182. It is remarkable that nothing is said here about a pit in which the corpses were laid. This is important as burning corpses in a pit is more difficult than on a flat surface. Later on, this was to play a role in the discussion about the mortal remains.
17. So far Trevor-Roper's report.

The survivors

In the years after the war, almost all the witnesses who had been present in Hitler's bunker had been interrogated. It took a long time, though, before information from the East reached the West. The witnesses in Western Europe who could have taken a good look at Hitler's corpse could be counted on the fingers of one hand. Prominent witnesses such as Joseph Goebbels and Martin Bormann had long since died. Hitler's most important associates who had experienced everything, Otto Günsche and Heinz Linge, were in captivity in the Soviet Union until 1955. Those who were within reach of the Allies had either gone into hiding or were telling stories that turned out to be incorrect. Even when the various reports of interrogations and other material are compared, a number of contradictions still stand out. The sometimes vague descriptions by Trevor-Roper are even contradicted, certainly in detail, or complemented by testimonies that only later became accessible to Western researchers.

Meanwhile, many survivors of the *Führerbunker* had written their memoirs, so the general public could learn what, according to them, had really happened in the bunker.[18] Of course, when read critically, contradictions stand out again. In one of the first books by a witness from the bunker who did live in the West after the war, Hitler's driver Erich Kempka, some issues were included that weren't entirely right. Five years after publication, he had to take some of it back as the most important witnesses of the events in the bunker suddenly returned from Soviet captivity.

The key witnesses were those who had been present in the room where the suicides had taken place, as well as in the garden where the cremation ceremony had taken place. On closer inspection, it turned out that Erich Kempka wasn't one of them. Rochus Misch, Hitler's telephone operator, who might have seen the bodies in Hitler's study from a distance, just like Kempka, hadn't been in the room himself either. As all the other eyewitnesses had passed away, there were only two people left in the 1950s who met the requirements: Heinz Linge and Otto Günsche. The former leader of the *Hitler Jugend*, Artur Axmann, did live in the West, although he had initially been declared dead. He had been in Hitler's room as well but he hadn't witnessed the cremation of the corpses.[19]

---

18. When writing this book, I made a choice of the existing material. In particular, I used the best-known books as, in addition to the news reels from the past, they still have the strongest influence on the 'general' opinion about Hitler's suicide.
19. The list of witnesses in the bunker is much longer, obviously. In so far as they are of any interest, they will be dealt with further down this chapter. Axmann, p. 446. Artur Axmann had been in the room after Hitler's suicide but he stayed inside the bunker when the corpses were cremated outside.

Thus, Trevor-Roper couldn't use the two key witnesses, Linge and Günsche. They were imprisoned in the Soviet Union and the Soviets had no intention of sharing the information they had with the West. That was blocked by Stalin and a political agenda.

Bezymenski and the results of the autopsies

In 1968, when Stalin had been dead for a long time and the testimonies of Günsche and Linge were well known in the West, the work of the so-called independent journalist Lev Bezymenski was published in Western Germany. It included, in addition to other matters, the record of the autopsies the Soviets had performed on the corpses that had been found during their first investigation in 1945. In a certain sense, in 1968 researchers were back at square one as to some issues because of the strange findings of this investigation.

The first investigation

The first description of a search for Adolf Hitler's corpse, which was conducted on 2 May 1945, was by a unit of Smersh, the Soviet counterespionage service established during the Second World War. The lieutenant colonel of the unit, Ivan Klimenko, had started a search in the vicinity of the *Reichskanzlei*, along with three Germans who knew the area. They were navy liaison officer Hans Erich Voss, mechanic Karl Schneider and kitchen chief Wilhelm Lange.[20] They identified the bodies of Joseph and Magda Goebbels. Klimenko decided to take the corpses with him in order to investigate them later elsewhere. The next day, other Soviet soldiers discovered the corpses of Goebbels' children and that of General Krebs. In the period that followed, the Soviets searched the bunker and its surroundings time and again. At that time, they naturally focused on the identification of Hitler's corpse. They succeeded. Parts of a jaw that had been discovered were identified by Hitler's dental technician.[21]

---

20. Kempka, from p. 121. In an appendix to Kempka's book is a long essay about the background of Kempka's story, written by Austrian extreme-right journalist and revisionist Erich Knud Kernmayer (Erich Kern). He indicates that a Soviet major named Boris Polewoj had looked at the entire bunker before Klimenko did. That took place on 2 May. Apart from the intention he might have had using this fact, it was taken from Cornelius Ryan's book *The Last Battle*. He states that Polewoj's team discovered the corpses of Joseph and Magda Goebbels along with their children in the bunker.
21. Kellerhoff, pp. 77–83

The autopsy on the other physical remains, the Goebbels family and the other alleged remains of Hitler, which were taken to the same laboratory in Berlin-Buch, was supervised by the Soviet-Jewish forensic pathologist Dr Faust Shkaravski. The conclusion of the autopsy was that corpse number twelve of those under investigation was that of a man between the ages of 50 and 60 and a height of 5ft 6in of whom the left testicle was missing. Based on the physical remains, the cause of death couldn't be determined, nor was there any question of severe injury or disease. The investigative committee did rule, however, based for instance on the smell of almonds on the corpses, that the cause of death of number twelve must have been cyanide.[22] It had to be Hitler.

In the extremely exhaustive report that can be found in Bezymenski's book, this corpse was described in such detail that it looked as if Hitler's almost complete body was in Soviet hands. Historians are doubtful though. This became apparent, for instance, from the comments of Anton Joachimsthaler, who said he didn't know 'which of the many corpses lying around at that moment was meant in the autopsy record. Certainly not the non-existent corpse of Hitler.'[23] It is remarkable that, based on the smell of almonds around the corpses, the autopsy record of number twelve, Hitler's, concludes that he died of cyanide poisoning. However, the fact that a corpse, after burning as long as Hitler's, could not smell of cyanide anymore was flatly ignored. Based on corpse number twelve and that of a woman, it was established that Hitler and his wife had died. The question remains though whether the Soviets had the correct corpses in hand.

Right after the war, contradictory statements were made about the same autopsy that were mainly politically motivated. As the corpses were being examined, Stalin wanted to exert pressure on the Western Allies with his unproved idea of Hitler's escape. The way he committed suicide, as reported by Linge and Günsche, was soon bent towards death by poison or a gun shot by an adjutant, as such a death was far less honourable than suicide by a bullet through the head.[24] The story about the missing testicle also fits neatly into this. Apparently, Stalin was much more interested in portraying Hitler as a coward with only one testicle than in unearthing the truth. It is therefore all the more strange that after Stalin's death, Bezymenski did publish a rather worthless report about the so-called autopsy on Hitler's corpse.

---

22. Marchetti a.o., 2005
23. Joachimsthaler, HE, p. 292
24. Kellerhoff, pp. 73–74

A second investigation

A second exhaustive Soviet investigation, this time headed by forensic pathologist Pyotr Semenovski, was conducted in April and May 1946, the results being published as late as 1996. This report, jointly compiled by a Soviet and a British journalist, came to be known as the *Myth Files*. It contained, for instance, the pictures of Hitler's skull that had been found in the garden of the *Reichskanzlei*. During this investigation, conducted no less than a year after Hitler's death, maps of the bunker were made, pictures taken, traces of blood were searched for and even the furniture and the spot where the corpses were found were thoroughly investigated. In a document of 30 May 1946 about the examination of the grave in which the remains are supposed to have been buried, it says that two other skull fragments were found, one of them with a bullet hole. The bullet would have entered either through the mouth or through the right temple. Pathologist Semenovski requested permission during his investigation to perform a fresh autopsy on the bodies that had been found earlier because he wanted to find out whether Hitler had indeed shot himself. Although the remains had been exhumed before and reburied, Semenovski wasn't granted permission to do so.

Of the body in the first investigation, only the jaws and teeth were transferred to Moscow. The other remains were buried. Yet, thanks to the fresh investigation in 1946, it was established that the blood type found in the bunker was the same as Hitler's.[25]

What happened to the physical remains?

As if things hadn't proceeded chaotically enough, the bodies mentioned in Bezymenski's report were reburied several times. In official literature, it is hard to find anything about it but with the emergence of the internet, anyone with a little interest in the case can trace Hitler's body on its way through East Germany.[26] Some say that the last grave in which the remains had been buried was cleared by the KGB in 1970; others claim this happened as late as 1982. Thereafter, the remains are supposed to have been cremated once again in the vicinity of Schöneberg and what was left of them was thrown

---

25. Marchetti a.o., 2005
26. *Pravda* sometimes published articles about the reburying of the corpses, for instance on its English website. On my website The Hitlerpages a list of locations can be found that are frequently mentioned in this connection. I do stress, however, that the chance of those being the actual mortal remains of Hitler is negligible.

from the Schweinebrücke into the River Ehle west of Biederitz.[27] Another version of this story came from Bezymenski again, who had stated in 1968 that Hitler's body had been cremated after the autopsy and the ashes had been dispersed in all directions. In 1992 he revoked this when he wrote that the remains had been reburied a few times and definitely burned in 1978.[28] It is very likely that there was nothing of Hitler in these remains.

With the disappearance of the remains, the discussion about Hitler's death didn't die down, of course. Although the lower jaw and other parts of the jaw were found to be Hitler's and the blood spatters could have been his, speculation still ran wild about the origin of a skull in Moscow.[29]

Contradictions and evidence

In the book *Das Ende Hitlers* by Anton Joachimsthaler,[30] all the witnesses and evidence of the last days of Hitler are dealt with exhaustively. The book is an important reaction to the years of speculation that circulated about Hitler's death. This was often the result of witnesses contradicting each other. Whereas one had heard a shot, another didn't hear anything. Whereas one said the bodies had been thrown into a pit to be cremated, another said it was done on flat ground. Various contradictory statements were made about many details surrounding Hitler's suicide that fuelled the idea in many people that Hitler wasn't dead after all.

Time

What stands out immediately when reading Trevor-Roper's report is that exact times aren't mentioned in passages where the suicide and its aftermath are being described. Apparently, Trevor-Roper wasn't sure about it, just like about other details.[31] He mentioned the times he had learned from guard Erich Mansfeld in a footnote. The bodies were set on fire at 1600 hours and burned until 1830. The remains were buried at 2300.[32]

---

27. www.hitlerpages.com
28. Joachimsthaler, HE, p. 293
29. More details below
30. The book *Hitler's End* by Anton Joachimstaler. Ian Kershaw says in his own book, footnote 155 on p. 1095 it concerns an extremely meticulous study of eyewitness accounts and the forensic evidence.
31. This appeared earlier on in the paragraph about the book by Trevor-Roper close to the fragment about who had been in Hitler's study.
32. Trevor-Roper, p. 182

Subsequent reports state different times. In the book by Erich Kempka, the bodies continued burning from 1400 hours until 1930. Linge said, however, that Hitler died at 1550[33] and that the bodies were still burning at 1930. He said further, 'others' later buried the remains in a shell crater.[34] It must be noted here that Linge didn't come back to take a look after assisting in setting fire to the bodies,[35] so he had learned from hearsay what had happened upstairs.

Artur Axmann said that 1530 was the moment when Günsche relayed the message that the Führer was dead.[36] That matches the time when, according to Mansfeld, the bodies were set on fire. It also matches the remark by Rochus Misch, who said he had seen Hitler alive for the last time at around 1500 hours. So, the bodies couldn't have been burning in the garden at 1400 as Kempka said.[37] Joachim Fest, the well-known biographer of Hitler, also mentions that time, 1530. At that moment, some thought they heard a shot and subsequently others went into the study to take the bodies upstairs.[38]

In *Das Buch Hitler*, based on the experiences of Linge and Günsche, in which the times are dealt with rather precisely, it says Eva Braun shook hands with Heinz Linge at 1510. Subsequently she went to see Magda Goebbels once more. At 1540, Linge was in the telephone exchange with a guard[39] and courier Krüger. Hitler went back to his quarters in the bunker after seeing Magda Goebbels. After two or three minutes, Eva followed her husband into his study.[40]

When comparing the times mentioned by Trevor-Roper, Kempka, Misch, Axmann, Linge and Günsche, it appears that in particular those mentioned by Kempka differ considerably from the others and those by Trevor-Roper are vague. The most important testimonies though, by Axmann, Linge and Günsche, are fairly consistent. Joachimsthaler therefore concluded that Hitler and Braun committed suicide between 1530 and 1550[41] and that the bodies were cremated at 1600 hours. This burning lasted until 1830 at least.[42] According to witnesses who came to take a look, there was nothing left of the bodies at that time.[43]

---

33. Joachimsthaler, HE, p. 177
34. Linge, pp. 158–164
35. Kershaw, Vergelding, p. 1098
36. Axmann, p. 445
37. Misch, p. 202
38. Pest, p. 137
39. Possibly Rochus Misch
40. *Das Buch Hitler*, p. 45
41. Joachimsthaler, HE, p. 177
42. Joachimsthaler, HE, p. 244
43. Joachimsthaler, HE, p. 247

In this connection, Joachim Fest points to the testimony of SS man Hermann Karnau, who established in the early evening that there was little left of the bodies.[44] If that is true, it is obvious that later on almost nothing was left of the corpses and that explains, in addition to Stalin's political agenda, the recurring question as to Hitler's death during the questioning of the witnesses in the bunker and the continual appearance of corpses that turned out not to be his. There simply wasn't enough of him left. In order to get certainty, it was of paramount importance to know how long the bodies had continued burning.

The shot and the weapon

Even before the corpses were laid down in the garden of the *Reichskanzlei*, many things had occurred that evoked much controversy later on. There was, for instance, the story by Traudl Junge, Hitler's secretary, who claimed to have heard a shot.[45] After Hitler had said goodbye to all his secretaries, Junge wanted to leave the bunker but she encountered the Goebbels' children on the stairs. As they hadn't eaten yet, she made them something to eat at a table on the landing. Around the moment of Hitler's suicide, a shot could be heard, causing Helmut, Goebbels' son, to shout 'Bull's eye!' Junge, of course, knew Hitler's intentions, in contrast to the boy, and she thought it had been the shot that killed him.[46]

Another witness, telephone operator Rochus Misch, didn't hear a shot either but wrote that somebody else might have heard one.[47] Driver Erich Kempka, who had been far off base as to certain points, did write in 1950 though that he, Bormann and Linge had heard a shot and subsequently entered the room.[48] But in a reprint of his book this remark was omitted and it said instead that he had heard Günsche say that Bormann, Linge and Günsche heard the shot themselves and then went into the room.[49] Kempka, by the way, revoked his initial statement in 1950[50] after he had learned Linge and Günsche had declared they had heard nothing.

---

44. Pest, p. 144
45. Joachimsthaler, HE, pp. 172–173. She wrote she had lunch with Adolf Hitler, Miss Manziarly, Miss Christian and with Eva Braun. It is questionable, however, whether Eva had been there. Trevor-Roper also claims she wasn't present.
46. Junge, p. 216
47. Misch, p. 204
48. Joachimsthaler, HE, p. 190
49. Kempka, p. 94
50. Joachimsthaler, HE, p. 190

It is difficult to judge whether the witnesses who did hear something had been mistaken as what they could have been heard. The *Kanzlei* was under continuous fire and it could have been that exploding artillery shells or something similar might have sounded like a shot, especially when deep down one is waiting for it. Probably, no one heard the shot. The witnesses who were closest heard nothing. Frau Junge was too far away to hear anything and Erich Kempka revoked his earlier statements. It would be strange to assume that those farther away would have been right in this case.

But if no shot was heard, then what had been the signal to cause people to enter Hitler's room? Heinz Linge, Hitler's private adjutant, who was always the one to enter Hitler's quarters in order to wake him up or bring him his breakfast, stated he had 'signed out' with Hitler for the last time and then went to the exit of the bunker. As he couldn't stay there for long, very imaginable in view of the situation, he went back to the anteroom of Hitler's study. There he smelt powder vapour. And that smell, and not the shot he heard, caused him to enter the study.

As he didn't want to go in alone, he called Bormann from the staff room, who apparently didn't know yet that Hitler and Braun had committed suicide, although he, together with a number of other prominent Nazis, sat close to Hitler's study. Bormann hadn't heard a shot either.[51]

Witnesses in the study

Hitler's quarters were located in a corner of the bunker in a square, consisting of four rooms similar in size. Facing the four rooms, Hitler's bedroom was at the back to the right. Adjacent to it was Hitler's study, where he committed suicide. In front of the study, on the left, was Hitler's living room with a staff room on the right that doubled as a chart room. Across the full width of the sitting room and chart room, there was a larger staff room that was also in use as a waiting room. From this room, one could turn to the right, straight up the stairs leading to the emergency exit; to the left there was a corridor leading to the *Kanzlei* via the front bunker. The latter was the usual way out.[52]

A description of the layout of Hitler's quarters is important as various witnesses from various positions and rooms had seen the bodies. This can lead to different interpretations, but many things have been written even

---

51. Linge, p. 163
52. Misch, maps between p. 192 and 193

about who had actually been in the study after the suicide and who went in first.

At the time of the suicide, Bormann, Goebbels, Axmann and a number of other witnesses must have been in the large staff room. Günsche stood guard at the door to the waiting room and Linge returned there a little later. As nobody heard anything from the study, everyone was waiting for things to happen. Eventually, it was Linge who, as has been said, entered the anteroom. There he smelled the powder vapour emanating from the study, which made him conclude it had happened.[53]

The early report by Trevor-Roper was still unclear about who entered the study and in what sequence. Erich Kempka's report isn't quite clear about this either but, after all, he hadn't been there when the first man entered the room. He learned from Günsche that Bormann, Linge and Günsche himself stormed into the room.[54] Traudl Junge, though, claimed Günsche had said Goebbels was the first to open the door. It isn't clear which door, the one to the anteroom or to the study.[55]

The report of the interrogations of Günsche and Linge by the Soviets had been presented to Stalin in the form of a secret document in 1948 or 1949. In it, the prominent role of Heinz Linge stands out in entering the room where the suicides had taken place. The report states that after he had been away for a while, he found Günsche at the door of the staff room, along with *SS-Obersturmführer* Frick. Linge told Günsche he thought it was over and entered the anteroom. There he smelt the powder vapour and he went back to the staff room. He reported to Bormann what he had smelled. Subsequently, Bormann and Linge entered Hitler's study. With regard to his function of private adjutant to Hitler, it is entirely logical Linge opened the door and not Bormann or anyone else.[56]

The descriptions in the secret Soviet files are in keeping with the stories Günsche and Linge told after their release from Soviet captivity. Their vision on the case didn't change, even when they arrived in the free West. Linge himself still stated he had entered Hitler's room with Bormann, who followed him in. There they saw that Hitler and Braun were dead.[57]

After Linge and Bormann had entered the room, various witnesses must have seen Hitler's body (in part) from different locations. Some entered the

---

53. Linge, p. 163
54. Kempka, p. 94
55. Junge, p. 219
56. *Das Buch Hitler*, p. 44
57. Linge, p. 163

190   The Hitler Myths

study themselves and must have seen the body, but others were watching from outside. Some had learned their information only by hearsay.

The corpses and the room

Utter confusion also arose about what was to be seen in Hitler's room. Witnesses contradicted each other and, of course, thorough police investigation, habitual when dealing with homicide, wasn't conducted. Instead, the traces of suicide were erased for a part. After all, the bodies were to be cremated. The fact that even in Hitler's room all traces were erased provides rich pickings for those devoted to conspiracy theories. Such as: was Hitler sitting in a chair or on the couch when he committed suicide? Had he shot himself through his mouth or did he have one of his adjutants shoot him? Was there perhaps a hole on both sides of his skull? Did he commit double suicide with a pill and a bullet? Did he fall forward or sideways? Where were the traces of blood? All these questions have received contradictory answers, given by witnesses who might have known something about it.

Driver Kempka wasn't clear about the position from where he looked into the room, probably to enlarge his own role. Wherever it was, he hadn't been in Hitler's study at the time the bodies could be seen there. His first testimony on this point wasn't entirely correct again. Trevor-Roper had to make do, however, with the testimonies of Kempka and of the secretaries, who hadn't seen anything themselves either. Based on these statements, Trevor-Roper concluded incorrectly that Hitler had shot himself through his mouth.[58]

In his book *Hitler's Last Witness*, Rochus Misch writes that he also took a look into the room from outside. He did admit he hadn't been able to see everything. When he stretched himself to look inside, he did see the dead bodies of Adolf and Eva[59] but later on, he couldn't say for sure whether Hitler was sitting on a chair or on the couch next to Eva; neither could he see whether there was blood on Hitler's head. He did see the head was slumped forward, though, and that was in keeping with other testimonies.[60] It must be noted here that the rooms in the bunker were so small that the furniture in Hitler's room stood close together. Thus, it would have been hard to see

---

58. Trevor-Roper, p. 178
59. Talking to the author, Rochus Misch admitted he had seen the corpses of Hitler and Braun.
60. Misch, p. 204

from a distance whether Hitler was sitting on the couch or in the chair standing askew to it.[61]

Furthermore, there were people who said they had been in the room after the bodies had been taken away. They too had seen things that could have been essential in a homicide investigation. Traudl Junge, for instance, stated that when she had 'gone down' once more, the brass jacket that had contained Eva's vial with poison had fallen to the ground.[62] Earlier on, someone had seen it lying on the table.[63] This jacket has never been found.

When more people, who had got their information mainly from hearsay, joined in the discussion, the number of contradictions became very much larger. Fortunately, after the war there were three witnesses still alive who had actually been in the room at the time when the bodies were still there. And those were, as we have seen earlier, Linge, Günsche and Axmann.

Even these three witnesses contradicted each other, though. It was mainly Axmann who had seen different things to the other two. He saw traces of blood on both Hitler's temples and, because his lower jaw had shifted slightly, he thought Hitler had shot himself through the mouth. No injuries could be seen on Eva's body. Later on, Axmann learned from Günsche that Hitler had shot himself through his right temple.[64] There was no difference of opinion between the major witnesses about Hitler's actual death but they did disagree on the method of suicide[65] and the spot where Hitler had been sitting.

Whereas Günsche said Hitler was sitting in a chair,[66] Linge and Axmann saw the bodies of Adolf and Eva slumped on the couch next to each other. As Linge must have taken the time to take a good look, the couch is more likely than the chair. Regarding the traces of blood on the armrest of the couch and the injury on the right temple, Linge and Axmann were probably right when they said Hitler had been sitting on the couch. According to Linge, however, Hitler hadn't shot himself through the mouth but through the head, contrary to what Trevor-Roper wrote and what Axmann thought. Eva had poisoned herself with cyanide, Hitler hadn't. Hitler's two weapons were on the floor and there was blood on the rug near the couch. The capsule that had contained the cyanide was on the table.[67]

---

61. Misch, p. 204
62. Junge, p. 217
63. Linge, p. 163
64. Axmann, p. 445
65. In the following paragraphs, the difference of opinion over where the bullet entered will be dealt with.
66. Joachimsthaler, HE, p. 184
67. Linge, p. 163

Linge indicated he hadn't seen Hitler's face that well, therefore he couldn't see to what extent the head had been damaged by the bullet.[68] This may seem strange in hindsight but both Günsche and Linge had such close ties with Hitler that his suicide must have left a deep impression. The image of the dead and subsequently burning Hitler must have been so unpleasant for both that they hadn't concerned themselves too deeply with all kinds of details.[69] Hitler was dead and in order to establish that they didn't need a forensic investigation.

Among the indirect witnesses in the bunker as well, the idea had taken root somehow that Hitler had shot himself through his mouth. How this conclusion, not established by an expert, could spread, is hard to determine afterwards. It could be that Axmann had already spoken about his idea in the bunker and that others had echoed him. In any case, Axmann and Kempka said Hitler supposedly shot himself through the mouth. Based on this, Trevor-Roper made it known to the world, and maybe Axmann thought it had really happened that way. Kempka, however, must have echoed someone's words. Later on, he did change his opinion on this point as in the first edition of his book in 1950 he mentioned the shot through the mouth but in the 1975 reprint this remark had been omitted.[70]

Axmann explained away Hitler's shifted lower jaw for himself with the possibility he had shot himself through the mouth, causing an explosion in Hitler's head. That way he sustained injuries on both temples, so Axmann thought. According to experts though, a shot through the mouth was no option.[71] If Hitler had done so, there should have been a hole in the back of his head and that, according to the witnesses, wasn't the case. We therefore have to assume that Hitler shot himself through his head and not through his mouth while sitting on the couch next to Eva. This was also indicated by the blood spatters on the couch.

The poison

Artur Axmann hadn't just claimed Hitler had shot himself through the mouth, he also claimed he had committed a double suicide, to be certain, by crushing a cyanide capsule first and then shooting himself. During the trial in Nuremberg, Axmann testified that Otto Günsche would have

---

68. Linge, p. 163
69. Joachimsthaler, HE, p. 183
70. Joachimsthaler, HE, p. 170
71. Joachimsthaler, HE, p. 188

told him so. After his release from the Soviet Union, Günsche denied ever claiming something like that and Axmann never mentioned it later on.[72] Yet, in 2002 Traudl Junge still stated it had happened the way Axmann had claimed.[73] In and of itself, this doesn't sound strange as in the meantime many publications appeared in which this double suicide was mentioned. One example is the book *Die Katakombe* by Bahnsen and O'Donnell from 1975. They concluded, for unclear reasons, that Hitler had simultaneously crushed a vial of poison and had shot himself.[74]

Hitler having taken poison was an idea that stemmed from two witnesses, Johan Rattenhuber and Harry Mengershausen. Joachimsthaler accused the latter many times of being a fantasist whose testimony should be judged with great suspicion. Rattenhuber still thought in 1955 he had smelled poison. Of the close associates, he was the only one who said this and, moreover, he hadn't been in Hitler's study himself. Many SS men also contradicted that there had been a smell of poison emanating from Hitler's body. Right after the suicide, nothing was said about Hitler's intoxication; not even by Rattenhuber. Various witnesses confirmed they did smell burnt almonds, prussic acid, near Eva's body. There was no question at all about that near Hitler's body.

In practice, it seems almost impossible to take prussic acid and shoot at the same time because the agent immediately stops all the important functions of the human body. Cyanide, often mentioned in this connection, is less effective than prussic acid and is sometimes mistakenly called the same thing. But then again, cyanide doesn't smell like almonds, so we can assume that many occupants of the bunker were given capsules containing prussic acid. The statement of Soviet author Byzemenski is very weird: he says that almonds could be smelled at Hitler's burnt body until four days after his death, which is absolutely impossible and an indication that the record of the Soviet autopsy is utterly unreliable.

It is also asserted that Hitler took poison and was subsequently shot by one of his adjutants or servants. But that was, as has been mentioned before, a fabrication by the Soviets that could be used to establish that Hitler was a coward who didn't die a soldier's death. The conclusion that Hitler died from a bullet and Eva from poison is by far the most likely.[75]

---

72. Joachimsthaler, HE, p. 182
73. Junge, p. 219
74. Bahnsen & O'Donnell, p. 277
75. Joachimsthaler, HE, chapter 4

The weapon

If Hitler's death could have been thoroughly investigated, without all kinds of things vanishing, then naturally an analysis would have been made of the weapon, the cartridge of the bullet and the ampoule or vial containing the poison Eva had taken. Both weapon and ampoule have never been found though. It has been said that among the corpses examined by the Soviets there was one with traces of glass in the mouth but it may be obvious that, after cremation, this could not have been either Eva or Adolf. Various witnesses saw the container of Eva's poison capsule in the room but that too vanished in the chaos directly after the suicide.

The weapon Hitler used to shoot himself to another world vanished, just like all the other arms in the room. Gerhard Welzin, Artur Axmann's adjutant, is supposed to have taken Hitler's weapons. However, he died in the Soviet Union so he never revealed in the West what happened to them. The cartridge from Hitler's gun has also been searched for but it too was untraceable. Heinz Linge is probably responsible for the removal of all these traces, along with the rug from Hitler's study.[76] The most important evidence that could be retrieved from the bunker later on were the remains of the blood that had dripped onto the couch.

The way up

After Hitler's body had been wrapped in a blanket it was carried outside, along with Eva's body, from the study through the anteroom and the staff room. Various witnesses were now able to see the bodies: Eva's uncovered and Hitler's wrapped in a blanket.

Erich Kempka declared he had seen more of Hitler's body than just his legs. He also saw his forehead, his hair and his left arm, which hung loosely from the blanket.[77] It is hard to determine whether he exaggerated his role as a witness again or he had really seen it like that. Researcher Trevor-Roper, using Kempka's testimony, concluded that only Hitler's legs could be seen.

It is unclear who was carried out first. According to Linge, it was Braun. Then the body of her husband followed.[78] There is something quite different in *Das Buch Hitler*: Goebbels, Krebs, Burgdorf, Axmann, Naumann and Rattenhuber went into the anteroom, where Linge and the SS men Lindloff and Reisser came in from the study with Hitler's body. Just his feet were

---

76. Linge, p. 164
77. Kempka, p. 94
78. Linge, p. 163

visible. Kempka was waiting in the staff room, where he took over Eva's lifeless body from Bormann. As Hitler's body was carried upstairs, Bormann and Kempka followed with Eva's body. Those present went with them.[79] In this book, the result of Linge's and Günsche's testimonies mind you, Hitler's body was carried upstairs first and later on Eva's. How can it be then that Linge stated it was Eva's body that was carried outside first. The possible confusion about this may be easy to explain as it isn't quite clear from Linge's statement whether he meant Braun's body was carried from the study to the anteroom first or was laid down in the garden first.

According to Kempka, when he and Günsche entered the garden, Braun's body was laid down next to Hitler's, a few yards from the emergency exit.[80] Bormann, Günsche, Linge, Schädle and Reisser poured part of the 200 litres of petrol on the bodies and then Günsche wanted to set them on fire with a hand grenade. In the meantime, Linge had found a piece of paper or a rag and lit the fire with it. The group remained standing behind the closed door for a while, which protected them from the flames. Then everyone went down again.

Here, Stalin's files go further than the statements from the biographies of Kempka and Linge. Attention is also paid to what Günsche did in Hitler's study, perhaps to zoom in on what happened to the evidence such as the weapon and the rug. Some curious things are also mentioned, though, which might have been interesting to Stalin in some way. According to these files, Günsche handed the weapon and Hitler's little whip to Axmann's adjutant *Leutnant* Hamann.[81] Subsequently Günsche ordered the runners Schwiedel and Krüger to burn the rug. The cartridge of the bullet couldn't be found. The painting of the Prussian king Frederik the Great that hung in his room was given to his pilot Hans Bauer, in keeping with Hitler's wish.

Kempka, who was now a direct witness to the events, indicated that in the course of the day the corpses were relit time and again.[82] After the bodies had been set on fire, Linge and Günsche didn't return to have a look.[83] The entire situation must have been very stressful for Hitler's closest associates anyway. Not only was their Führer dead, the man they had worked with for years, but they also were in a hurry to get away before the Soviets arrived at the *Kanzlei*. Despite all the uncertainties and contradictions that again existed on this point, the witnesses agreed on two things: Hitler was dead and his body, along with that of his wife, were burned in the garden of the *Reichskanzlei*.

---

79. *Das Buch Hitler*, pp. 448–449
80. Kempka, p. 96
81. Gerhard Welzin is also mentioned as the person who took the weapons
82. Kempka, pp. 98–99
83. Kershaw, Vergelding, p. 1098

Petrol

If someone wants to say something about what remained of Adolf and Eva, it is important to know how much petrol there was in and around the bunker. Most sources mention the amount of 200 litres that Kempka would have arranged. Both Linge and Günsche claimed they had ordered Kempka accordingly. Heinz Linge said, for instance, that Hitler himself had ordered him to obtain woollen blankets and petrol and he subsequently called Kempka to get it.[84] Kempka himself said Otto Günsche had ordered him to do so.[85] The name Bormann was also mentioned. He would have been the one to ask Günsche to obtain the fuel. Subsequently Günsche is supposed to have called Kempka. The former would also have been the one who had sent away the guards in and around the bunker.[86]

Naturally, these kind of weird discrepancies provoked much discussion. Why wouldn't Linge and Günsche have known who had called Kempka? Because they were lying? Because such an order was never made? Because Hitler had escaped? A remark by Hitler's pilot Hans Bauer may shed some light on the matter. He said that the *Chef*[87] had ordered him, as he had told many others, to see to it that the corpses would be cremated.[88] So Hitler, probably in order to be certain, had asked various people to burn the corpses. But of course, this doesn't explain why Linge claimed he had called Kempka as he himself said Linge hadn't. When the book in which Linge claimed this was published he had already passed away and so he couldn't answer any questions about it.

The volume of petrol is important when determining the possible burn time of the bodies as the longer they burned, the less could have been left over. The volumes mentioned were relatively close to the amount of the 200 litres claimed by Kempka. Moreover, in addition to the fuel Kempka came up with, Günsche and Linge had also taken a lot of it from the engine room, according to Joachimsthaler. Petrol was taken to the bunker from the old *Kanzlei* as well. Joachimsthaler concludes that at least 300 litres of fuel had been present in and around the bunker. So much that even a number of cans were left over.[89] This meant there was more than enough to cremate the bodies with and it was possible to keep the fire going for a long time. But in order to have the bodies consumed completely, the fire must also have been hot enough.

---

84. Linge, p. 158
85. Kempka, p. 90
86. *Das Buch Hitler*, p. 44
87. Many of Hitler's subordinates called him *Der Chef* (the chief)
88. Bahnsen & O'Donnell, p. 171
89. Joachimsthaler, HE, pp. 241–242

Cremation in a pit

Kempka was rather meticulous as to the spot where Hitler and his wife were cremated: some 3 yards to the right of the exit, near a concrete mixer.[90] He writes in his report that the fire was relit time and again and kept burning from 1400 hours until 1930. It was already apparent that Hitler was still alive at 1400 and that Kempka was mistaken about many things. He wasn't responsible, though, for another misconception: the one about the pit in which Hitler and Braun had been cremated. Kempka had indicated the spot clearly and hadn't said anything about a pit. Yet Bahnsen and O'Donnell echoed the testimony of Harry Mengershausen, who thought he had seen from a distance of seventy yards that the bodies were placed in a grave, about 3ft deep, subsequently doused with fuel and set alight.[91] This again led to a discussion about Hitler's death and this uncertainty could also be used as proof of his escape. The difference of burning material in a pit or on a flat surface is very important as burning in a pit proceeds very much slower than on a flat surface.

Linge and Günsche, however, stood close to the bodies, just like Kempka, and they said Hitler and Braun were placed on a sandy surface, close to the emergency exit of the bunker.[92] In this connection they never mentioned a trench, a shell crater or any other hole, according to Joachimsthaler. Not even later on. Only in the report of Linge's experiences, edited by historian Werner Maser, is it mentioned that Hitler's body was placed in a shallow pit next to Braun's. Whether Maser was entirely correct here or if he put words in Linge's mouth, something he did regularly, isn't entirely clear.[93]

The misconception about the pit has probably been maintained by the interpretation of the pictures showing the spot where Hitler was burned.[94] Sometimes, but not always, a pit can be seen in a chaotic environment. When these pictures were taken, however, the corpses were no longer there

---

90. This concrete mixer can be seen on many photographs of the remains of the garden of the Reichschancellry. It indeed stood near the entrance of the bunker.
91. Bahnsen & O'Donnell, p. 281
92. Joachimsthaler, HE, p. 234. From this page on, Joachimsthaler also shows Mengershausen is a very unreliable witness.
93. Linge, p. 164. When Linge's book was published in 1985, he had already passed away. Maser could be responsible for this mistake. In the book, Maser frequently puts his own theories into Linge's mouth; for instance about the visit Hitler paid to Ardooie in 1940, something Maser needed for his theory about the child Hitler could have fathered during the First World War. The confusion about Linge's phone call to Kempka and Linge carrying the body outside, mentioned earlier, stem from this book, edited by Maser.
94. Like the photographs in the books by Rochus Misch and Anton Joachimsthaler.

and of course, the pictures show the situation after the burning and not the spot Günsche, Linge and Kempka found when they still had to cremate the corpses.

The idea of Hitler and Braun being cremated in a pit means that their corpses couldn't have perished completely as they hadn't burned enough. Those assuming this apparently prefer to rely on unreliable Mengershausen than on the other three witnesses, of whom Linge said that the flames had flared up.[95] If it was true that the corpses had burned so well, then they had to have been placed on a flat surface. And if that were true, almost nothing of them must have remained. The parts of the jaw that were found, with a gold bridge, could have endured the fire, owing to the gold alloy of which it had been made.[96]

Of course, bodies have been found in pits but that doesn't mean (if they were the corpses of Adolf and Eva) that they were also burned in the pit they were found in. Yet many assume this without there being any reason for it. Even the Soviets, who had had time enough to search the grounds thoroughly, did nothing to deny this. This is not so difficult to understand, according to Joachimsthaler. Of course, the Soviets could have easily found out whether or not the corpses had been burned in a pit by having Linge and Günsche make a clear statement about it, but they didn't. Instead, they claimed time and again they had discovered an almost complete corpse that was Hitler's. If they had admitted the corpses had been burned on a flat surface and there had been enough fuel, it would have become clear immediately that the corpse on which they had performed an autopsy could never have been Hitler's and that there could have been no question whatsoever of a cyanide smell near the corpse.[97]

Autopsy and the retrieved remains

In the book by Lev Byzemenski of 1968 in which the autopsy report was included, it appeared that in the Soviet Union it was assumed that Hitler's mortal remains still existed, even after the cremation in the garden of the *Reichskanzlei*. But this, of course, was because of the strange and mendacious report of Byzemenski in which he claimed that fragments of glass of a cyanide capsule had been found in Hitler's mouth and that his body still smelled of almonds. This meant Hitler had died like a coward and not like

---

95. Joachimsthaler, HE, p. 244
96. Joachimsthaler, HE, p. 272
97. Joachimsthaler, HE, p. 242

someone who had shot himself to death. It is impossible that the totally charred corpse of Hitler still smelled like almonds, as has been confirmed by experts.[98]

The Soviets discovered a lot of bodies in the vicinity of the *Reichskanzlei* as many people had died in the area. Those bodies were also thrown into pits or buried. How the Soviets subsequently arrived at the conclusion that one of those bodies was Hitler's isn't clear. After all, none of the witnesses in Soviet hands was asked to identify a body and, apart from the fantasist Mengershausen, no one had seen the body they eventually claimed was Hitler's.[99]

In the record of the Soviet autopsy a corpse is described that was in a state similar to that of Joseph Goebbels, of whom the remains were easily identifiable, even in photographs. The bodies of Adolf and Eva, however, had been burning much longer and much more fuel had been used. Therefore, not much more can have been left of these corpses than charred bones that easily fell apart – or at least they must have burned much more than the corpses of Goebbels and his wife, of whom it was already said that her body had been burned beyond recognition.[100]

One of the reasons for assuming that almost nothing had been left of Hitler's corpse was the testimony of SS man Hermann Karnau. He said that when he went to bury the remains, the skeletons had crumbled completely. He suspended his attempts when more heavy shelling started. Karnau said he hadn't seen any bones, just ashes that had probably been dispersed by the shelling.[101] According to Otto Günsche, SS man Lindloff would have buried the remains. At least, that is what Lindloff had reported. He could neither testify about this nor about the state of Hitler's remains as he died on 2 May 1945 after escaping from the bunker.[102]

Trevor-Roper said the remains were buried by a few SS men at 2300. Maybe Lindloff had been one of them. Erich Kempka, by the way, managed to name a location: close to his home next to the garden of the *Kanzlei*. However, Kempka revoked this statement later when he said that nothing had been done to erase the traces of the cremation. The Soviet artillery fire saw to that.

During an interview with the BBC in 1955, Linge said he thought the Soviets had never found Hitler's body. He had been interrogated about the

---

98. Joachimsthaler, HE, pp. 199–201
99. Joachimsthaler, HE, p. 238
100. Joachimsthaler, HE, p. 245
101. Joachimsthaler, HE, pp. 245–246
102. Joachimsthaler, HE, p. 249

issue so many times when he was still in prison that he assumed that was the case. In the same interview, he did say though that Hitler had been buried in a simple grave in the garden of the *Kanzlei*.[103] It isn't clear if this is true. Linge hadn't been there and neither had Kempka but maybe a few SS men had buried some ashes and a few parts of his jaw.

The skull and the jaw

Little is left of the remains that the Soviets had claimed were Hitler's. The most important objects, a skull that is supposed to be his, the lower jaw and some loose parts of the jaw – the last of which his dentist's assistant had identified as being from the Führer – had ended up in Moscow. After the war, little information about these remains was shared with the West. As late as 1995, Professor Zyagin of the Russian Federal Forensic Institution claimed, after examining the skull, that the 'bullet could have been fired in the mouth or below the chin. This had made it possible to shoot and bite simultaneously.'[104] So, the idea of a double suicide still played a role. The same year, the German magazine *Der Spiegel* had the skull investigated as to its authenticity. Forensic anatomic pathologist Otto Prokop concluded the skull had probably belonged to a much younger person. As the Soviets refused to co-operate in a genetic comparison of the material of the skull to Hitler's still surviving next of kin, irrefutable evidence that the skull had belonged to someone else couldn't be found.[105] If it were true what Prokop said, the discussion about the bullet hole in the skull that would prove Hitler had shot himself through the mouth was redundant.

In May 2000, the skull fragment was displayed at an exhibition in Moscow, at which Hitler's remains were shown together with all kinds of material from the bunker. The most important evidence of Hitler's death, the jaw, was not part of it; just a picture. In 2003, historic journalist Sven Felix Kellerhof wrote in a booklet about the *Führerbunker*: 'The skull fragment that was on display at an exhibition in Moscow in 2000 is in all probability not Hitler's.'[106] Notwithstanding this – in hindsight, correct – assessment, the most recent analysis of 2009 of the same skull 'shed quite another light on Hitler's death', according to the international press. The part of the skull found during the second investigation by the Soviets was, as requested by the

---

103. BBC, 1955, YouTube
104. Marchetti e.a., 2005
105. Der Spiegel, nr. 1812000
106. Kellerhoff, pp. 77–83. Kellerhoff was not the only one who thought so.

History Channel, examined in that year by Professor Linda Strausbaugh of Connecticut University and archeologist Nick Bellantoni. DNA matching proved the skull couldn't have been Hitler's. The skull with the bullet hole belonged to a female between the ages of 20 and 40. It couldn't have been Eva Braun's either as she, according to witnesses, hadn't shot herself through the head. After examination, the blood that had been found on the couch turned out to be that of a man.[107]

At the end of the day, those who had predicted it wasn't Hitler's skull had been right after all. Much was published in the press about the spectacular information that the History Channel had unearthed, so many more people who hadn't seen the broadcast found out that the so-called Hitler skull was that of a woman. The question was, however, whether the misidentification of the skull had made the facts about Hitler's death in 1945 less secure. Holocaust historian Christopher Browning of North Carolina University commented: 'If the History Channel says that all we know since 1945 is in doubt, then that is an incorrect conclusion.' The investigator, Professor Strausbaugh herself, said something similar. According to her, the investigation didn't contradict the fact that Hitler died in the bunker, though it was hard to determine to whom the skull really belonged, she said, as the remains in Moscow hadn't been catalogued well enough.[108]

Byzemenski suggested that the jaws that were Hitler's had been broken off the skull by the Soviets themselves. Even assuming, for the sake of argument, that the jaws did indeed belong to the skull, this remains a strange story because why would the Soviets have smashed Hitler's skull to pieces?

The jaws turned up among the remnants of the thirteen to fifteen corpses that had been buried in the vicinity of the bunker and were included in the famous autopsy record of the Soviets. The jaws themselves were identified as Hitler's. Immediately after the war, Hitler's teeth were identified by Hitler's dentist's assistant, Käthe Heusermann, and dental technician Fritz Echtmann. Shortly after the suicide, they analysed Hitler's jaws and parts of Eva's teeth that were recognised as well. As a reward, they spent some ten years in Soviet captivity. For a dental assistant and a dental technician, this was a very severe sentence that can only be explained by the wish of the Soviets to keep their findings under wraps. Initially, the Western world wasn't informed about this important piece of evidence of Hitler's death.[109]

---

107. Jane Mills, AFP, 28 September 2009
108. Jane Mills, AFP, 28 September 2009
109. Joachimsthaler, HE, pp. 272–273

The lookalike and the secret passage

After the war, a story was told that there had been a Hitler lookalike in the bunker who was kept prisoner without anyone knowing about it. As the Soviets were getting too close, Hitler escaped through one of the passages connecting the bunker to the outside world. The lookalike remained in the bunker and died there instead of Hitler himself.

The story about the lookalike is suspect because it turned up only after the Soviets had shown a body that was supposed to be Hitler's but wasn't.[110] When that bubble was burst, the Soviets fabricated the stories about a lookalike and Hitler's escape through a secret passage. Although the real witnesses in the bunker, such as Heinz Linge, considered the story ridiculous, it kept popping up. In his interview with the BBC in 1955, Linge said he had never seen a Hitler lookalike[111] and, moreover, there were no witnesses who confirmed there had been a double. If indeed somebody had to take over Hitler's role, then he must have been smuggled into the bunker at some moment and there must have been witnesses who knew about the presence of this double, if only because he had to eat at some time. As is usual in a conspiracy theory, though, it was claimed these witnesses probably didn't survive the war or didn't want to speak about it later on. The secret passage Hitler is supposed to have used to escape was never there, by the way. The maps showing the various passages connecting the bunker to the outside world turned out to be forgeries.[112]

There is no evidence for the stories of the lookalike and Hitler's escape through a secret passage. The analysis by Anton Joachimsthaler, which boils down to Hitler's body being consumed by fire for the most part and the heavy shelling of the garden of the *Reichskanzlei*, remains the most likely after this and all other spectacular assumptions.

What do we know for sure?

Despite all the diversionary stories, we can conclude that Adolf Hitler and Eva Braun committed suicide on 30 April 1945 between 1530 and 1550 hours. The shot with which Hitler killed himself wasn't heard. Witnesses who claimed they did hear a shot must have been misled by other sounds. Heinz Linge and Martin Bormann were the first witnesses to see that Hitler

---

110. The pictures of the corpse of the lookalike, who seems to resemble Hitler only by his small moustache, can still be found on the internet.
111. BBC, 1955, YouTube
112. Joachimsthaler, HE, p. 40

had shot himself through the right temple. Adolf was sitting on the right and Eva on the left of the couch. Eva had crushed an ampoule with prussic acid and had fallen sideways against Adolf. Blood from Adolf's bullet wound had dripped onto the armrest of the couch and onto the floor. The gun had also fallen to the ground. The corpses of Hitler and Braun were carried out into the garden of the *Kanzlei* and cremated on a flat surface outside the emergency exit of the bunker. There was enough fuel at hand. During the cremation and the next day, artillery fire in the vicinity of the bunker was continuous. It isn't strange that almost nothing was left of Hitler's corpse, given the duration and intensity of the fire and the shelling. What had remained were the blood spatters found in Hitler's study, and it turned out they could have been from a man like Hitler. The most important pieces of evidence are the maxillary bridge in Hitler's upper jaw, the lower jaw with a number of teeth and two maxillary bridges that were Hitler's, as confirmed by a dental assistant and a dental technician.[113] These bridges, made of a gold alloy, must have survived the fire. The upper and lower jaws are kept in Moscow.

All of this can be concluded from the eyewitness accounts of Heinz Linge, Otto Günsche and Artur Axmann in particular, and from the statements of many other people who survived the bunker, helped carry and cremate the corpses or were eyewitnesses. Unless we assume that Hitler has been running around in Argentina without jaws, we have to conclude he did commit suicide on 30 April 1945.

In the maze of indications, lies and theories, it still is difficult to find one's way. Right after the war, the direct witnesses had either died or disappeared, and those surviving were imprisoned in the Soviet Union. With the degree of distrust between East and West and the whims of that other dictator, Stalin, sharing of information was poor or heavily biased. Linge and Günsche were treated so heavy-handedly in order to force them to a confession Stalin could use to prove his claim that Hitler was still alive, it is remarkable they never gave in.

The fairy tale about Hitler's survival, meanwhile, has taken root among the general public, never to disappear again. In keeping with most myths about Hitler, all the old stories, true or not, popped up on the internet from the 1990s onward. In particular, the discrepancies that occurred in all areas of the investigation are still the connecting points for conspiracy devotees. Was it so strange then that witnesses said different things? Not everyone had been in Hitler's study and the location alone, from where one looked

---

113. Joachimsthaler, HE, p. 261, 263

at for instance the burning corpses, evokes differences in interpretation. Although who was present when and what was done isn't entirely clear, this is very likely more the result of poor memory than proof of Hitler's survival.

Any uncertainty about both Hitler's death and his alleged escape could be taken away if we had DNA at our disposal of before and after the alleged death or escape that could then be compared. Even then, a theory could certainly be constructed to prove this wrong and that Hitler did indeed escape. Hitlerbunker expert Sven Kellerhoff remarked correctly that where this kind of story is concerned, people are apt to believe the fairy tale. Apparently, rumours are much more interesting than plain reality.[114]

The most important point in doubt is the skull with the bullet hole that the Soviets claimed to be Hitler's but which turned out to be of a woman. To historians, however, it was no news that the skull wasn't Hitler's and it didn't cause the investigators to doubt his death. There were jaws that did belong to Hitler. And blood spatters as well. The most important evidence of all comes from the witnesses who said, unanimously and after all those years, that Hitler and his wife had killed themselves in his study and that subsequently their corpses were cremated in the garden of the *Kanzlei*. And those witnesses had known Hitler intimately.

In 2018, a few years after the publication of the Dutch version of this book, researchers from Versailles Saint-Quentin-en-Yvelines University were granted permission to examine both the skull and the jaws once again. Their conclusion went further than this chapter because they claimed that the skull could also belong to Hitler. It was difficult to ascertain whether the skull belonged to a man or a woman, nor could the person's age at the moment of death be established. So, it could have been Hitler's. Research of the jaws proved once again that these were from Hitler. More analysis of DNA material would be required to establish the relationship between the skull and the jaws.

---

114. Kellerhoff, p. 15, 18

Chapter 16

Was the Führer Bunker Really That Strong?

The myth of Hitler's bunker in Berlin

What happened inside the Führerbunker on the last day of Hitler's life was a source of inspiration for conspiracy devotees but the bunker itself was too. The subterranean fortification is supposed to have been connected to Tempelhof airfield, to the Reichstag building, long since out of service, and various ministerial departments. With a ceiling more than 30ft thick, everyone inside was supposedly safe from bombardment. But how safe was the bunker really and what was true of the stories about the secret connecting passages between the bunker and the outside world?

Since 1935, the foundation of a banquet hall and a shelter, meant to protect against aerial attacks, was located behind the old *Reichskanzlei*, where once Otto von Bismarck and Paul von Hindenburg had resided. In 1943, an expansion to this bunker was constructed for better protection against British bombing raids. The combination of both would become known as the *Führerbunker*. Hitler would commit suicide in the most recent and deepest part of it.

The front and main bunker

It wasn't strange at all that in 1935, well before the Second World War, the first bunker was constructed. It had transpired from the First World War that because of the deployment of aircraft and zeppelins, wars wouldn't just be waged at the front. When Hitler wasn't pleased with the buildings on Wilhelmstrasse where he had lived and worked since 1933 and had them converted, the opportunity was taken to construct a bunker beneath an extension in the garden that would protect the Führer from aerial attacks. This could be considered proof of the possibility that Hitler had plans for war at a very early stage but it is hard to say whether this was the real reason for its construction.

Hitler could reach the ground floor by way of a balcony adjacent to his private quarters in the old *Reichskanzlei* and an indoor staircase to the dining room. After the construction of the banquet hall with the bunker beneath it, from 1935 he could quickly reach the safety of the bunker via the same route. The walls of the shelter, later called the front bunker, were 16 to 20in thick and the ceiling was about 5.2ft thick.[1]

The thickness of the concrete was sufficient for the first aerial attacks on Berlin in 1940 but when the city was being bombed again in 1943, Hitler ordered the existing bunker to be expanded with a second, much stronger, bunker.

Dimensions

When the second bunker was ready, nothing could be seen of it in the garden of the old *Kanzlei*, which now bordered on the new one on Vossstrasse apart from a few small buildings: a square one used as an emergency exit and two conical ventilation structures with a pointed roof. One of them could also be used as a watchtower.

After the war, all kinds of statements were made about this secretive and unknown bunker that weren't all true. Apparently, so little was known about how deep it lay and the thickness of the concrete walls that guesses ran wild. In 2003, Sven Felix Kellerhof published a booklet about the bunker, containing a number of remarkable statements about its depth and strength. A Soviet eyewitness who visited the bunker after the war said, for instance, that the roof was 12ft beneath the surface and that the ceiling had a thickness of no less than 26ft. Hitler's secretary, Traudl Junge, thought it was even thicker, no less than 36ft. According to her, the roof would have risen 3ft above ground. According to a tourist guide, the bunker lay at 39ft below the surface but it didn't say whether the roof or the floor was meant.[2]

According to Albert Speer, the bottom of the bunker was indeed a little more than 40ft below ground level and his estimates about depth and thickness of the walls corresponded best with the actual dimensions. It can be expected of an architect, though, to have an eye for such matters. Hugh Trevor-Roper was way off base with his idea that the bunker lay 50ft beneath the surface.[3]

---

1. Kellerhoff, p. 35
2. Pastfinder 1933–1945
3. Trevor-Roper, p. 96

The truth about the dimensions could, of course, only be established by taking measurements on the spot. In 1973, the GDR department of Homeland Security did just that. According to the record, the highest part of the bunker was covered with 3ft of earth,[4] the roof slab was 13ft thick, the inside height 10ft and the bottom slab 8ft thick.[5] So, the top slab was twice as thick as the one of the old front bunker and the 13ft side walls were eight times thicker. The 20in interior walls were almost as thick as the exterior walls of the front bunker.[6] The bottom of the main bunker, where Hitler had his quarters, was just 8ft below the bottom slab of the front bunker. So, the main bunker was considerably stronger than the old one but the extreme dimensions mentioned about the top slab were complete nonsense.

Subterranean passages

From the bunker, various passages are supposed to have led to all sorts of locations in the vicinity. There was one leading to the *Tiergarten*, one ran below the Wilhelmstrasse and ended up in the Ministry of Propaganda, one ran to the Ministry of Foreign Affairs, which bordered on the old *Reichskanzlei*, and one connected to the so-called Van der Lubbe passage between the *Reichstag* and the *Reichspräsidentenpalast* on Wilhelmstrasse.[7] Especially in regard to the tall stories about Hitler's alleged escape, the facts about the existence of these kind of passages are very interesting. The fact that various groups escaped from the bunker through the *Reichskanzlei* after Hitler's death and not through a subterranean passage leads to the assumption these passages weren't actually there. The passage that allegedly connected the *Reichstag* to the buildings on Wilhelmstrasse and which would have connected to a passage from the bunker probably didn't exist either. In a footnote, Kellerhof points out it would have hardly been expedient for Hitler to have a subterranean connection to the *Reichstag*, which hadn't been in use since 1933.[8] To put it even stronger, such a connection could even pose a threat if the enemy were to discover the passage. Investigation by East Germany had to provide an answer.

---

4. Kellerhoff p. 16. This is an estimate as during the 1950s earth slides had occurred in the area around the bunker.
5. Kellerhoff, p. 15–16. He names many more witnesses and numbers but the picture from various sources is clear.
6. Kellerhoff, p. 44
7. Kellerhoff, p. 17. He mentions more likely witnesses here and on p. 18
8. Kellerhoff, p. 10

Soil research in no-man's-land

After the war, the bunker was in the Soviet part of Berlin. This meant it soon became more difficult for westerners to visit the bunker. As the Soviets wanted to get rid of this magnet for tourists, they attempted to blow up the bunker as early as 1947. Luck wasn't with them as only the visible buildings were damaged. The bunker was made inaccessible though. In the late 1950s, when the new *Reichskanzlei* and been blown up and cleared away, the East German government made a renewed attempt at removing the bunker. This time they also failed to break up the concrete slab, in any case, not on the top side. The remnants of the bunker were now covered in sand, which can be seen in various pictures.[9] Further demolition of the bunker wasn't necessary as from 1961 onwards the area was part of the no-man's-land east of the wall. From the west as well as from the east, no one could reach the bunker any more, except the East German authorities. This was an advantage as well. In the area where hardly any buildings were still standing, extensive research could be conducted relatively easily into the existence of eventual passages, contrary to the situation later on.[10] After rumours about the existence of these passages, it was decided in the GDR in the 1970s to investigate whether or not they were still there, because if there was a secret passage from east to west this, of course, had to be closed off. Naturally, the *Führerbunker* was also included in this investigation. Various cellars and bunkers were found in the area but the conclusion as to eventual secret passages was clear: there wasn't a single connecting tunnel between east and west and other secret passages weren't found either.

Apartment buildings

In the 1980s, the East German government decided to erect apartment buildings on the Wilhelmstrasse on the exact location where the old *Reichskanzlei* had once stood. Construction was commenced in 1988 and that year offered the last possibility, albeit for the time being, to enter the bunker. How he managed it isn't clear but photographer Tom Posh of the British war magazine *After the Battle* was given permission to enter the site to take pictures. He was also allowed to enter the *Führerbunker*. A few other East Germans were granted the same opportunity, including for instance

---

9. For instance, on the back cover of the war magazine *After the Battle*, nr. 61/1988
10. The area around the Vossstrasse has meanwhile been filled with modern buildings, which obviously makes soil exploration impossible.

the artisan Erich Schreider. As the bunker was now being demolished for a large part, their work was of historic value.

Posh's report in *After the Battle* is therefore extremely interesting. He tells he was allowed to enter the bunker on 7 April 1988, in which work had been going on for three months to remove the various layers of reinforced concrete. The man who opened the gate of the entrance said it had taken four days to drain the front bunker to make it accessible. Once inside, Posh found various objects from 1945 such as a typewriter, wine bottles, a German army helmet and a cook book. In the room where once the Goebbels' children had been killed he found their bunk beds.

When Posh went towards the staircase to the main bunker, he had to abort his search as the stairs were completely flooded. Despite all the attention by the press, which could have caused the East Germans to prohibit any further searches, Posh was allowed to enter for a second time on 26 April. This time, the main bunker had been drained as well but Posh still didn't get much further than the stairs. It turned out that the explosions in 1947 had certainly damaged the interior. The ceiling had come down, making it impossible to enter the main bunker.[11] So, it remained a mystery what was left in it after all those years.

The end of a myth

When the Berlin Wall fell in 1989, the apartments were not yet ready but as a result of the construction, the Hitlerbunker had as good as disappeared from the face of the earth.[12] According to *After the Battle*, the roof slab of the main bunker eventually collapsed. It had taken months of work to demolish it. That wasn't caused by the top layer being 49ft thick, as a slab of reinforced concrete of 11ft was difficult enough. Sand and other material was dumped between the remnants of the exterior walls and the bottom slab. What remains of the bunker is now beneath a parking lot near a T intersection for the apartments. Almost right over the spot where Hitler had his quarters there is now a barrier at the entrance to the parking lot. Beyond it, there isn't only the parking lot but a small playground as well for the youngest inhabitants of the apartments. What had once been the garden of one of the most important buildings in Germany has now been turned into a spot where cars are parked, people take a walk and children play. Just an inconspicuous sign with information is a reminder of what once took place below ground.

---

11. *After the Battle*, nr. 61/1988
12. This part is based on Kellerhoff, pp. 84–98.

Chapter 17

What Happened to Hitler's Remains?

The myth of the Schweinebrücke

Hitler was dead. His remains, if they belonged to him at all, had been examined by the Soviets time and again. Subsequently, they had been buried somewhere in East Germany, together with the remains of other inhabitants of the bunker. Naturally, this situation couldn't last forever. If old or new followers of Hitler found out the chances were that they would turn his burial site into a memorial. Therefore, the Soviet secret service decided to have the remains disappear for good. This was certainly strange because why had the so-called skull of Hitler and his identified jaws been transferred to Moscow and why had the rest of the corpse been cremated?

In the chapter about Hitler's suicide, it says that not much was left of the corpses of Adolf and Eva after they had been cremated. Not everything about it has been said though. The entire route of the remains of the various inhabitants of the bunker including, some say, those of Hitler as well, can be traced through East Germany on various websites. That *only* the remains of the Goebbels family and a few other people are probably meant is often omitted.

A garden in Berlin-Buch

When the shelling of Hitler's *Reichskanzlei* had stopped in May 1945, there were several corpses in the garden. These included those of Adolf and Eva and almost the entire Goebbels family. The corpses, or what was left of them, were transferred to a pathology clinic in the suburb Berlin-Buch, where autopsies were performed. Subsequently, they are supposed to have been buried in the garden of the clinic. How long they remained there is hard to say but it is supposed to have only been for a short while. They were soon exhumed and relocated. The parts of Hitler's jaws and the skull, which was assumed at the time belonged to Hitler, were no longer among the remains.

Finow, Rathenow and Magdeburg

The remains were reburied in the vicinity of a base of Smersh, the Soviet counterespionage service, near Finow in East Germany. They didn't remain there for long either. It is completely unclear why. The reason they were taken shortly afterwards to Rathenow, yet another city in Brandenburg, to be reburied there, is unknown. In Rathenow they remained for a short while as well. It seems that they had been exhumed once more as early as February 1946 and they were subsequently taken to Magdeburg. On the Smersh base on what is now the Klausenerstrasse they were buried for the umpteenth time in the courtyard. There they would remain for twenty-four years, until April 1970.

The Schweinebrücke

In 1970 it was decided to exhume the remains once again. The head of the Soviet secret service, Juri Andropov, is supposed to have been responsible for this. It is said Andropov was afraid it would become known who had been buried there as construction was to start on the premises. The remains now had to be destroyed permanently. Agents of the KGB took them to an open field near Schönebeck, where they were subsequently burned. What was left after this cremation was either thrown into a canal near Biederitz or dumped into the River Ehle. One of the versions is that the ashes of Hitler and others had been thrown into the Ehle from a small bridge. Entirely in keeping with a good Hitler myth, this little bridge was named *Die Schweinebrücke* or Pigs Bridge.

With the destruction of the material, a lot of evidence for Hitler's death or, of course, the evidence that there hadn't been any of his remains among them, were gone forever.

A myth with a nucleus of truth

If it were true that there were still remains of Hitler among the material disposed of and if it were true that they had been thrown into the river from the little bridge, then the ashes of a man who, in his own myth *Mein Kampf* and by a 'lucky twist of fate'[1] had been born in a village on the border between Austria and Germany, was eventually thrown from the even more symbolic *Schweinebrücke* and had disappeared in another river. But there is

---

1. *Mein Kampf*, p. 1

hardly any proof that it had been indeed Hitler's remains that had been reburied in the states of Brandenburg and Saxe-Anhalt. It is crucial here that the material that was supposed to be Hitler's was in Moscow at that time and that nothing of him was found later on. Among the remains that had been buried for the first time in Berlin-Buch, there had been no corpse of Hitler.[2] Moreover, reliable sources that explain why the remains were moved around time and again are hard to find. An article about this from 2009 on the website of the German paper *Die Welt*, for instance, is based on statements by the head of the KGB archives in Russia, who doesn't do much else than what his predecessors did, namely create confusion.[3]

It speaks for itself that human material from the garden of the *Reichskanzlei* was taken to a clinic where an autopsy could be performed.[4] The reburial in Finov and Rathenow has also been confirmed by historian Joachim Fest. But it is still a mystery about what exactly happened in the vicinity of Magdeburg in the 1970s. Fest confirms that material was burned in the vicinity of Magdeburg but he also states it was very likely there was nothing of Adolf Hitler or of his wife in the caskets containing the physical remains.[5]

---

2. The chapter 'Did Hitler commit suicide' contains more than enough reasons for strong doubts.
3. The chief of the archives, Vasil Khristoforov, claims, among other things, that the American researchers who investigated the DNA of the skull, ostensibly belonging to Hitler, never received this DNA.
4. Berlin-Buch is also mentioned in *Der Untergang* by Joachim Fest, p. 186.
5. Fest, p. 187

Chapter 18

Hitler's Testament

The intriguing story of his last will

'On April 30, 2011, it was exactly 66 years ago that British soldier Herman Rothman (now aged 86) penetrated the bunker to find Adolf Hitler. He had just killed himself however, but Rothman found his testament.' This could be read on the website of the German newspaper the Berliner Kurier from 29 April 2011 onwards. A curious story. On the day of Hitler's suicide, Rothman, a Jew who had escaped from Berlin, supposedly returned there, reached the bunker and found Hitler's testament while everyone who could do so fled the other way, out of the bunker and out of Berlin.

There isn't a single serious source dealing with Hitler's testament that mentions this absurd story. It must have been a fantasy of the journalist that lay at the roots of this incredible piece of journalism. Rothman had made headlines as he had written a book about his role in finding Hitler's testament. In it, he told the real story. The spectacular adventure of a British soldier entering Hitler's bunker although it was still crowded with Germans doesn't appear in it. Directly after Hitler's death nobody, not even Rothman, knew that Hitler had left one text behind: his testament was signed on 29 April 1945 at 0400 hours, one day before his suicide.

Hitler's secretary

Hitler dictated his testament to his secretary, Traudl Junge, the day before he was to marry Eva Braun. Shortly before the ceremony, around midnight, Junge was sitting in Hitler's room with a shorthand notepad. After Josef Goebbels had added a statement of his own, she typed the text. According to Rochus Misch, she did so while sitting in the telephone exchange with him.[1] However, Junge said this was done in the common room near Goebbels'

---

1. Misch, p. 199

quarters.² Both spaces were close to each other. The testament was copied, signed in triplicate and subsequently distributed in 'various directions'. According to Junge, three men would see to it that Hitler's testament was smuggled out of Berlin: his Luftwaffe adjutant *Oberst* von Below, Heinz Lorenz and Bormann's associate, Wilhelm Zander.³

Junge made a mistake here though. It wasn't von Below but Willi Johannmeier who went on his way with a copy of the will. Von Below left the bunker the same day but much later than the couriers. He had also something else with him but this was a letter from Hitler to *Feldmarschall* Wilhelm Keitel, not a copy of the will.⁴ Junge probably misunderstood this.⁵ The names of the three men with the testaments were known long before publication of Junge's memoirs in 2002. Army adjutant Willi Johannmeier was to take a copy of the will to *Generalfeldmarschall* Ferdinand Schörner in Czechoslovakia. Zander, *SS-Standartenführer* and Bormann's adjutant, was to report to Admiral Dönitz in northern Germany with a copy of the will in which he had been appointed president. It was expected of the deputy *Reichspressechef* that he would then take the will to Munich. There, the documents would be preserved for posterity. Lorenz had the original will with him.⁶ All three couriers were to hand over the document in person.

The content of the will

Hitler's will consisted of a personal and a political part. In the first part he thanked Eva for her loyalty. She was to join him in death as his wife, in keeping with her own wish. It must have been strange for Junge to take this dictation. The document continues with Hitler's possessions: about paintings that had to go to Linz; about Martin Bormann, who was to be his executor-testamentary; and about next of kin and associates who were to receive unspecified goods and money after his death.

According to Kershaw, the political testament is no more than a self-justification but he also sees a reference to the Endlösung.⁷ Hitler says he

---

2. Junge, pp. 212–213
3. Junge, p. 214
4. Kershaw, Vergelding, p. 1083
5. The Wikipedia page in German has repeated Junge's mistake about Hitler's testament. Von Below is not mentioned on the English page about Heinz Lorenz.
6. Trevor-Roper, pp. 165–167. Ian Kershaw and Herman Rothman confirm that these three people were involved. The latter and his team were probably an important source for Trevor-Roper.
7. Kershaw, Vergelding, p. 1078

didn't want the war himself: international Jewry was responsible for that. Next he repeats his warning towards the Jews he voiced years ago. Didn't Hitler say once that the race responsible for this murderous battle would atone for it?[8] Apparently, Hitler wanted to stress once more that his prediction had come true but with this he did acknowledge in so many words that he knew very well what had happened to the Jews? Further, Hitler named the members of the new government: Dönitz was to become *Reichspräsident* and Goebbels *Reichskanzler*. Göring and Himmler were banished from the party.

The original will contained an appendix by Josef Goebbels in which he indicated that he was going to ignore an order by his Führer for the first time in his life. He wasn't going to take up his new job as head of the government and he wasn't going to leave the capital either but was going to end his life at the side of his leader. Goebbels said about his children, who could not speak for themselves yet, that if they had been old enough, they would without any doubt have agreed to his decision. A few days later, soldiers found the corpses of the entire family in the garden of the *Reichskanzlei*.

Escape from Berlin

The couriers left the bunker in Berlin at 0800 hours[9] with their escort, *Unteroffizier* Hummerich. Ian Kershaw called it an 'extremely dangerous and useless mission'[10] and as the Soviets had surrounded the city completely, the men themselves must have doubted their chances of survival. Johannmeier and Zander, still in uniform, left the *Reichskanzlei* through the garages on the Tiergarten side. It isn't quite clear how but the foursome managed to cross the city swarming with Soviet soldiers to end up on the west side of Berlin. From Pichelsdorf, the men sailed in two boats to the Wannsee, where they hid in bunkers throughout the day. At dusk, they left in the direction of the *Pfaueninsel*, an island in the River Havel. It was 30 April, the day of Hitler's death.

On the island, the men managed to obtain civilian clothing and to make radio contact with Dönitz. They gave their position and asked for an aeroplane to rescue them. The plane didn't arrive at once and the island was shelled by the Soviets instead. The four men fled from the island in a canoe and ended up on a yacht that was drifting around. Eventually, the plane arrived and two men even managed to reach it but as they wanted to fetch

---

8. Kershaw, Vergelding, p. 1079
9. Joachimsthaler, HE, p. 149
10. Kershaw, Vergelding, p. 1082

Johannmeier, who had guided the plane in with a torch from the yacht, they came under fire and the pilot took off without his intended passengers.

At that moment, the couriers could do nothing more than stay on the island. When things had quietened down a few days later, they left in the direction of Potsdam and from there they attempted to reach the River Elbe. The British zone was beyond the river and when they had reached it, Hitler's will ended up in the western part of Germany in triplicate. However, no one else knew about the existence of a will and, according to Johannmeier, Lorenz and Zander, their mission had become useless after Dönitz had surrendered. Therefore, the men decided to hide the documents and continue their lives one way or another. Zander sent his documents to Bavaria in a suitcase, where they were hidden somewhere near Tegernsee. Using the alias Friedrich Wilhelm Paustin, he tried to start a new life. Johannmeier went to his next of kin in Iserlohn in Westphalia. He put the copy of the will in a bottle and buried it in the back garden of his family. Lorenz adopted a new identity and for the time being went through life as a journalist from Luxembourg.[11]

How the testaments were found

How events with the testaments unfolded further is told by, among others, Hermann Rothman, a soldier in the British army who, as a Jewish boy, had escaped from Berlin to England and was, of course, fluent in both German and English. In the army, Rothman had been given a job as interpreter, interrogating German prisoners in a camp in Fallingbostel in northern Germany. When in the autumn of 1945, the phone rang at 0500 and Rothman had to report to the office, he became part of the Hitler history. A man had been apprehended under extremely suspicious circumstances and the documents he carried had to be translated. It turned out to be Heinz Lorenz, Goebbels' chief of press, travelling under his alias as a journalist from Luxembourg. A report of the British secret service said that he was living in the British zone under a false name, Georg Thiers. As the war had ended a few months earlier, Lorenz decided the time had come to make the important documents public. To that end, he contacted the British in Hanover, telling them he had important information about details from the Hitlerbunker. As he couldn't say much more without blowing his cover, he was arrested. The circumstances of his arrest are not entirely clear. It was also said he was arrested while trying to cross the border between the Soviet

---

11. Trevor-Roper, pp. 167–168

zone and a western sector in Berlin but what he was doing there isn't entirely clear and a connection between the story of the contact with the British in Hanover and his arrest remains unclear in Rothman's book. Anyway, Lorenz ended up in Fallingbostel, where he admitted he wasn't Georg Thiers and the original will and Goebbels' appendix were found in the shoulder lining of his coat. It was soon found out that there had to be two other copies of the will.

The search for the other two men could now start. Zander wasn't with his wife, who had gone to her parents in Hanover. She said she thought her husband wasn't alive anymore. He was living in Aidenbach, however, in the home of Martin Bormann's secretary. On his arrest, he told the agents he had sent the documents to friends in Bavaria in a suitcase. When they were found, it turned out they contained Hitler's wedding papers as well.

Johannmeier was found in the house of his parents in the British zone in Iserlohn, Sauerland. Although he denied it initially, he eventually admitted he was in possession of one of the copies of the will. He had buried them in the garden of his parents in a bottle.[12]

A chaotic end

The interpreters and interrogators in Fallingbostel were given strict orders by the British authorities to keep the findings secret. This could only be maintained for a short while as American newspapers suddenly reported that Hitler's testament had been found. The US authorities who were aware of the case had proved to be more loose-lipped. Further secrecy by the British became senseless, of course.

Today, various versions of both testaments, the wedding papers, Goebbels' appendix and pictures of accompanying notes by Burgdorf and Bormann, can be found on many internet sites and many publications appeared about the contents. The original version of the testament, carried by Lorenz, is in the Imperial War Museum in London, while both copies can be found in the US National Archives in Washington DC.

The period at the end of the war was chaotic and that makes it imaginable that, with regard to Hitler's testament, small mysteries continue to exist. Traudl Junge was responsible for the notion that von Below had a copy of the will but this misinterpretation was understandable. Moreover, some confusion existed about where the various testaments had to go to, but that

---

12. Rothman, pp. 98–110

has been cleared up in the meantime as well.[13] At the end of the day, the only thing remaining is the weird story in the *Berliner Kurier*, in which Rothman more or less achieved the unachievable. It was utterly impossible for a British soldier to enter Hitler's bunker on 30 April, and anyone writing about Hitler should have known that. Goebbels committed suicide as late as 1 May and on 2 May, the Soviets captured the *Reichskanzlei*. If the Germans were still defending the bunker, how then could Rothman have entered it to find the testament? In Rothman's own book he doesn't say anywhere, of course, that on 30 April 1945 he had been anywhere near the bunker. This story then is a journalist's fabrication as well. The testament had been taken away on 29 April by Lorenz, Johannmeier and Zander and Rothman was only responsible for the translation of it.

---

13. Joachimsthaler, p. 149. General Burgdorf sent Willi Johannmeier to Generalfeldmarschall Schörner, Martin Bormann sent Wilhelm Zander to Dönitz and Joseph Goebbels had Heinz Lorentz go to the Braune Haus (brown house) in Munich.

Chapter 19

Was Hitler a Demon?

The Führer as the symbol of the ultimate evil

The famous American author Will Smith triggered a global row in 2007 when he remarked about Adolf Hitler that even he wouldn't wake up with the idea to go and do the utmost worst that day that he could think of. Smith thought Hitler had a kind of peculiar lopsided logic, fooling himself that what he was doing was the right thing to do.[1] This statement had been twisted in the headlines of various internet messages in such a way that Smith would have said literally that even Hitler thought to do well. It is an idea that has also been discussed seriously by renowned historians, psychologists and philosophers since the end of the Second World War.

Discussions about Hitler have always been in the extreme. In pre-war Germany he was the infallible genius and the servant of providence who came to save Germany. In foreign countries people talked about Hitler as if he were the Satan himself, and his devilish image in particular dominated all of Europe after the war. This demonisation of Hitler is brilliantly illustrated in the novel *Siegfried* by Harry Mulisch in which the leading character undertakes an ambitious search for the person Adolf Hitler. In this book he digs so deep into this matter that he even meets his end. Hitler is called a nonentity, a manifestation of the Nothing and a meta-natural phenomenon in the novel: 'After the death of God, Nothing stood at the door and Hitler was his only son.'[2]

Will Smith's example shows that Hitler is still the icon of evil for many people. Even the most cautious suggestion that Hitler thought of himself to be good is sure to trigger immediate disapproval. That is understandable because if Hitler were someone of extraterrestrial evil, he stands so far away from normal people that it causes some sort of peace of mind. And although a satanic Hitler is much more frightening than a human Hitler, the first image

---

1. Quoted on websites such as people.com, huffingtonpost.com and dailymail.co.uk.
2. Mulisch, p. 177

is apparently preferred over the image of a Hitler who resembles us more than we would like. But what was Hitler really? A servant of providence, the only son of the satanic Nothing or a human being of flesh and blood who perhaps thought he did well himself? And that is precisely the key question of a 'dangerous' discussion about Hitler.

Teppichfresser

A well-known but never entirely clarified misunderstanding about Hitler involves his nickname *Teppichfresser* or carpet-eater. One of the first sources of this nickname must have been William Shirer, an American journalist who was correspondent in Berlin until 1940. He heard the nickname for the first time in 1938 in Bad Godesberg, where a meeting between Adolf Hitler and the British Prime Minister Neville Chamberlain was to take place about the Czechoslovakian issue. Hitler wanted to annex parts of Czechoslovakia, whereas Chamberlain only wanted peace in Europe. Prior to the meeting, Hitler is supposed to have been so edgy, he was close to a nervous breakdown and Shirer learned from his German companion that the Führer frequently rolled about the floor during a bout of rage, chewing up the carpet.[3] There is no real evidence for this story. Shirer had also never seen Hitler do this and since then the story has usually been presented by historians as a curiosity. The Jewish-German philosopher and author Victor Klemperer considered the story a legend,[4] and that is probably true. Another, more plausible, explanation for this nickname pointed to Hitler pacing around while dictating, resulting in traces of wear in the carpet. Perhaps this typification of Hitler was subsequently misunderstood and added to the popular stories about the bursts of anger of the Führer.[5]

In the meantime, dozens of years have passed but the story still circulates. It is sometimes used as proof of Hitler's so-called psychic disorder or his demoniacal possession. The same quote about Hitler as a *Teppichfresser* appears on the websites of various Christian organisations. He is supposed to have earned this nickname as he, in his satanic frenzy, tore up entire rugs. 'The extraordinary physical force he displayed is a clear sign of influence by the powers of the dark.'[6] This statement can also be found on the forum

---

3. Shirer, p. 349
4. Klemperer, p. 69
5. Kershaw, HM, p. 187
6. www.franklinterhorst.nl, groups.omnichat.com, www.stormfront.org

of the ultra-right website Stormfront, where a somewhat puzzled forum member asks about the truth of the matter.

Another version, equally unbelievable, is told on the internet by a forum user who claims his story is first-hand knowledge, as is usual with many Hitler myths. Apparently, this isn't quite right. In the 1960s, the *brother* of said internet user was engaged to a *girl* whose *mother* had been Hitler's housekeeper. The mother would have stated that Hitler, when having a bout of rage, fell down on the floor chewing up the carpet.[7] It is striking that on the same website there is a similar story but this time about the *grandfather* of an unknown forum user. With that, we're back at the alleged origin of the story: unfounded gossip.

Stories like this tell little about who Hitler was. The satanic powers attributed to him only distort the image we have of him. The literal demonisation[8] and the identification of Hitler with a supernatural form of evil can lead to the result that people who dare call Hitler a person who perhaps thought to do well are immediately driven into the politically incorrect corner. This was already apparent from the worldwide reactions to Smith's comments but it also applies to those who thought that Hitler was presented as being too much of a human being in the movie *Downfall*.

Demonisation – Lukacs about religion

Demonising Hitler isn't only unrealistic, it is also a way – albeit unwanted – to exonerate him. If Hitler were possessed by the devil, then he was, for a part anyway, not responsible for his actions. Historian John Lukacs therefore pointed out the necessity of a Christian viewpoint of Hitler regarding the far too easy mystification of evil. In doing so, he criticised the statement of Pope Pius XII, who spoke about the 'satanic ghost image of National Socialism'.[9] It is hard to blame believers to believe in the devil but Lukacs stresses that the tendency to attribute 'demonic or satanic characteristics' to Hitler can be rejected within religion as well. The 'satanic ghost image' the Pope spoke about had, after all, a human embodiment; just like the

---

7. andrewhammel.typepad.com
8. Someone who is being 'demonised' is compared to a demon, a devil. It was said about the Dutch politician Pim Fortuyn that he was being demonised. Actually, he was compared to Hitler. It is probably revealing that a step was missed here. Hitler is probably so strongly identified with the devil that it was not understood that Fortuyn was being 'Hitlerised' and not literally 'demonised'. But what is the difference when we carry an image of Hitler, the devil, in our own heads?
9. Lukacs, p. 253

antichrist, the predicted manifestation of evil in the Bible that will not appear as a gruesome monster but will appear as an idol being worshipped by a mass of followers.[10] In the prologue to his book about the history of Hitler, Lukacs says: 'It is all too true that with demonising Hitler, a lot of questions are being ignored and the whole "Hitler problem" is being swept under the rug.'[11]

Historians about evil

Of course, research by historians, psychologists and philosophers about the nature of Hitler's evil continued nonetheless, despite all the complaints about the explanations themselves. The question of what Hitler thought about himself was the subject of an important exchange of views. That exchange was dealt with extensively in Ron Rosenbaum's book *Why Hitler* and in other books.

During the research for his book, Rosenbaum asked various people who explain Hitler, these questions: 'Do you consider Hitler evil?' and 'Did he know he did wrong?', and got very different responses.[12] The biographer of Hitler, Alan Bullock for instance, reacted with: 'If he wasn't, then who was?' but Bullock indicated that Hitler wasn't some sort of occult Messiah or demon, but a shrewd and capable politician. Historian Yehudi Bauer, an expert on the subject of the Holocaust, believes: 'Hitler stands for the *near extreme evil*.'[13] Yet Bauer considers Hitler's homicidal attitude 'unusual' but unfortunately 'not abnormal'.[14] Another biographer of Hitler, Hugh Trevor-Roper, answered Rosenbaum's question whether Hitler was aware of the evil he did: 'Oh no, Hitler was convinced of his sincerity.' And Efraïm Zuroff, head of the Simon Wiesenthal Centre's main office, said: 'Of course not! Hitler thought he was a doctor! That he was killing bacteria.[15] As to theologian Emil Fackenheim: 'Hitler was way out of any known category of humanity and there was an enormous void between usual evil and Hitler's "radical evil".'[16]

The assumption that Hitler thought himself to be sincere in one way or another is imaginable. Some assume though, he actually was.[17] This is

---

10. Lukacs, pp. 253–254
11. Lukacs, p. 10
12. Rosenbaum, p. 20
13. Rosenbaum, p. 19
14. Rosenbaum, p. 345
15. Rosenbaum, p. 20
16. Rosenbaum, p. 345
17. Will Smith was incorrectly blamed for the latter.

Was Hitler a Demon? 223

exemplified by author David Irving. He uses, for instance, Hitler's missing order for the *Endlösung* to prove the idea that he didn't know anything about what happened to the Jews. Irving did call the death of so many Jews criminal but not genocide as the Jews in the camps had supposedly mainly died of hunger and diseases. In his view, that means it wasn't premeditated murder that was going on in Auschwitz. 'It was just like killing by neglect. Hitler was so sloppy he didn't realise it could have been the result of his speeches. You can also look at it that way.'[18] The mood of destruction and aggression on the Eastern Front could also have been caused by the Allied bombing of Germany, he claimed.[19] In the opinion of Irving and his kindred spirits, Hitler wasn't so bad, apparently. It was Irving himself who made his role as a serious historian utterly untenable. John Lukacs, for instance, typified the amateur historian Irving as someone who 'evolved from young Germanophile to rehabilitator of Hitler and subsequently to his unshakable admirer and follower'.[20]

Witnesses of Hitler's evil

The people who had known Hitler in life also had different views on who he was and on his degree of evil. A small number of them, including Albert Speer and secretary Traudl Junge, displayed some kind of repentance.[21] In 1969, for instance, Speer said that when he had been admitted to a sanatorium in early 1944, he turned away from Hitler. When Hitler came to visit him, he would have suddenly noticed his tacky head, his broad nose, the yellowish colour of his skin and his puffy face.[22] This physical aversion may have been caused by something else though. Hitler had put his rival, Xavier Dorsch, once Speer's subordinate, in full charge of the most important government organisation for construction, the *Organisation Todt*. Speer took this very personally and therefore he said about Hitler's visit: 'As if friendship can be turned on and off with the flick of a switch.'[23]

---

18. Rosenbaum, p. 300
19. Rosenbaum, pp. 298–300
20. Lukacs, p. 220
21. Gilbert, p. 21. There were more 'converts' but sometimes it is difficult to take them seriously. It turned out that Hans Frank, the lawyer and former Governor-general in the occupied territories in Poland, and as such responsible for the deportation of Jews, had converted to the Catholic faith during the International Military Tribunal in Nuremberg.
22. Fest, OV, pp. 113–114
23. Fest, OV, pp. 114–115

The definite turning point in Speer's vision of the Hitler years came, as he himself said, on 29 November 1945 when during the Nuremberg trial against the Nazis, a film was shown about the concentration camps. From that moment on, Speer took into account he could well be sentenced to death 'and couldn't discover nothing unjustified in that'.[24] His vision caused arguments and vehement rows with the other Nazis standing trial, in particular with Hermann Göring. Speer said about him: 'Göring should have been enraged when Hitler led the entire country straight into the abyss. (...) Instead, he sedated himself with morphine and scoured all of Europe for works of art.'[25] All sorts of things can be said about Speer's role but in any case, he publicly revised his view on Hitler and National Socialism, contrary to Göring who never showed repentance. After the war, others left unspoken what they thought of Hitler or indicated they mistrusted Speer's change of opinion or called it hypocritical.

Long after the war, there were various persons from Hitler's circle, apart from Göring, who either never condemned him or still admired him.[26] A rather interesting statement about how Hitler dealt with evil was made by his hardly remorseful secretary, Christa Schröder, during a talk with David Irving, when she told him that Hitler is supposed to have told her after the Night of the Long Knives: 'You see, Fräulein Schröder, I have taken a bath and I am just as clean as a newborn baby.' For Hitler's former secretary, this must have been proof of his cruelty.[27]

Traudl Junge remained troubled with the two sides of Hitler until long after the war. The Hitler she had known had been the man who seemed to care about her well-being but also the man she had begun to hate near the end of the war and the man who 'inflicted suffering on millions of people with his boundless destructive drive'.[28] Junge would never get free from her past with Hitler, although she rejected National Socialism very strongly after the war. She doesn't tell the story of a satanic Hitler though, but of a human being of whom she, even initially, didn't see the bad characteristics.

Rochus Misch, the last witness of Hitler's death, who passed away in 2013, did away with both Hitler's positive enlargement as well as the negative in his biography by saying: 'I have neither seen a monster, nor an *Übermensch* (...) In private, Hitler was a normal man, the simplest man I knew. Only

---

24. Fest, SH, p. 412
25. Fest, SH, p. 414
26. Lukacs, pp. 217–219
27. Rosenbaum, p. 294. During an interview, David Irving told this story to Ron Rosenbaum. Rosenbaum questions his source but considers the story credible.
28. Junge, p. 246

outwardly did he play his role of Führer, then everything had to proceed according to protocol and the staging had to be perfect.'[29] In his view, Hitler was a normal human being, not the chosen one or a devil.

Various Nazis who stood trial in Nuremberg after the war made statements about who Hitler had been in talks with psychiatrist Leon Goldensohn. Hitler's successor, Karl Dönitz, didn't believe Hitler had ordered the extermination of the Jews,[30] but he also said: 'Hitler was good, although I thought so until all those cruelties came to the surface after the war.' It may be likely that Dönitz' statements were part of a defensive tactic during his trial, yet he paints a picture of an ambiguous Hitler, like so many others who knew him. A Hitler who appeared to be good but turned out to be very cruel at the end of the day. But even Dönitz didn't mention a satanic or extraterrestrial Hitler.

During a talk with Goldensohn, *Feldmarschall* Wilhelm Keitel was asked whether he saw Hitler as the devil. He answered: 'Yes, he was a demonic man with extraordinary will power; once he had something in his head, he had to achieve it, no matter what.' But Keitel's remarks show the two sides of Hitler as well: 'He was charming, he loved kids and he enchanted women. But in political matters he met everything head on.'[31]

Prison psychologist Gustave Gilbert also talked with the defendants in Nuremberg. Hans Frank, the governor-general of the occupied territories in Poland, mentioned Hitler's satanic evil during such a conversation but he nuanced it with a somewhat strange remark: 'In the beginning, I had an alliance with the devil. Later on, I noticed he actually was a tough psychopath devoid of feelings.'[32]

According to the defendants, Hitler was brutal, satanic and he had an enormous will power, but he also was modest, charming and intelligent. Even after his death, it remained impossible to see him as a normal human being. This applied to the Allies, who emphasized his satanic side in particular, as well as to the Nazis, who continued pointing to his genius. Those who stood trial in Nuremberg could hardly do anything else but adopt the idea that Hitler had something demonic. They had seen film fragments of concentration camps and it was impossible to play down those stark images. They thought that perhaps they even stood a chance of evading the death penalty. Yet some of them refused to let Hitler down. At the end of the day,

---

29. Misch, pp. 66–67
30. Goldensohn, p. 43
31. Goldensohn, p. 198
32. Gilbert, p. 23

most defendants had followed him until the bitter end and it would be a sign of cowardice to distance themselves from him.

Psychologists about Hitler

In order to penetrate into Hitler's mind, the remarks of close associates of the dictator are perhaps not sufficient but, unfortunately, we haven't got much more than these statements at our disposal to use in order to analyse him. The possible analysis of Hitler, conducted after the First World War in a psychiatric ward of a hospital north of Berlin, has not been preserved,[33] and the report drafted by psychologist Walter C Langer on behalf of the American authorities during the Second World War was based on statements by acquaintances of Hitler or even on written sources.[34]

Nonetheless, the American report is an interesting document. It says about Hitler, for instance, that he undoubtedly believed in his own greatness. He was convinced of his mission and thought – and said so numerous times – that he was being protected and guided by Providence. This even went so far that he saw himself as the Messiah. And although his appearance was hardly impressive, the report mentions the hypnotic quality of Hitler's look and his capacity to captivate huge crowds by his manner of speech, although he repeated himself often during his speeches. The report also shows a Hitler, though, who couldn't work according to a schedule, went to bed and got up whenever he liked, was a bad sleeper, held up his friends until well into the night, hated being alone, had an aversion towards desk work and details, couldn't concentrate, couldn't listen, was often bad tempered and was hesitant when having to make important decisions.

The report concludes that Hitler suffered from 'hysteria, bordering on schizophrenia'. The notion that Hitler was paranoid was rejected, which means in the end, according to Langer, he wasn't crazy but a neurotic, suffering from hysterical attacks. It seems that for a disorder like this the term hysteria is no longer used today but at the time of the Second World War it meant a brain disorder causing physical complaints as well, including Hitler's 'vague' complaints about pain, or his 'blindness' caused by stress he

---

33. Horstmann, p. 12. In the chapter about Hitler's illnesses, this has been dealt with more exhaustively.
34. Contributors to the American analysis of Hitler, *A Psychological Analysis of Adolph Hitler, His Life and Legend* by Walter C Langer, were, for instance, Ernst Hanfstaengl, Otto Strasser, Hermann Rauschning, William Patrick Hitler, Dr Eduard Bloch, Princess Stephanie von Hohenlohe, Friedelinde Wagner and Kurt Lüdecke. People such as Heinrich Hoffmann and Ernst Röhm and many others are also quoted.

suffered from at the end of the First World War. Moreover, Langer assumed continuous conflicts were milling about in Hitler's head causing him to become confused, fearful and doubtful. In the end, Langer arrived at about the same conclusion as the high-ranking Nazis standing trial in Nuremberg: Hitler was ambiguous. He had a soft, hesitant and sentimental side and another cruel, energetic and aggressive side.

From this point on, Langer starts speculating at random: the first, soft version of Hitler would have been Hitler himself and the second, energetic and harsh version was the Führer in him, manifesting himself, for instance, during his speeches. The first Hitler transformed into the second just prior to a speech. Descriptions from Hitler's youth, such as those of August Kubizek, do show Hitler as a talkative young man who sometimes needed an audience, even if it consisted of just one person. The report also mentions moments on which Hitler talked much without the necessity of a transformation. It mentions, for instance, the unspoken agreement with people who met Hitler in private: one of them always had to stay awake in order to listen to him. That the talkative Hitler perhaps concentrated more on a speech, doesn't mean there were literally two Hitlers.[35]

In the fifth part of his report, in which the actual psychological analysis of Hitler is dealt with, Langer goes even further, making parts of it nearly ludicrous. According to him, what for instance must have been decisive for the development of Adolf Hitler is that young Adolf had watched his parents having intercourse. Where Langer got that from is a mystery but he assumed Adolf felt himself a lonely boy in a cruel world who later on bent all the emotions he felt for his mother towards Germany. And that is a pretty clever conclusion for someone who has never spoken to the person in question. Furthermore, Langer wrote that Hitler had already thought of himself as the chosen one after the death of the three children his mother had given birth to prior to him and the death of his younger brother afterwards. This feeling was strengthened by the big difference in age of Hitler's parents. According to Langer, such a difference would often lead to a Messiah complex as the thought that an old father could never be the real father would always be in the back of a child's mind. And, therefore, children would think more easily they were the result of a supernatural conception as their father could not have been the actual procreator.

The only proof for all these findings is the report itself, which has perhaps been written in the spirit of psychiatry and psychology of that time. Of course, it is splendid material to quote from if you want to substantiate an

---

35. The report does not mention the concentration but only a transformation.

interesting myth. As if the report wasn't speculative enough already, Langer also claims that Hitler's eyes were a possible substitute for his sexual organ, that the possibility existed that Hitler practised masochism and that his hatred of Jews was in fact a projection of his self-hatred. All three conclusions are Langer's own findings and impossible to prove. His report was actually an attempt to explain the man Hitler but it was mainly based on statements by people who had fled from him. Langer's own, far-fetched conclusions actually make the report unsuitable for serious analysis.

Modern psychology

Meanwhile, dozens of years have passed and the knowledge of men's motives and the nature of human evil are no longer dominated by the sociological and Freudian vision of them. In his book *The Violent Brain*, professor of neurocriminology Adrian Raine reports about his investigation into the roots of the so-called criminal brain. He shows that some mutant genes cause uncontrolled and wild aggression and that others are associated with planned psychopathic behaviour. For instance, head injury can cause coarse unorganised violence, whereas a criminal with a well-organised prefrontal cortex can regulate his violence in such a way that he can get away with murdering people for years.[36] For the sake of clarity, his book doesn't deal with Hitler but with criminality in general although certain well-known elements that, according to Raine, do belong to asocial behaviour, clearly apply to Hitler, like poor achievements at school, poor judgment of moral issues, asocialism, trouble with authority, an impulsive lifestyle and being good at lying.[37] Whether, apart from these factors, Hitler suffered from a brain disorder that, according to Raine, often causes a turnaround in aggression and criminality has never been established by physicians.

Hitler's brain could well resemble the brain of white-collar criminals, as described by Raine, who possess the ability to function successfully as leaders without their fraudulent activities becoming known. But the Hitler presented to us in the history books also shows various similarities with paranoid schizophrenics of whom distrust manifested as 'you have to get them before they get you' and 'megalomania' are important traits of character.[38]

How Hitler's criminality is explained mainly depends on which examples are being emphasized from his extensively described life. When

---

36. Raine, respectively p. 79, 8, 101, 102–103
37. Raine, p. 114, 130–131, 132, 197, 217
38. Raine, p. 295

focusing on his aggression, his bouts of rage, the death of Geli Raubal and the millions of deaths for which he was responsible, then he could have been the 'aggressive criminal' who hardly thinks before engaging a challenger and leaving traces of blood everywhere without considering the consequences. Focusing on his doubts when making important decisions or his shy retreat at moments he felt like the underdog, then he looks more like the 'thinking criminal' who commits his crimes for years on end without anyone finding out.

The free will

In his work, Raine also describes the issue of free will. If criminal behaviour can be determined by neurologic or biologic disorders then the question arises whether a perpetrator is free in his choice of evil. As soon as we apply this to Hitler, we enter forbidden territory, according to some. Just thinking about it is, according to them, a 'transgression of almost Biblical proportions'.[39] French philosopher and journalist Claude Lanzmann, who produced the documentary *Shoah* about the Holocaust, considered it undesired, based on whatever explanation, to try and understand the evil Hitler did. He said about it: 'You can take all causes, all explanations (...) and they can all be true. But (...) even if they are necessary, they aren't sufficient. One day, you'll have to start murdering (...) on a massive scale.'[40]

The possibility that genes, brain damage or tumours can determine someone's actions must be a terrible idea for Lanzmann: before you know it, you encounter excuses for the most horrible crimes. Because when certain factors, which can hardly be influenced by Hitler or any other hardened criminal, played a role then, judicially speaking, perhaps there would have been mitigating circumstances.[41] Raine doesn't go so far, however, as to say everybody has an excuse for his actions. 'Some people are almost completely free in their actions, whereas others may have relatively less freedom.'[42] When according to them, a fatal mix of poor biologic, genetic or social environmental factors play a role, someone may not even have the possibility to control his aggression or rage, whereas someone with a healthy brain and who grows up in a caring environment does have control over himself.

---

39. Rosenbaum, p. 13
40. Rosenbaum, p. 16
41. Raine, pp. 396–397. Raine emphasizes, however, that anger and reprisal have also evolved into pillars of our society. 'If we start forgiving psychopaths, we would be trampled to death.'
42. Raine, p. 379

Because biologic and genetic defects have not been established and a number of social factors are extremely questionable, we can only conclude that Hitler must have had full control over his brain.

Numb or sadistic?

Scientist and psychologist Kathleen Taylor pointed out that 'We want the people we call evil to have nothing in common with us: empathy alone can make our thoughts and feelings look dangerously like his.'[43] This could be the reason why we demonise Hitler and why we have a problem with anyone suggesting he wants to peel off some of Hitler's extraterrestrial evil. Demonising is safe because almost nobody wants to look like Hitler. And certainly not like David Irving, who started to feel sympathy for Hitler by identifying himself too much with him.

Taylor says it is simplistic and dangerously misleading to call an army 'satanic' that enters the city and creates a bloodbath.[44] That is more understandable than it seems at first sight. One can't separate the word 'devil' from its metaphysic meaning, even if one just wanted to use the word to label a bad person. Perhaps we manage to create a distance between ourselves and Hitler or other criminals but, even then, there is no question of real safety because devils don't disappear. Hitler, by the way, has long since left us. During the Nuremberg trial, the defendants weren't devils but men who were considered responsible for their actions. Even 'deranged' Rudolf Hess was sentenced to life imprisonment.

Nazis carrying out the *Endlösung* also had a moral. Taylor explains this by dwelling on two characteristics that lie close together: numbness and sadism.[45] For instance, she calls the extermination of the Jews heartless but not necessarily sadistic because the Nazis did this for the purpose of their Thousand Year Empire. 'Sadism evoked aversion in many – even within the murderous *Einsatzgruppen* (...) The inflicted suffering can even be shocking. Yet we consider sadism, not numbness as the moral lowest point of human evil.'[46] Rudolf Höss, camp commander of Auschwitz, for instance answered a question by psychiatrist Goldensohn in Nuremberg prison whether he was a sadist: 'No, during my whole tenure as camp commander I have never beaten a prisoner. When I saw a guard mistreating a prisoner I tried to replace him

---

43. Taylor, p. 21
44. Taylor, pp. 26–27
45. Taylor, p. 68
46. Taylor, p. 73

by another guard.⁴⁷ Shortly before, Höss had reported extensively how and in what numbers he had Jews gassed and their bodies cremated. But beating? That was a bridge too far, even for him ...

Was Hitler 'truthful'?

Whatever we may think of him, Adolf Hitler could well have thought of himself that he was a good and sincere man. In order to present himself as truthful or even consistent, he did his best, for instance, to date his hatred of Jews as early as possible. He had adopted the notion of the Jews wanting to dominate the world at an early age, he said, and he continued believing in it until the end of his life. So, he was open and honest about his hatred and therefore straightforward in his own, for most people, rejectable way.

An interesting possibility as a result of the thought experiment about the sincere and true Hitler was voiced by Ron Rosenbaum on the occasion of a talk with Hugh Trevor-Roper. Rosenbaum compared the thought of the true Hitler in his hatred of Jews to a case that was held before a Californian court once. Two brothers were pronounced guilty of manslaughter instead of murder of their parents because they sincerely thought their parents were going to kill them. Based on this jurisprudence, Hitler could have argued, provided he had been indicted for genocide in California, that he was 'sincerely convinced the Jews tried to destroy him and that he therefore had murdered them out of self-defence'.⁴⁸ Regarding the massive scale of the Holocaust, this wouldn't have affected the eventual verdict, which in Nuremberg would have been the death penalty anyway, but the idea that Hitler was a 'true believer' is, bizarre as it may seem, an argument his lawyers could have used to defend him in court.⁴⁹

A play run out of hand?

Ian Kershaw doubts the unshakable belief Hitler had in himself as he assumes he was acting most of the time. Kershaw points, for example, to the statements about Hitler by the *Gauleiter* of Hamburg, Albert Krebs, who thought he manipulated the masses he addressed without internal involvement or sincerity.⁵⁰ Laurence Rees differentiated this: 'Hitler has

---

47. Goldensohn, p. 339
48. Rosenbaum, p. 120
49. Rosenbaum, p. 120
50. Kershaw, Hoogmoed, p. 368

always been accused of being an "actor" but a crucial aspect of his attraction in the early years was that his followers in the beer halls (…) thought he was "authentic" through and through.'[51] These statements by Rees and Kershaw don't necessarily contradict each other when we consider a statement by Alan Bullock: 'He was a great actor who strongly believed in the play.'[52] Even assuming there is some opportunism involved in his choice of certain viewpoints, it could still be that, in the end, Hitler started believing in his own propaganda and that he was completely mesmerised by his own acting.[53] Kershaw admits this too. He says that Hitler, from 1935–36 onwards, believed more and more in the myth of the Messianic Führer created by the Nazis themselves.[54] The Nazi propaganda was so much in Hitler's favour that the population got the idea that he was all right but the party, in particular the various high and low-ranking officials, were not because they were involved in all sorts of shady matters such as self-enrichment.[55]

Explanations and problems

Claude Lanzmann is opposed to any explanation of Hitler's hatred of the Jews. Thereby, he adopts a fairly rigorous point of view. He says delving into the psyche of the Nazis should be avoided. Those who do so, soon foster revisionist ideas, he says: ideas in which excuses are conscientiously sought for the actions of the Nazis with the goal of rehabilitation. Lanzmann even mentions the 'obscenity of understanding' as he sees any attempt at understanding Hitler or the Holocaust as obscene.[56] Of course, this goes way too far. It would make the work of historians impossible. But Lanzmann isn't entirely wrong here as explanations of his behaviour exonerate the perpetrator for a part in the eyes of many, and where Hitler is concerned, we don't want that.

Normalisation

Professor Alvin Rosenfeld wrote as early as 1985 that the mythological Hitler is more alive than the historical Hitler.[57] However, the importance

---

51. Rees, p. 34
52. Rosenbaum, p. 140
53. Rosenbaum, p. 140
54. Kershaw, THM, pp. 81–82
55. Kershaw, THM, pp. 103–104
56. Rosenbaum, pp. 315–331
57. Rosenfeld, p. 13

of normalising Hitler and not portraying him any longer as the embodiment of evil or as a demon is explained very well by a subtle argumentation by John Lukacs about Hitler's so-called derangement. He points out that by saying Hitler wasn't completely sane, you not only label the Third Reich as a period of madness but you also make Hitler unaccountable for his actions. Hitler wasn't ill though, and he was no extraterrestrial evil being. There is ample evidence for this, even medical, Lukacs emphasizes. Hitler did do bad things but that is, according to Lukacs, just as human as doing the right things. 'He also was brave, self-assured, steady on many occasions, loyal to his friends and those who worked for him, self-disciplined and modest as to material needs.'[58] And precisely that is the nucleus of Lukacs' vison on Hitler's evil. Hitler was a normal human being with a myriad of good and bad characteristics and because he had many talents, he also was fully accountable for the abuse thereof.[59]

The idea of Hitler belonging to an outside category of humanity is only good for our peace of mind as the possibility of someone like him arising in the near future is, of course, smaller than if Hitler had been a normal human being. Now that the war is a long time behind us, Lukacs says about this: 'The notion that Hitler wasn't a demonic – that is to say a non-human and non-historical – phenomenon but a historical figure with human characteristics and gifted with recognisable talents, isn't only shared by some historians but to a growing number of people as well.'[60] But has this vision penetrated everywhere? Hitler wasn't alone in his evil. He had many willing helpers and it would be very far-fetched to call all these men and women demons as well. Unfortunately, genocide is human behaviour and crimes committed by someone can't all be attributed to his superiors and not at all to an alleged extraterrestrial entity. Man himself choses between good and evil, that is the foundation of our entire judicial system. To people suffering from a brain disorder, brain injury or a genetic aberration, a limitation of the free will could be applied but something similar has never been established beyond any doubt in Hitler. Hitler wasn't crazy, so he was fully accountable for what happened inside the Third Reich.

---

58. Lukacs, p. 51
59. Lukacs, pp. 51–52
60. Lukacs, p. 16

Bibliography

Axmann, Artur, *Hitlerjugend, 'Das kann doch nicht das Ende sein'*, Karl Müller Verlag, Erlangen
Bahnsen, Uwe & O'Donnell, James P., *Die Katakombe, das Ende in der Reichskanzlei*, Rowohlt Taschenbuch Verlag, Reinbek bei Hamburg, 2004 (original publication 1975)
Basti, Abel & Helsing, Jan, van, *Hitler überlebte in Argentinien*, Amadeus Verlag, Fichtenau, 2011
Beevor, Antony, *Berlijn, de ondergang 1945*, Olympus, Amsterdam, 2005
Beevor, Anthony, *De Tweede Wereldoorlog*, Ambo, Amsterdam, 2012
Beier-Lindhardt, Erich, *Ein Buch vom Führer für die deutsche Jugend*, Gerhard Stalling Verlagsbuchhandlung, Oldenburg/Berlin, 1939
Below, Nicolaus von, *Als Hitlers Adjudant 1937–45*, Pour le Mérite, Selent, 1999
Bruppacher, *Adolf Hitler und die Geschichte der NSDAP, Eine Chronik, Teil 1, 1889–1937*, Books on Demand GmbH, Norderstedt, 2008
Bullock, Alan, *Hitler, leven en ondergang van een tiran*, A.W. Bruna & zoon, Utrecht, 1953 (1958 reprint)
Capelle, van, H. & Bovenkamp, van de, A.P., *Hitler aan het Westfront*, De Lantaarn, Ede, 2014
Conradi, Peter, *Hitlers Klavierspieler*, Scherz Verlag, Frankfurt am Main, 2007
Cumbey, Constance, *The Hidden Dangers of the Rainbow, the New Age Movement and Our Coming age of Barbarism*, Huntington House, year of publication unknown
Debaeke, Siegfried, *Hitler in Vlaanderen*, De Klaproos, Brugge, 2011
Eberle, Henrik & Uhl, Matthias, *Das Buch Hitler*, Gustav Lübbe Verlag, Bergisch Gladbach, 2005
Fest, Joachim, *Der Untergang, Hitler und das Ende des Dritten Reiches* (DU), Rowohlt Taschenbuch Verlag, Reinbek bei Hamburg, 2003
Fest, Joachim, *Onbeantwoorde vragen, Gesprekken met Albert Speer* (OV), De Bezige Bij, Amsterdam, 2006
Fest, Joachim, *Speer, architect van Hitler* (SH), De Boekerij, Amsterdam, 2004
Fleischmann, Peter, *Hitler als Häftling in Landsberg am Lech, 1923/24*, Verlag Ph. C.W. Schmidt, Neustadt an der Aisch, 2015
Fontaine, P.F.M., *De onbekende Hitler*, Ambo, Baarn, 1992
Fromm, Bella, *Bloed en banketten, Society reporter in Berlijn*, Balans, Amsterdam, 1991
Gellately, Robert, *Pal achter Hitler, Openheid en onderdrukking in Nazi-Duitsland*, Sdu Uitgevers, Den Haag, 2001
Giebels, Lambert, *Hitler als kunstenaar, Wenen 1907-München 1919*, Balans, Amsterdam, 2012
Gilbert, G.M., *Dagboek Neurenberg, 1945/46*, Strengholt, Naarden, 1985 (1st printing 1947)
Goebbels, Joseph, *Tagebücher, Band 4: 1940–1942, herausgegeben von Ralf Georg Reuth*, Piper Verlag, München-Zürich, 2003
Goldensohn, Leon (edited by Gellately, Robert), *Neurenberg – Gesprekken, Nazi's en hun psychiater Leon Goldensohn*, Meulenhoff, Amsterdam, 2004

Gordon, Mel, Erik Jan Hanussen, *Hitler's Jewish Clairvoyant*, Feral House, Los Angeles, 2001
Gun, Nerin E., *Eva Braun, maitresse en vrouw van Adolf Hitler*, Uitgeverij de Forel, Rotterdam-Nieuwendijk, 1968
Haffner, Sebastian, *Kanttekeningen bij Hitler*, Mets & Schilt, Amsterdam, 2002
Haidinger, Martin & Steinbach, Günther, *Unser Hitler, die Österreicher und ihr Landsmann*, Ecowin Verlag, Salzburg, 2009
Hamann, Brigitte, *Hitlers Wien, Lehrjahre eines Diktators* (HW), Piper, München/Zürich, 2007
Hamann, Brigitte, *Het Wenen van Hitler* (WH) (Ned. editie van *Hitlers Wien*), Omniboek, Utrecht, 2014 (1e druk 1998)
Hamann, Brigitte, *Winifred Wagner oder Hitlers Bayreuth* (WW), Piper Verlag, München, 2003
Hamann, Brigitte, *Hitlers Edeljude, das Leben des Armenarztes Eduard Bloch* (HE), Piper Verlag, München, 2010
Hant, Claus P., *Young Hitler, a non-fiction novel*, Quartet Books, London, 2010 (appendix The Thule Society)
Hertog, den, Peter, *Hitlers schutkleur, De oorsprong van zijn antisemitisme*, De Arbeiderspers, Amsterdam, 2005
Herz, Rudolf, *Hoffmann & Hitler, Fotografie als Medium des Führer-Mythos*, Klinkhardt & Biermann, München, 1994
Hitler, Adolf, *Mijn kamp*, De Amsterdamsche Keurkamer, vijfde druk, Amsterdam
Hoffmann, Heinrich, *Hitler wie ich ihn sah, Aufzeihnungen seines Leibfotografen* (HH), Herbig/Winkelried Verlag, Dresden, 1974
Hoffmann, Peter, *The History of the German Resistance 1933–1945* (HP), McGill-Queen's University Press, Montreal & Kingston-London-Buffalo, 1996 (1e druk 1969)
Horstmann, Bernhard, *Hitler in Pasewalk*, Droste Verlag, Düsseldorf, 2004
Jetzinger, Franz, *Hitler's Youth*, Greenwood Press, Westport, Connecticut, 1976 (1e druk 1958)
Joachimsthaler, Anton, *Hitlers einde, De legendes, het bewijs, de waarheid* (HE), Omniboek, Kampen, 2009
Joachimsthaler, Anton, *Hitlers Weg begann in München, 1913–1923* (HW), Herbig Verlag, München, 2000 (extended version of *Korrektur einer Biographie*)
Joachimsthaler, Anton, *Korrektur einer Biographie, Adolf Hitler 1908–1920* (KB), Herbig, München, 1989
Johnson, David, *The Man Who Didn't Shoot Hitler, The story of Henry Tandey VC and Adolf Hitler, 1918*, Spellmount, Gloucestershire, 2014
Junge, Traudl, *Tot het laatste uur, Het intrigerende levensverhaal van Hitlers secretaresse*, Tirion, Baarn, 2002
Katz, Othmar, *Prof. Dr Med. Theo Morell, Hitlers Leibarzt*, Hestia Verlag, Bayreuth, 1982
Kellerhof, Sven Felix, *Mythos Führerbunker*, Giebel Verlag, Berlijn, 2003
Kempka, Erich, *Die letzten Tage mit Adolf Hitler*, Verlag K.W. Schütz KG, Preußisch Oldendorf, 1975
Kershaw, Ian, *Hitler, Hoogmoed 1889–1936 & Vergelding 1936–1945*, Spectrum, Utrecht, 1999
Kershaw, Ian, *Hitler, de Duitsers en de holocaust* (HDH), Spectrum, Houten, 2009
Kershaw, Ian, *Keerpunten* (KP), Spectrum, Utrecht, 2007
Kershaw, Ian, *The Hitler Myth, Image and Reality in the Third Reich* (HM), Oxford University Press, Oxford New York, 1987

Kershaw, Ian, *Tot de laatste man, Duitsland 1944–1945* (LM), Spectrum, Houten-Antwerpen, 2011

Kirsten, Holm, *Weimar im Banne des Führers, die Besuche Adolf Hitlers 1925–1940*, Böhlau Verlag, Köln-Weimar-Wien, 2001

Klemperer, Victor, *Lingua tertii imperii, Die Sprache des Dritten Reiches*, Reclam Verlag, Leipzich, 1991

Koch-Hillebrecht, *Hitler, ein Sohn des Krieges, Fronterlebnis und Weltbild*, Herbig, München, 2003

Kopleck, Maik, *Pastfinder Berlin 1933–1945*, CH Links Verlag, Berlin

Kubizek, August, *Adolf Hitler, mein Jugendfreund*, Leopold Stocker Verlag, Graz/Stuttgart, 2002

Kuch, Kurt, *Bei Hitlers, Zimmermädchen Annas Erinnerungen*, Verlag Josef Kleindienst, St. Andrä-Wördern, 2003

Langer, Walter C., *A Psychological Analysis of Adolph Hitler: his life and legend*, M.O. Branche Office of Strategic Services, Washington, D.C., 1943

Lehrer, Steven, *Hitler Sites, A city-by-city guidebook*, McFarland & Company, Jefferson, North Carolina, London, 2002

Linge, Heinz, *In het voetspoor van de Führer, Onthullingen van Hitlers privé adjudant uitgegeven door dr. Werner Maser*, Uitgeverij Kadmos, Utrecht, 1985 (originele uitgave 1982)

Lukacs, John, *Hitler en de geschiedenis, Hitlers plaats in de 20th eeuw*, Standaard Uitgeverij, Antwerpen, 1999

Machtan, Lothar, *Hitlers intieme kring, De politieke en psychologische ontwikkeling van Adolf Hitler*, Uitgeverij Contact, Amsterdam/Antwerpen, 2001

Maser, Werner, *Hitlers brieven en notities* (BN), Aspekt, Soesterberg, 2004

Maser, Werner, *Hitlers Mein Kampf, Geschiedenis, Fragmenten, Commentaren* (HMK), Uitgeverij Aspekt, Soesterberg, 2004 (eerste Duitse druk: 1966)

Maser, Werner, *Adolf Hitler, Legende Mythos Wirklichkeit* (ALW), Bechtle Verlag, München-Esslingen, 1971 (16ᵉ druk 1997)

Melching, Willem, *Hitler, Opkomst en ondergang van een Duits politicus*, Uitgeverij Bert Bakker, Amsterdam, 2013

Meyer, Adolf, *Mit Adolf Hitler im Bayerischen reserve-Infanterie-Regiment 16 List*, Verlag Georg Aupperle, Neustadt-Aisch, 1934

Misch, Rochus, *De laatste getuige, Onthullend oorlogsdagboek van Hitlers koerier en lijfwacht*, Fontaine uitgevers, 2008

Moorhouse, Roger, *Hitler, de aanslagen*, Nieuw Amsterdam Uitgevers, Amsterdam, 2007

Mulders, Jean-Paul, *Op zoek naar de zoon van Hitler*, Uitgeverij Aspekt, Soesterberg, 2009

Mulisch, Harry, *Siegfried, Een zwarte idylle*, De Bezige Bij, Amsterdam, 2001

Neumann & Eberle, *War Hitler Krank?, ein abschließender Befund*, Gustav Lübbe Verlag, Bergisch Gladbach, 2009

Ortner, Helmut, *Moordenaar in toga, Roland Freisler, rechter in dienst van Hitler*, Just Publishers, Meppel, 2014

Plöckinger, Othmar, *Geschichte eines Buches: Adolf Hitlers 'Mein Kampf'* (GB), R. Oldenbourg Verlag, München, 2006

Plöckinger, Othmar, *Unter Soldaten und Agitatoren, Hitlers prägende Jahre im deutschen Militär 1918–1920* (US), Ferdinand Schöningh, Paderborn-München-Wien-Zürich, 2013

Price, Billy F., *Adolf Hitler als Maler und Zeichner*, Gallant Verlag, Zug/Schweiz, 1983

Raine, Adrian, *Het gewelddadige brein, De biologische wortels van crimineel gedrag*, uitgeverij Balans, 2013

Rees, Laurence, *Het charisma van Adolf Hitler, Hoe hij miljoenen naar de afgrond leidde*, Ambo, Amsterdam, 2012

Rosenbaum, Ron, *Waarom Hitler? Een zoektocht naar de wortels van het kwaad*, Prometheus, Amsterdam, 1999
Rosenfeld, Alvin, *Imagining Hitler*, Indiana University Press, Bloomington, 1985
Rothman, Herman, *Hitler's Will*, The History Press, The Mill, Brimscombe Port, Stroud, Gloucestershire, 2014 (1st printing 2009)
Russell, Stuart, *Frontsoldat Hitler, der Freiwillige des Ersten Weltkrieges*, Zeitgeschichte in Bildern, Arndt-Verlag, Kiel, 2006
Ryback, Timothy W., *Hitlers privébibliotheek*, uitgeverij Balans, Amsterdam, 2008
Schilperoord, Paul, *Het geheim van Hitlers Volkswagen, het geesteskind van de Joodse ontwerper Josef Ganz*, Just Publishers, Meppel, 2014
Schirach, von, Henriette, *Der Preis der Herlichkeit*, Herbig, München, 2003
Schroeder, Christa, *Er war mein Chef*, Herbig, München, 2004 (1st printing 1985). Nederlandse uitgave: Schroeder, Christa, *Hij was mijn Führer*, Just Publishers, Meppel, 2011
Schwarz, Birgit, *Geniewahn: Hitler und die Kunst*, Böhlau Verlag, Wien-Köln-Weimar, 2011
Shirer, William L., *The Rise and Fall of the Third Reich, A History of Nazi Germany*, Ballantine Publishing Group, 1998
Sigmund, Anna Maria, *Des Führers bester Freund* (FF), Ullstein Heyne List GmbH, München, 2003
Sigmund, Anna Maria, *Die Frauen der Nazis* (FN), Wilhelm Heyne Verlag, München, 2005
Solleder, Fridolin, *Vier Jahre Westfront, Geschichte des Regiments List*, R.I.R. 16, Verlag Max Schick, München, 1932
Speer, Albert, *Erinnerungen*, Ullstein Verlag, Berlin, 2005 (1e druk 1969)
Taylor, Kathleen, *Het wrede brein, Waarom in elk van ons een moordenaar schuilt*, Uitgeverij Lannoo nv, Tielt, 2010
Trevor-Roper, Hugh, *The Last Days of Hitler*, seventh edition, Pan Books, London, 2002 (eerste publicatie 1947)
Ullrich, Viktor, *Hauptstadt der Bewegung, München 1919–1938, Zeitgeschichte in Farbe*, Teil 1, ARNDT-Verlag, Kiel, 2006 & Teil 2, 2007
Ullrich, Volker, *Adolf Hitler, opkomst, deel 1: De jaren van opkomst 1889–1939*, De Arbeiderspers, Antwerpen-Amsterdam, 2013
Unruh, Karl, *Langemarck, Legende und Wirklichkeit*, Bernard & Graefe Verlag, Koblenz 1986 (3rd printing 1997)
Weber, Thomas, *Adolf Hitler en de Eerste Wereldoorlog*, Nieuw Amsterdam, Amsterdam, 2010
Weinberg, Gerhard L., *Hitler's Second Book, the unpublished sequel to Mein Kampf by Adolf Hitler*, Enigma Books, New York, 2003 (original publication in German in 1961)
Weiss, Ernst, *De ooggetuige*, Van Gennep, Amsterdam, 2007
Wiedemann, Fritz, *Der Mann der Feldherr werden wollte, 1914–1918, 1934–1939*, Verlag für politische Bildung, 1964
Williams, John F., *Corporal Hitler and the Great War 1914–1918, the List regiment*, Frank Cass, London and New York, 2005
Wilson, A.N., *Hitler*, Het Spectrum, Houten-Antwerpen, 2012
Zdral, Wolfgang, *De Hitlers, De onbekende familie van de Führer*, Aspekt, Soesterberg, 2006
Zentner, Christian, *Adolf Hitlers Mein Kampf, Eine kommentierte Auswahl*, Ullstein Buchverlage, Berlin, 2009 (1e druk 1974)
NN, *Adolf Hitler in Bilddokumenten seiner Zeit*, Band 1-5, Verlag für geschichtliche Dokumentation, Hamburg, 1979
NN, *Frülingssturm, Ein Führer-Hauptquartier in Niederösterreich, Mönichkirchen, 12. bis 25. April 1941*, Kral Verlag, Berndorf, 2013

NN, *Hitlers tafelgesprekken, 1941–1944*, introduction by Bert Natter, De Prom, Amsterdam/Antwerpen, 2005

NN, *Mythos Germania, Schatten und Spuren der Reichshauptstadt*, Edition Berliner Unterwelten, Lehmanns Media, Berlin, 2009

Articles and other sources

'Adolf Hitler: Vater eines Sohnes', Werner Maser, in: *Zeitgeschichte* okt. 1977 – sept. 1978, Heft 1-12, 1977

'Anti-Joodse 'Protocollen van Zion' duiken steeds opnieuw op', Jakob Hoekman, in: *Reformatorisch Dagblad*, 31 January 2011

'Blutfahne der NSDAP', Bernard Schäfer, in: Historisches Lexicon Bayerns (website)

'Das kann doch nicht unser Hitler sein!', citaten van Fritz Wiedemann, in: *Der Spiegel* nr. 47, 1964

'De mythe van Langemarck, sporen van de Eerste Wereldoorlog in Berlijn', Kammelar, Rob & Wielinga, Menno, www.wereldoorlog1418.nl, 2012

'Der Mann in der Menge', Hoffmann, Heinrich, in: *Illustrierter Beobachter, Adolf Hitler, ein Mann und sein Volk*, Verlag Franz Eher, München, 1936

'Der Schimmelreiter meldet', Hans Mend, in: *Der Gerade Weg*, 9 October 1932

'Der Schimmelreiter vom Listregiment meldet sich', Hans Mend, in: *Der Gerade Weg*, 4 December 1932

'De vroege jaren, 1918–1914', in: *Historia*, Oorlogen & Veldslagen 5, Het Derde Rijk, 2014

'De weg uit de crisis, 1933–1939', in: *Historia*, Oorlogen & Veldslagen 5, Het Derde Rijk, 2014

'Did Hitler shake hands with black 1936 Olympic hero Jesse Owens?', Allan Hall, in: Mailonline, 11 August 2009

'Ein verlässlicher Augenzeuge', Waldemar Besson, in: *Die Zeit*, 5 February 1965

Encyclopedie: Protocollen van de Wijzen van Zion, Tussen Waarheid en Waanzin: een encyclopedie der pseudo-wetenschappen, zoals gepubliceerd op www.kwakzalverij.nl, 23 October 2009

Examen geschiedenis en staatsinrichting CSE GL en TL, VMBO-GL en TL, tijdvak 1, 2011, Cito, Arnhem

'Het geheim van Hitlers Volkswagen', Paul Schilperoord, in: *Wereld in Oorlog* nr. 39, 2014

'Het 'Wirtschaftswunder' van Nazi-Duitsland 1933-1939', AW Sijthoff, in: *Forum der Letteren*, Leiden, 1971

'Hitler aan de crystal meth, voor tirades en tegen pijn', in: *Trouw*, 14 October 2014

Hitler, Adolf, 'Mijn politieke testament', www.go2war2.nl/artikel/1331/Hitlers-politiek-testament-29-04-1945.htm?page=2, STIWOT, 2002-2013

'Hitler aurait eu un fils avec une Française' op de website van *Le Point* (Le Point.fr), 17 February 2012

'Hitler, de eenzaamste man aan de frontlijn', Peter Giesen, in: *de Volkskrant*, 2 April 2011

'Hitler wasn't a socialist. Stop saying he was', in: *The Telegraph*, Tim Stanley, 26 February 2014, http://blogs.telegraph.co.uk/news/timstanley/100261121/hitler-wasnt-a-socialist-stop-saying-he-was'Ich fand Hitlers Testament', Bernd Peters, in: *Berliner Kurier*, 29 April 2011

'Is this Hitlers Mercedes?', Hugo Guy, in: *Daily Mail* (online), 10 July 2012

'Knöcherne Beute', Klussmann, Uwe, in: *Der Spiegel* nr. 18, 2000

'Liebe in Flandern' in: *Der Spiegel* nr. 46, 1977

'Nieuw bewijs: Hitler had zoon die tegen hem vocht in WOII', op website *Algemeen Dagblad*, 17 February 2012

'Ohne Maske, ohne Mythos, privat', in: *Der Spiegel* nr. 28, 1949

'Russische Agenten haben angeblich Hitlers Kiefer', in: *Die Welt*, 8 December 2009

'Sergej Nilus und die 'Protokolle der Weisen von Zion', Überlegungen zur Forschungslage, Michael Hagemeister', in: W. Benz, *Jahrbuch für Antisemitismusforschung* 5, pp. 127–147

'The Armistice', Editor: Winston G. Ramsey, in: *After the Battle* nr. 14, Battle of Britain International Ltd, 1976 (This article contains passages from *The Rise and Fall of the Third Reich* van William L. Shirer)

'The Berlin Führerbunker: the thirteenth hole', Andrew Mollo, in: *After the Battle* nr. 61, 1988

'The death of Adolf Hitler – Forensic Aspects', Marchetti, Daniela e.a., September 2005, Facolta di Medicina e Chirurga, Roma

'The Protocols of the Elders of Zion: Between History and Fiction', Michael Hagemeister, in: *New German Critique*, vol. 103, vol. 35, no. 1, Spring 2008, pp. 83–95

'The remains of Adolf Hitler: A biomedical analysis and definitive identification', Philippe Charlier a.o., in: European Journal of Internal Medicine, May 2018

'The story of a car', Ludwig Kosche, in: *After the Battle* nr. 35, 1982

'Todesurteile wurden zur billigen Ware', in: *Der Spiegel* nr. 15, 1981

'Vor dem 'Volksgerichtshof', Schauprozesse vor laufender Kamera', Pr. Dr Johannes Tuchel, in: *Das Jahrhundert der Bilder 1900-1945*, Gerhard Paul (Hrsg.) Göttingen, 2009 (digitale versie via Gedenkstätte Deutsche Wiederstand in 'bezit' auteur)

'Was Adolf Hitler in Vlaanderen in juni 1940', Erik Dewitte, ongepubliceerd, in bezit van auteur, artikel van inwoner van Izegem, nabij Ardooie

'Wie Ich die Leiche Hitlers fand', Iwan Klimenko, in: *Der Spiegel* nr. 19, 1965

'Will Smith "incensed" over claims he praised Hitler', www.dailymail.co.uk, Richard Ferrer, 2007

'Will Smith Explains Hitler Quote', www.people.com, Karen Salkin, 2007

'Will Smith, Hitler and the Holocaust's Unanswerable Question', www.huffingtonpost.com, 2007

'"Zo sterk als een buffel, en koelbloedig onbevreesd", Hitlers privé-chauffeur Julius Schreck (1898-1936)', Martijn Steenbergen, in: *Wereld in Oorlog* nr. 40, 2014

'UK should consider ban on Mein Kampf, says Scottish Labour MP', in: The Guardian, 26 January 2015

Documentaries etc.

Der Führerbunker 1935–1942, eine virtuelle Rekonstruktion, Keystone animation, Christoph Neubauer Verlag, 2007 (DVD)

Hitler, eine Bilanz, 1. der Privatman, 2. der Verführer, Guido Knopp, ZDF-video, München, 2001

Hitlers Hidden Drug Habit, Channel 4, 2014

Stond een Jood aan de wieg van de VW?, Erwin Hoffman, in: Netwerk, 22 November 2005

Olympia, Leni Riefenstahl, 1938 (film)

Index

Acker, Lucien van, 46
Alt, Rudolf von, 97
Aly, Götz, 83
Amann, Max, 25, 33, 35, 45, 73
Andropov, Juri, 211
Axmann, Artur, 179-81, 186, 189, 191-5, 203, 234

Bachmann, Anton, 27, 114
Bahnsen, Uwe, 193, 196-7, 234
Basti, Abel, 48, 118, 177, 234
Bauer, Eleonora, 117
Bauer, Yehuda, 117
Bauer, Hans, 195-6
Bechstein, Lotte, 112
Beethoven, Ludwig von, 95-6
Bellantoni, Nick, 201
Below, Nicolaus von, 214, 217, 234
Bezymenski, Lev, 182-5
Bismarck, Otto von, 99, 205
Bloch, Eduard, 69, 131, 138, 158, 160, 226, 235
Blomberg, Werner von, 150
Böcklin, Arnold, 98-9
Bormann, Martin, 98, 115, 126, 149, 152-3, 175, 179-81, 187-89, 195-6, 202, 214, 217-8
Brahms, Johannes, 95-6
Brandmayer, Balthasar, 22, 25
Brandt, Karl, 164-5, 169-70
Braun, Eva, viii, ix, 109, 116-7, 119-20, 123-5, 127, 133, 174, 177-8, 186-7, 201-2, 213, 235
Braun, Fanny, 123
Braun, Gretl, 126, 133, 180
Braun, Ilse, 117, 125
Browning, Christopher, 201

Bruckmann, Elsa, 112
Bruckner, Anton, 95-6, 106
Bullock, Alan, 36, 50, 159, 222, 232, 234
Burgdorf, Wilhelm, 179-80, 194, 217

Carlyle, Thomas, 100
Chamberlain, Neville, 220

Dewitte, Erik, 45-6, 239
Dirksen, Viktoria, 112
Dönitz, Karl, 174, 214-6, 218, 225
Dorsch, Franz Xavier, 223
Duyck, Walter, 46

Eberle, Henrik, 134, 156-70. 172, 234, 236
Echtmann, Fritz, 201
Eckart, Dietrich, 115
Eggers, Karl, 57
Eher, Franz, 26, 73, 238
Eisner, Kurt, 50, 52, 72
Engelhardt, Philipp, 27, 32

Fackenheim, Emil, 222
Falcén, Mafalda, 177
Fegelein, Hermann, 180
Fest, Joachim, 98-9, 103, 186-7, 212
Feuerbach, Anselm, 97-8
Forster, Edmund, 161
Franco, Francisco, 176
Frank, Hans, x, 2, 8, 10, 148, 223, 225
Frankenberger, family, 2, 3, 8-10
Frederik II, king, 195
Frey, Alexander, 36
Frick, Helmuth, 189

Ganz, Josef, 94, 237
Giebels, Lambert, 89, 93, 100, 105, 107
Giesing, Erwin, 169
Giesler, Hermann, 101
Gilbert, Gustave, 149, 225
Glassl, Anna, 7
Godin, Freiherr von, 34
Goebbels, Helmut, 187
Goebbels, Joseph, 57, 68, 76, 78, 85, 96, 108, 142, 151, 153-4, 167, 179, 181, 199, 218
Goebbels, Magda, viii, 118, 179, 182, 186
Goedsche, Hermann, 77
Goethals, Joseph, 42, 46
Goldensohn, Leon, 148, 225, 234
Göring, Hermann, 36, 72, 91, 148, 153, 171, 224
Grimminger, Jakob, 58
Grützner, Eduard von, 97
Guderian, Heinz, 164
Gun, Nerin, 116, 126, 235
Günsche, Otto, 178-9, 181, 192, 196, 199, 203
Güstrow, Dietrich, 159
Gutmann, Hugo, 335

Hakvaag, William, 104
Hamann, Brigitte, 13-14, 16, 65, 139, 160
Hamann, Leutnant, 195
Hanfstaengl, Ernst, 95, 112-13, 115, 122, 129, 131-2, 171, 226
Hanfstaengl, Helene, 132
Hanisch, Reinhold, 115, 132, 140
Hansen, Theophil, 101
Hasselbach, Hans Karl, 164, 169
Haug, Jenny, 117
Hâusler, Rudolf, 111, 113
Heiden, Konrad, 128
Helsing, Jan van, 48, 118, 177, 234
Hepp, Ernst, 21, 32
Hertog, Peter den, 170-1
Hess, Rudolf, 33, 62, 70, 72-3, 91, 115, 230
Heusermann, Käthe, 201
Heydrich, Reinhard, 148

Hiedler, Georg, 2, 4-8, 48
Hiedler, Nepomuk, 2, 4, 6, 8, 48
Himmler, Heinrich, 57-8, 147-8, 153
Hindenburg, Paul von, 205
Hitler, Alois (Adolfs half-brotther), 11
Hitler, Alois (Adolfs father), 1,2
Hitler, Paula, 16, 47
Hitler, William Patrick, 48, 131, 226
Hoffmann, Carola, 112
Hoffmann, Heinrich, 20, 52, 97, 105, 117-8, 124-6, 226
Hoffmann, Henriette (von Schirach), 118, 173, 237
Horstmann, Bernard, 161-2, 226, 235
Höss, Rudolf, 148, 230
Hümer, dr., 136-7
Hummerich, corporal, 215
Hüttler, Andreas, 48
Hüttler, Walter, 48

Irving, David, 167, 223-4, 230

Jahoda, family, 140
Jetzinger, Franz, 8, 13-14, 90, 136
Joachimsthaler, Anton, xii, 35, 37, 40, 43, 50, 105-6, 176-7, 183, 185, 197, 202
Johannmeier, Willi, 214, 218
Joly, Maurice, 77
Junge, Traudi, 179

Karnau, Hermann, 180, 187, 199
Katukov, Michail, 175
Katz, Ottmar, 166
Keitel, Wilhelm, 153, 214, 225
Kellerhoff, Sven Felix, v, 200, 206, 235
Kempka, Erich, 176, 179, 181, 186-9, 194, 199
Kennedy, John F., xi
Kershaw, Ian, xii, 5-6, 8-9, 36, 40, 44, 48, 50-1, 66, 74, 79, 82, 93, 98, 107, 111, 119, 123, 142, 144, 146, 150-1, 158, 162, 165, 167-8, 185, 214-15, 231
Klimenko, Ivan, 182, 239
Klotz, Clemens, 103
Knopp, Guido, 53, 239
Krebs, Albert, 231

Krebs, general, 175, 182
Krüger, courier, 186
Kubizek, August, 5, 16, 92, 95, 110, 113, 115, 130, 132, 137, 139, 227
Kujau, Konrad, 71

Lambert, Angela, 127, 133
Lammers, Hans, 153
Lange, Wilhelm, 182
Langer, Walter Charles, 131, 226-8, 236,
Lanzmann, Claude, 229, 232
Lauer, Erich, 72
Léhar, Franz, 96
Ley, Inge, 117
Ley, Robert, 117
Lindloff, Ewald, 194, 199
Linge, Heinz, 42, 44, 46, 127, 133, 169, 176, 179, 181, 186, 188-9, 194, 196, 202-3
Liptauer, Suzi, 117
List, Guido von, 69
Liszt, Franz, 95
Lobjoie, Charlotte, 41-2, 44-7
Lorenz, Heinz, 214, 216
Loret, Jean-Marie, 43, 46-8
Lüdecke, Kurt, 131, 226
Lukacs, John, xii, 133, 221, 223, 233

Machiavelli, Niccolo, 77
Machtan, Lothar, 30, 113, 131
Makart, Hans, 97
Mansfeld, Erich, 180, 185
Marx, Karl, 65
Maser, Werner, 13-14, 33-4, 37, 41, 43, 46, 105, 127, 197, 236, 238
Matzelberger, Franziska, 7
Maurice, Emil, 115, 121
May, Karl, 100
Meisner, Otto, 72
Melching, Willem, 80, 83-4
Mend, Hans, 22, 24, 29, 34, 37, 114, 131, 238
Mengershausen, Harry, 193, 197
Meyer, Adolf, 22-3, 31, 36
Misch, Rochus, 181, 186-7, 190, 197, 213, 224

Mitford, Unity, 117
Montesquieu, Charles de, 77
Morell, Theodor, ix, 156, 164
Mulders, Jean-Paul, 11, 47
Mulisch, Harry, 219
Müller, Adolf, 62
Müller-Schönhausen, Johannes von, 174
Mussolini, Benito, 73-4, 138

Napoleon III, emperor, 77
Nasse, prof. H., 105
Naumann, Werner, 179
Negri, Pola, 117
Neumann, Hans-Joachim, 157
Neumann, Josef, 115
Nietzsche, Friedrich, 100
Nüll, Eduard van der, 101

O'Donnell, James P, 193, 196-7, 234
Ohlendorf, Otto, 149

Padua, Paul Mathias, 97
Paustin, Friedrich Wilhelm, 216
Picker, Henri, 99
Plaim, Anna, 125, 127
Plöckinger, Othmar, 53, 62, 73
Pölzl, Johanna, 14, 16
Pölzl, Klara, 1, 7
Price, Billy F., 94
Pröhl, Ilse, 62,
Prokop, Otto, 200

Rabitsch, Hugo, 90
Raine, Adrian, 228
Rasputin, Grigori, 165
Rattenhuber, Johann, 179
Raubal, Angela, 16
Raubal, Geli, 31, 62, 115, 119-20, 124, 128-9, 131, 141, 229
Rauschning, Hermann, 119, 130-1, 226
Rees, Laurence, xii, 150, 231
Reisser, Hans, 194-5
Reiter, Mimi, 118, 120, 124, 133
Retcliffe, Sir John, 77
Riefenstahl, Leni, 100-1, 239
Röhm, Ernst, 115, 128, 143, 226

Romedor, Walburga, 14-15
Rosenbaum, Ron, xii, 3, 128, 130, 222, 224, 231
Rosenberg, Alfred, 78, 98
Rosenfeld, Alvin, 232
Rothman, Herman, 213-4
Rothschild, baron, 2
Russell, Stuart, 38, 44, 46
Rutz, Korbinian, 31, 39
Ryback, Timothy, 165

Schacht, Hjalmar, 84, 87
Schädle, Franz, 195
Schaub, Julius, 71-2
Schicklgruber, Maria Anna, 1, 4, 11
Schirach, Baldur von, 73
Schirach, Henriette von, 173
Schleehuber, Michael, 31
Schleicher, Kurt von, 162
Schmidt, Ernst, 30, 45, 52, 114
Schneider, Karl, 182
Schnell, Georg, 33
Schönerer, Georg, 69, 136, 144
Schopenhauer, Arthur, 140
Schörner, Ferdinand, 214
Schreck, Julius, 115, 239
Schreider, Erich, 209
Schröder, Christa, 72, 100, 224
Schwarz, Birgit, 93, 99
Schwiedel, Werner, 195
Semenovski, Pyotr, 184
Semper, Godfried, 101
Shakespeare, William, 100
Shirer, William, 220
Shkaravski, Faust, 183
Smelik, Klaas, 78-9
Smith, Will, 219, 222, 239
Spaun, Fridolin von, 150
Speer, Albert, 36, 73, 95-6, 99, 101-3, 105, 125, 153, 168, 206, 223, 234
Stalin, Joseph, 149
Stefanie (girl from Linz), 110, 120, 137
Stettner, Josef, 32
Stolzing-Cerny, Josef, 62
Strasser, Gregor, 142

Strasser, Otto, 68, 122, 128, 131, 226
Strausbaug, Linda, 201
Strauss, Johann, 96
Streicher, Julius, 23
Stuart-Houston, Alex, 48
Stumpfegger, Ludwig, 170

Tamms, Friedrich, 105
Tandey, Henry, 28, 235
Taylor, Kathleen, 230, 237
Thiers, George (Heinz Lorenz), 214, 216
Trambauer, Heinrich Wilhelm, 57
Trevor-Roper, Hugh, 178, 206, 222, 231
Troost, Gerdy, 97
Troost, Paul Ludwig, 97, 101, 103, 117

Ullrich, Volker, 81, 87, 237

Veit, Aloisia, 159
Verdi, Guiseppe, 95, 231
Voss, Hans-Erich, 179, 182, 206, 208

Wagner, Adolf, 56, 58, 98
Wagner, Friedlinde, 131, 226
Wagner, Richard, 61, 75, 92, 95, 96, 98, 113, 115, 137
Wagner, Siegfried, 61
Wagner, Winifred, 72, 75, 117, 235
Waite, Robert, 109
Wasner, Eugen, 160
Weber, Thomas, xii, 26, 28, 35, 36, 38, 44, 51, 114,
Weinberg, Gerhard L, 71-5, 237
Weiss, Ernst, 162
Welzin, Gerhard, 194-5
Wiedemann, Fritz, 20, 25, 238
Winter, Anna, 123
Wolf, Hugo, 96

Zander, Wilhelm, 214, 218
Zdral, Wolfgang, 6
Zehnpfennig, Barbara, 64
Zoller, Albert, 72
Zuroff, Efraim, 222
Zyagin, Victor, 200